Finding Your *Famous* {& Infamous} ANCESTORS

Uncover the celebrities, rogues, and royals in your family tree

{Rhonda R. McClure}

BETTERWAY BOOKS
CINCINNATI, OHIO

www.familytreemagazine.com

Other fine Betterway Books are available from your local bookstore or on our Web site at www.familytreemagazine.com.

06 05 04 03 02   5 4 3 2 1

Library of Congress Cataloging-in-Publication Data

McClure, Rhonda R.
  Finding your famous (& infamous) ancestors / Rhonda R. McClure—1st ed.
    p. cm.
  Includes bibliographical references and index.
  ISBN 1-55870-654-2 (alk. paper)
    1. United States—Genealogy—Handbooks, manuals, etc. 2. Celebrities—Genealogy—Handbooks, manuals, etc. I. Title: Finding your famous (and infamous) ancestors. II. Title.
CS49.M35   2003
929'.1'072073—dc21   2003052272
                                                                         CIP

Editor: Sharon DeBartolo Carmack, CG
Associate editor: Erin Nevius
Production coordinator: Sara Dumford
Cover designer: Lisa Buchanan
Interior designer: Sandy Conopeotis Kent
Icon designer: Cindy Beckmeyer

About the Author

Rhonda R. McClure is a professional genealogical researcher, lecturer, and author. She has been involved in research for 20 years and has spent the last 15 years using online genealogy to facilitate and enhance her research endeavors. For the last three years she has devoted most of her time to researching the ancestry of celebrities and historical personalities. The family trees she compiles have been published on *Genealogy.com*. She is a contributing editor to *Biography*, writing the "Celebrity Roots" column that reveals the fascinating connections between celebrities and other famous individuals. Her most recent periodical endeavor is "Generations," her column in *The History Channel Magazine*, where she is a contributing writer. She has written extensively for a variety of genealogical periodicals. This is her eighth book and her second for Betterway Books. She lectures frequently around the country, where she often incorporates some of her unique celebrity research scenarios into her presentations.

Table of Contents At a Glance

Table of Contents

to prevent family discomfort over an embarrassing relation. In some instances, however, no amount of time can cushion the shock that the discovery of an ancestor who committed heinous deeds may provoke. This chapter will also explore ethical questions regarding the airing of dirty family laundry.

12 Telling All, *208*

This chapter looks at the legal and ethical issues of sharing the information you have found, and reiterates that the feelings of living persons who might be hurt by the discovery of rogues in the family must be considered. Other critical issues discussed are whether to publish or post information about living persons—famous or not—and the dangers of publishing fanciful family tales and unproven connections with famous individuals.

Introduction

Celebrity. There is something that fascinates all of us about the rich, the famous, and the infamous. We read biographies and watch documentaries and made-for-TV movies about these people. And for those with the same last name as a celebrated individual, there is always the hope that a relation can be claimed.

Over the last few years, I have spent a lot of time researching the family trees of celebrities who have been highlighted in *Biography* episodes as shown on A&E cable TV. The trees are available online and coincide with the individual highlighted in given episodes. While most of them are performers or actors, I have also researched the roots of famous sports personalities and politicians, as well as a few of the more colorful and infamous through history.

One of the things I have discovered is that anyone can be related to a celebrity. Seldom will the relationship be found through the sharing of a surname. Usually the relationship is found only after following the twisting, turning paths that are your family tree and that of the celebrity. Sometimes finding the connection requires tracking the extended family's lines as well.

In addition to admitting my own fascination with many of these famous individuals, I will say that researching their trees has sparked a different interest in them. As I have read about the struggles and hardships of some of their ancestors, I find myself more intrigued by the stories of these ancestors than in the glitter of the celebrity himself. Once, while researching a number of boxers, I marveled at the difficult lives they led until they were "discovered" and became famous for their abilities. While a few couldn't quite blunt the hard edge they were forced to hone while they were growing up, others not only rose above their beginnings but then turned around and tried to help others living in the same area and economic situation.

The world of technology that genealogists now claim for their own goes a long way in aiding the research of personal family histories, whether our own or that of the famous. The Internet has brought many useful research tools into the homes of genealogists, and those who find themselves interested in proving a connection to someone famous will appreciate the records and resources that are available online and accessible any time.

Genealogy has become an increasingly popular hobby. Today you can go into any book store and find a number of books introducing you to the fascinating world of researching your family tree. Most of these books have one thing in common, however: they deal only with how to research your own lineage. What if you want to find out if you are related to someone famous? Few books explain how to work on lines to which you are not directly related. As you read this book, you will be introduced to the concept of researching the family tree of someone you haven't even met. Let's face it, few of us will have the opportunity to meet these celebrities, so we have to depend on other sources of information.

Most other genealogy books do not talk to you about reading biographies, or using the information found in a *Who's Who* compilation. After all, few of us know that we have any famous ancestors who might show up in such works until we get started on the search. Even if family legend claims that you are related to someone famous, you may not have any idea how to go about proving it. For this, not only do you need to research your family history, but you must also research the family tree of the celebrity.

Researching a celebrity offers benefits and challenges. The fact that a person is famous may mean that there is more information available on that person than on your ancestor. Family historians everywhere find the occasional brick wall; researching a famous cousin may aid you in breaking through that brick wall. People far and wide have researched celebrities for a variety of reasons. Biographers may have written not only their subject's life, but also about the person's family tree. Such information may be just what you need to break through a barrier on your own line.

So, how do you research the celebrity? And how do you take what you know about your family and make the connection? This book will walk you through a variety of records unique to researching celebrities, as well as showing you how to use traditional records that genealogists commonly employ as they try to push back their ancestry one generation at a time.

The biggest difference between simply researching your family tree and trying to find a connection with a famous person is that instead of concentrating on direct lineage—as we are wont to do when trying to reach as far back in our own history as possible—your search will now encompass more branches of the family tree. This book will introduce you to *cluster genealogy*: a method of researching not only a direct line but also anyone else connected with that family line, including siblings and spouses. Such an approach to family history will give you a better understanding of the research process so that work on your own lines will be more productive. So often we seem to do research with blinders on, overlooking important resources or records as we move from one person per generation to the next. Cluster genealogy brings you a well-rounded, more complete picture of your family history. It is also the way in which you may find a relationship to a famous individual.

Few of us descend directly from a famous figure. However, through the cluster approach to genealogical research, you may discover that you have an illustrious cousin. Don't worry if you have never even heard of cluster genealogy before. This and other research approaches will be completely discussed so that you will understand them and feel comfortable using them, even if you're just researching your own family rather than a famous person.

I have discovered, however, that none of us is an island unto himself. You may not have any idea that you have a connection to anyone famous, and then all of a sudden you stumble on something that sets you wondering. It has happened to many of us. Sometimes it is the infamous that we discover.

Handling such individuals can be tricky. You may be fascinated with what you are finding, but the rest of the family isn't. You may not know what happened, just that the family never talks about Uncle Ralph. How do you go about finding out what happened or why he is such a big family secret? What would the family say if they knew you were looking for Uncle Ralph in prison records? This book will introduce you to a variety of sources that may hold the clues you need to uncover the truth about your relatives. We'll also discuss how to handle sensitive family issues that may arise from your research.

Finally we will examine what you can do with the information you find on the famous and infamous. Are there laws that protect such information, or can you share all on the Internet? Can you find a photo of a celebrity online and use it on your Web site? Should you post everything you find when you have uncovered some of the more unscrupulous characters that hang from the tree? These are some of the questions that we'll consider.

Join me now as I introduce you to the world of tracing not only your own family history, but that of the famous. Find out how to get started and where to turn, both online and off. Learn what you can do with the information you have found. And enjoy the glimpses into celebrity genealogy that have been included.

You Think Who Is Related to You?

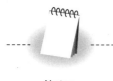

Notes

We all have family stories, some that have been handed down for generations and some that have come about only recently. Most of these family stories either tell of the amazing or daring feats of an ancestor or make some claim to a relationship to someone famous.

I have been involved in genealogical research for almost twenty years now, and the last fifteen of those years have been spent involved in online genealogy communities and Internet research. It has been through this capacity, as a sysop or author, that I have had the opportunity to conduct a lot of correspondence with other researchers, much of it inquiring about relationships to people of famous or historical importance.

Many of the people start out their letter with "The family says we are related to. . . ." The individuals that people claim relationship to run the gambit—some are Hollywood movie stars, others are historical icons, some think they have a connection to royalty. While it is never out of the question, the problem that most of the people face with this type of research is that they have not done any or enough research on their own lineage, so all they have to go on is the family story.

Before getting into the hows and wheres of researching your family history or that of the celebrity of interest, **let's look at some of the more popular family traditions or stories that have been passed along to those trying to make the connection.** As each "story" is discussed, you will be introduced to some of the records and resources that I will explain in greater detail later in the book.

ROYALTY AND NOBILITY

There is something fascinating about royalty. While the United States fought a war to gain independence from a monarchy, and those who became citizens of the United States forfeited any title, it is the inhabitants of the United States who seem most intrigued by the royals. We clamor to get a glimpse whenever we can.

Many people think they are related to one royal house or another, and service that you and George W. Bush are "like that." However, once you find the connection you may find that the research done on the president benefits your own research. While having a presidential lineage may prove interesting, more often it's the sources I've used developing that lineage that are important—helping lead me down new paths in my own research.

Like any research, it is necessary to know your subject. For instance, people write to me and tell me that they are descended from George Washington. This just isn't possible. While he apparently "slept" everywhere, if you can believe all the "George Washington slept here" signs that can be found at historical homes, the only children that George Washington had were his wife's from her first marriage. He never fathered any children of his own, at least none that have been proven. While it isn't possible for the individual to be descended from George, it may be possible to be related to him. After all, if you can trace your ancestry back to the early colonial days, you will find you have many interesting famous cousins, including a president or two. Perhaps George is one of them.

RELATED TO A SIGNER OF THE DECLARATION OF INDEPENDENCE

One can't help but wonder if people would be as eager to claim a signer of the Declaration of Independence if things had gone differently during the American Revolution. But America did get its independence, and as such the names on that document are now some of the most often claimed ancestors. Many people have been told for years how they descend from one signer or another. In my days of accepting clients, in the space of just a couple of years I had two different clients request research to prove their connection to a signer, but unfortunately in both cases the research disproved the family story.

The signers and their descendants have been pretty well researched and published in *Descendants of the Signers of the Declaration of Independence* by Rev. Frederick Wallace Pyne (Picton Press, seven volumes). Volume seven includes the descent of those signers from North Carolina, South Carolina, and Georgia, and this was one of the published resources utilized in regard to Goldie Hawn's potential descent from Edward Rutledge. There was concern when I did not find her listed in the index, as the descents were brought forward into the 1980s. **Family traditions usually have a thread of truth in them** and there is indeed a Rutledge lineage in Goldie's past, but unfortunately it does not appear to connect to Edward's either as a descendant or cousin, though more extensive research would be necessary in England to rule that out. See Figure 1-1 on page 9 for an ancestry of Goldie Hawn.

Important

MILITARY HEROES

The family trees I compile on celebrities are posted on a commercial Web site. On the main celebrity trees page, there is a link with an e-mail address.

DECLARATION DESCENDANTS

© *Mario Anzuoni/Splash News*

In his book, *Roots of the Rich and Famous*, Robert Ralsey Davenport (Dallas: Taylor Pub., 1998) shares a story apparently from Goldie Hawn about her descent from John Rutledge, a signer of the Declaration of Independence. According to the book, Goldie gave her son the middle name of Rutledge in honor of this connection. I researched the tree of Goldie Hawn and discovered that something wasn't quite right.

First, John Rutledge was not the signer of the Declaration of Independence; instead it was his brother Edward. In fact, Goldie's father is named Edward Rutledge Hawn. So, the first question had been answered, the family story was more likely that the family thought they were descended from Edward, which would make sense since he was the signer.

The next step was to build a genealogy for Goldie, especially when published Rutledge genealogies on Edward did not reveal a connection to Goldie. It was five generations back that I discovered the Rutledge surname, a Mary L. Rutledge, born about 1826 in Alabama. Online research showed a possible ancestry for Mary, and I began to work in original records to see if the ancestry was correct. The more I researched, the more I realized that Goldie's Rutledge line traces back to a Joseph Rutledge, born about 1744 in Amelia County, Virginia, and died about 1814 in Greenville, South Carolina. He married Mary Paschal and is Goldie's third great-grandfather.

Since Edward Rutledge was born in Charleston, South Carolina on 23 Nov. 1749, it is not possible for Joseph to be a descendant of Edward's. It may still be possible for Goldie and Edward to be cousins, though it looks like the connection would have to be at least three more generations back.

A GENERAL'S GENEALOGY

Lee Marvin has always been a man's man and is best known for his roles in military movies. It shouldn't be surprising when you look at some of his cousins. He can claim two of America's best known generals: General George Washington, later President Washington, is his second cousin, six times removed. General Robert E. Lee, for whom he was named, is his first cousin, four times removed.

People are encouraged to write me with suggestions of people whose ancestry they are interested in seeing explored. While some of the messages I get

ANCESTRY OF GOLDIE HAWN

This ancestry appears to disprove the family tradition that Goldie Hawn is a descendant of Edward Rutledge, signer of the Declaration from South Carolina. The table shows the ancestry by generation, with Goldie Hawn as the first generation and her parents as the second. To find the parents of Edward Rutledge Hawn, take his number (2) and multiple by 2 (which gives you 4) and find 4 in the third generation—Otto, his father, and add one to the father's number to find the mother who is 5—Clara. Continue to multiply and add to find the parents of each person in the additional generations.

Generation 1

| 1 | **Goldie Hawn** was born in Silver Spring, Maryland, 21 Nov. 1945. She married William Louis Hudson in Takoma Park, Maryland, 1976. She is the companion of Kurt Russell. |

Generation 2

| 2 | **Edward Rutledge Hawn** was born in Arkansas, 28 Sept. 1908. He married Laura Steinhoff in Washington, District of Columbia, 30 Apr. 1936. Edward died 7 June 1982 in Los Angeles County, California. |
| 3 | **Laura Steinhoff** was born in Pennsylvania, 27 Nov. 1913. She died 27 Nov. 1993 in Los Angeles County, California. |

Generation 3

| 4 | **Otto Delphia Hawn** was born in Bollinger Co., Missouri, 18 July 1879. He married Clara Estelle Johnson in Newport, Arkansas, 7 June 1904. Otto died 24 July 1930 in Little Rock, Pulaski, Arkansas. |
| 5 | **Clara Estelle Johnson** was born in Arkansas, Oct. 1881. She died Jan. 1969 in Little Rock, Pulaski, Arkansas. |

Generation 4

8	**Aaron Madison Hawn** was born in Castor, Bollinger, Missouri, 12 Mar. 1851. He married Nannie Ada Hevrin in Bollinger Co., Missouri, 8 Sept. 1878. Aaron died 25 June 1901 in Marquard, Madison, Missouri.
9	**Nannie Ada Hevrin** was born in Harrodsburg, Mercer, Kentucky, 13 Apr. 1861. She died 29 Dec. 1936 in Denver, Colorado.
10	**Henry Spencer Johnson** was born in Alabama, ca. 1847. He married Mary F. Hall in Saline Co., Arkansas, 2 Nov. 1877. Henry died before 1900.
11	**Mary F. Hall** was born in Missouri, Nov. 1853. She died after 1910.

Generation 5

16	**Samuel Hahn**
18	**G.W. Hevrin** married Elizabeth Ann [--?--].
19	**Elizabeth Ann [--?--]**
20	**Henry Johnson** was born in South Carolina, 1820. He married Mary L. Rutledge in Perry Co., Alabama, 13 Oct. 1842.
21	**Mary L. Rutledge** was born in Alabama, ca. 1826. She died before 9 Feb. 1870.

Generation 6

| 42 | **Paschal Rutledge** was born in Virginia, ca. 1786. He married Mary Lester in South Carolina, ca. 1813. |
| 43 | **Mary Lester** was born in South Carolina, 1788. She died before 9 Feb. 1870. |

Generation 7

84	**Joseph Rutledge** was born in Amelia Co., Virginia, ca. 1744. He married Mary Paschal. Joseph died ca. 1814 in Greenville, South Carolina.
85	**Mary Paschal**
86	**Archibald Lester** married Elizabeth Crynes.
87	**Elizabeth Crynes**

Figure 1-1

are predictable, I will say that I have been surprised by how many people have a family story claiming they are related to General Robert E. Lee.

Deciding whether or not a military hero is a famous or infamous individual will sometimes depend on which side your family was on during the battle in question. For instance, a Georgia family might take exception to discovering that they are related to General Sherman. He could be the relative no one talks about.

Pick any war and you will find military heroes who everyone wants to be related to. Some of those heroes are women—many people have written asking for additional information on Betsy Ross or Clara Barton. Clara is another of those that you can't descend from because she had no children, but you could find she is a cousin.

RED CROSS ROOTS

Clara Barton was born in 1821 in Massachusetts and died in 1912 in Maryland. She is best known for her nursing of troops during the Civil War and the founding of the American Red Cross. Somehow it seems fitting that actress Michael Learned, who played a nurse on television in the show *Nurse* after her more famous role as Olivia Walton, should be her fourth cousin, five times removed.

There is a lot of misinformation that floats around about early military heroes. It becomes ever more important that you verify any information found so you are not led astray and wind up losing your connection because you have researched the wrong lineage on the famous person.

THE WILD WEST

Like royalty, there is a fascination with the Wild West. I have spent many hours reading about the Wild West and some of its more colorful characters. I have compiled genealogies on Wyatt Earp, Doc Holliday, Jesse James, and Wild Bill Hickok, to name just a few. They fascinate me. I am not alone— I know colleagues who have spent time researching these individuals and others who helped carve out the more fantastic section of the West.

Like researching the presidential pedigrees and military heroes of long ago, there are often times when the information shared by the historians is not quite accurate. Sometimes it is a misinterpretation of the records, and other times it is based on hearsay that was taken as fact and not verified.

In addition to those famous men, there are also many famous, or infa-

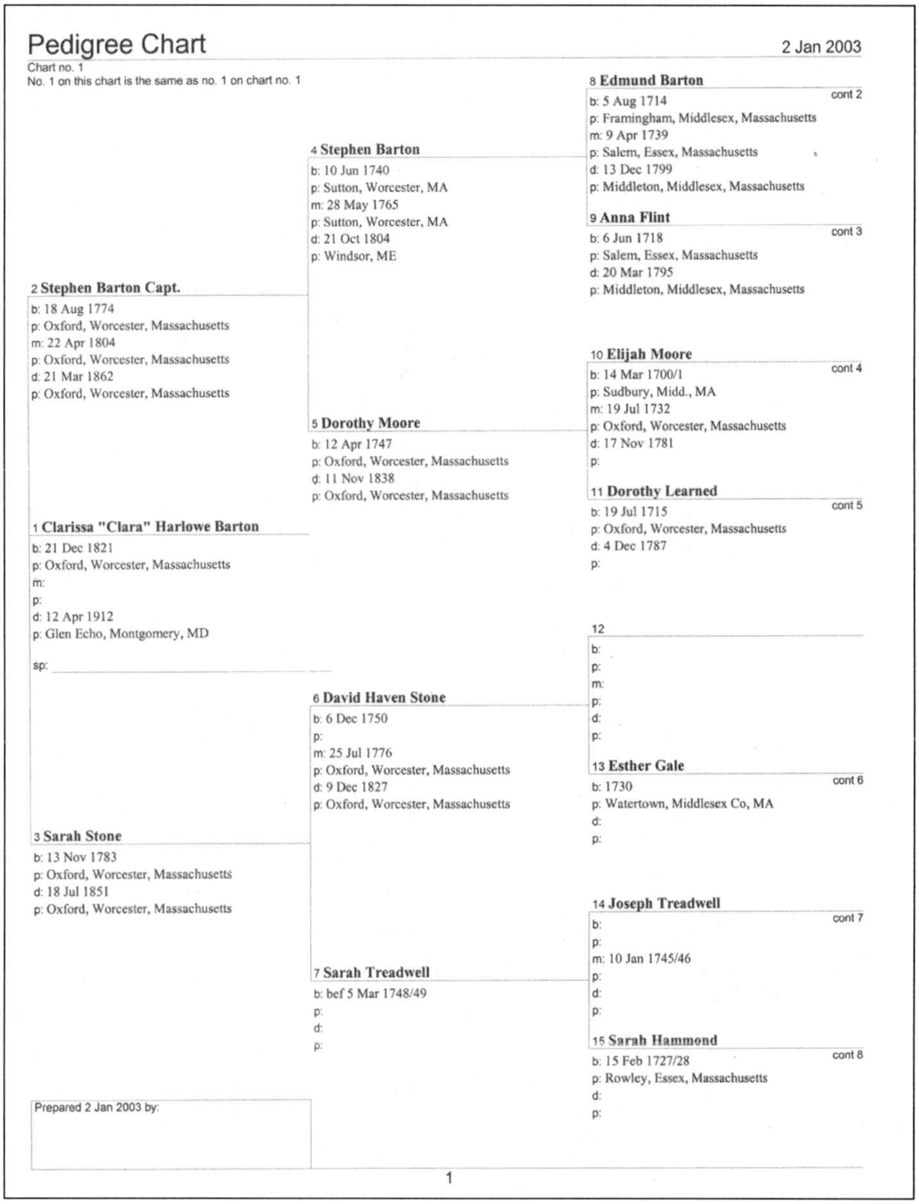

Figure 1-2
Clara Barton's pedigree chart.

Pedigree Chart

Chart no. 1
No. 1 on this chart is the same as no. 1 on chart no. 1

2 Jan 2003

4 Stephen Barton
b: 10 Jun 1740
p: Sutton, Worcester, MA
m: 28 May 1765
p: Sutton, Worcester, MA
d: 21 Oct 1804
p: Windsor, ME

8 Edmund Barton   cont 2
b: 5 Aug 1714
p: Framingham, Middlesex, Massachusetts
m: 9 Apr 1739
p: Salem, Essex, Massachusetts
d: 13 Dec 1799
p: Middleton, Middlesex, Massachusetts

9 Anna Flint   cont 3
b: 6 Jun 1718
p: Salem, Essex, Massachusetts
d: 20 Mar 1795
p: Middleton, Middlesex, Massachusetts

2 Stephen Barton Capt.
b: 18 Aug 1774
p: Oxford, Worcester, Massachusetts
m: 22 Apr 1804
p: Oxford, Worcester, Massachusetts
d: 21 Mar 1862
p: Oxford, Worcester, Massachusetts

5 Dorothy Moore
b: 12 Apr 1747
p: Oxford, Worcester, Massachusetts
d: 11 Nov 1838
p: Oxford, Worcester, Massachusetts

10 Elijah Moore   cont 4
b: 14 Mar 1700/1
p: Sudbury, Midd., MA
m: 19 Jul 1732
p: Oxford, Worcester, Massachusetts
d: 17 Nov 1781
p:

11 Dorothy Learned   cont 5
b: 19 Jul 1715
p: Oxford, Worcester, Massachusetts
d: 4 Dec 1787
p:

1 Clarissa "Clara" Harlowe Barton
b: 21 Dec 1821
p: Oxford, Worcester, Massachusetts
m:
p:
d: 12 Apr 1912
p: Glen Echo, Montgomery, MD

sp:

6 David Haven Stone
b: 6 Dec 1750
p:
m: 25 Jul 1776
p: Oxford, Worcester, Massachusetts
d: 9 Dec 1827
p: Oxford, Worcester, Massachusetts

12
b:
p:
m:
p:
d:
p:

13 Esther Gale   cont 6
b: 1730
p: Watertown, Middlesex Co, MA
d:
p:

3 Sarah Stone
b: 13 Nov 1783
p: Oxford, Worcester, Massachusetts
d: 18 Jul 1851
p: Oxford, Worcester, Massachusetts

7 Sarah Treadwell
b: bef 5 Mar 1748/49
p:
d:
p:

14 Joseph Treadwell   cont 7
b:
p:
m: 10 Jan 1745/46
p:
d:
p:

15 Sarah Hammond   cont 8
b: 15 Feb 1727/28
p: Rowley, Essex, Massachusetts
d:
p:

Prepared 2 Jan 2003 by:

1

WILD RELATIONS

Dennis Hopper was born in Dodge City, Kansas, a part of the West that tempted so many pioneers, so perhaps it is fitting that he can claim Daniel Boone as an uncle, his fifth great-granduncle to be precise. Synonymous with Boonesboro, Kentucky, the town he founded after hacking a trail through the Cumberland Gap, Daniel Boone is almost as famous a movie star as Dennis Hopper, having been portrayed by many different actors over time.

\di'fin\ vb

Definitions

SOILED DOVE

A *soiled dove* is a slang term for a prostitute. It was usually given to those who worked in saloons and halls of the Wild West because they were often making their living in the boxed seat areas that were above the main stage and seats.

Notes

ENCHANTED ANCESTORS

Today we often claim witches proudly by joining a lineage society, such as the Sons and Daughters of the Victims of Colonial Witch Trials, P.O. Box 164, Stoneham, MA 02180.

Internet Source

For a great Web site about witch hunts around the world, check out The Killings of Witches Web site <www.illusions.com/burning/burnwit1.htm>.

mous, women who made a name for themselves in the Wild West. Of course, since they were women, it is probable that their name changed at some point. Most of the women of this time would get married, although some would just change their names. Some were "soiled doves" while others were just running away from sad home lives. For those who made it a point to be inconspicuous, it can sometimes be difficult to find the information you need to jump-start your research. Of course, if they were famous despite their colorful past or profession, then it is likely that you will find something written about them somewhere.

DESCENDED FROM A WITCH

While not always an appreciated ancestor, most of the accused witches throughout history were actually just poor individuals who were different enough to be outside the accepted norm of a community. Many of the accused witches in the United States can be found in New England during the 1600s, the most famous being those accused during the Salem Witchcraft Hysteria of 1692.

While today's population no longer sees this as a stigma, you will find that some family histories written in the late 1800s or early 1900s will hide the fact that someone was accused of witchcraft. Today's family histories seem to revel in laying claim to a witch.

Perhaps the lack of stigma comes from the many individuals who do descend from one or more of these witches. For instance, Walt Disney, famous for his family entertainment and a certain mouse named Mickey, is a sixth great-grandson of the Rev. George Burroughs, an accused witch who was hanged in 1692, one of the few men executed for witchcraft.

While Salem is by far the most famous town with a history of witches, it is not the only one. Many towns, in New England especially, had accused witches, so even if your ancestry does not trace back to Salem there is still a possibility that you are related to a witch.

CRIMINALS

While you could certainly consider witches criminals, since some were incarcerated and some were put to death, they are such a unique group that I kept them separate. There are many criminals both past and present, and some families fear a criminal relation while others take interest in the connection.

How upset you and your family are over finding a criminal ancestor depends on how close the relationship is and how recently the crime was committed. Someone related to Lizzie Borden now may find it easier to handle than the Bordens of Fall River probably did in 1892 (like actress Elizabeth Montgomery—see Figure 1-3 on page 15). Also the nature of the crime will affect the acceptance or rejection by the family. In some instances

---

DESCENDANT LIST—GEORGE BURROUGHS

1. George Burroughs (about 1650–19 Aug. 1692)
sp-Hannah (–)
  2. Hannah Burroughs (27 Apr. 1680–5 Aug. 1746)
  sp-Jabez Fox (–)
    3. Thomas Fox (6 Dec. 1706–13 Mar. 1793)
    sp-Mercy Lawrence (–)
      4. Mercy Fox (10 Mar. 1740/41–)
      sp-Moses Johnson (26 July 1737–3 Aug. 1815)
        5. Fanny Johnson (16 May 1764–27 Apr. 1801)
        sp-John Call (14 Oct. 1761–1 June 1831)
          6. Eber Call (14 July 1791–)
          sp-Violette Lawrence (about 1792–12 June 1870)
            7. Charles Call (22 Mar. 1822–6 Jan. 1890)
            sp-Henrietta Gross (27 July 1837–21 Feb. 1910)
              8. Flora Call (22 Apr. 1868–26 Nov. 1938)
              sp-Elias Disney (6 Feb. 1859–13 Sept. 1941)
                9. **Walter Elias Disney** (5 Dec. 1901–15 Dec. 1966)
                sp-Lillian M. Bounds (15 Feb. 1899–16 Dec. 1997)
                9. Roy O. Disney (24 June 1893–)
                9. Herbert Disney (8 Dec. 1888–)
                9. Raymond Disney (30 Dec. 1890–)
              8. Charles Henry Call (6 Oct. 1870–)
              8. Grace Call (25 Jan. 1873–)
              8. Julia Call (23 Aug. 1876–)
              8. Laura M. Call (about 1857–)
              8. Harry Call (about 1858–)
              8. Ada Call (about 1860–)
              8. Alice Call (about 1862–)
              8. Mary Call (about 1864–)
              8. Jessie Call (about 1866–)
           6. Hannah Call (14 Apr. 1787–)
          6. Ira Call (22 Dec. 1785–)
          6. Levina Call (26 Mar. 1789–)
          6. Olive Call (24 June 1793–)

The above indented descendant chart shows that Walt Disney is the sixth great-grandson of George Burroughs, accused and hanged during the Salem witch trials. George has the distinction of being the only minister accused.

---

it is knowledge or fear of such a relationship that causes family members to get upset when you mention you are now researching your family tree.

MOVIE STARS AND SINGERS

By far the most popular requests I receive are for the lineages of different movie stars and singers. They can be more interesting than royalty—they come into our homes via the television or appear larger than life on the

FAMILY FALSEHOODS

Clare Boothe Luce has long had family issues. There is conjecture, due to a lack of a marriage certificate and the fact that at the time of her birth her parents weren't married, that they never bothered to marry after all, even though Clare's brother was born the year before her. However, her Boothe ancestors were strict—in fact, one was a minister. It is said that he changed the spelling of his surname, adding the "e," to differentiate himself from those Booths who were actually related to John Wilkes Booth, after John assassinated President Lincoln. Research later disproved this story, but it did make for an interesting anecdote in the many biographies that have been published about Clare over the years.

MURDEROUS COUSIN

Elizabeth Montgomery, born 15 April 1933 and known around the world for her portrayal as the stylish witch Samantha Stephens, from her TV series *Bewitched*, also played the part of Lizzie Borden in *The Legend of Lizzie Borden*. Research shows that Elizabeth and Lizzie were sixth cousins once removed. In the movie version Lizzie really did do it. I wonder how Elizabeth would have felt if she knew she was playing her own cousin.

Digital Press Photos

movie screen. They are popular. Everyone wants to say they know a celebrity, and to be related to one is even better, so many people claim they are related to this actress or that singer.

While it doesn't change the fact that the celebrity doesn't even know you, there is something special about being able to claim a celebrity as your cousin, even if that relationship is so remote you need all your fingers and toes to figure it out.

Of course researching such a connection usually requires that you not only research your own lineage, but also that of the celebrity. While some have been done and can be found in the various compiled pedigree databases, you will find that the information is sometimes full of errors. Other times you will need to create the search from the very beginning—the celebrity—just as you will have done with your own research.

Important

HE WAS THERE

Another type of story that we often find passed down through the generations is the story of how your great-great-great-grandfather was there

	ANCESTRY OF ELIZABETH MONTGOMERY
	Elizabeth's connection to Lizzie Borden is through her Luther lineage. John Luther (#1,296) in Generation 11 is the common ancestor, and is Lizzie Borden's seventh great-grandfather and Elizabeth's eighth great-grandfather.

Generation 1

1	**Elizabeth Montgomery** was born in Los Angeles, Los Angeles, California, 15 Apr. 1933. She married Fred Gallatin Cammann in New York, 27 Mar. 1954. Elizabeth was divorced from Fred Gallatin Cammann in Las Vegas, Clark, Nevada, Aug. 1955. She married Gig Young 28 Dec. 1956. Elizabeth was divorced from Gig Young in Mexico, Jan. 1963. She married William Milton Asher in El Paso, El Paso, Texas, 26 Oct. 1963. She married Robert Foxworth 28 Jan. 1993. Elizabeth died 18 May 1995 in Beverly Hills, Los Angeles, California.

Generation 2

2	**Robert Montgomery** was born in Fishkill Landing, Dutchess, New York, 21 May 1904. He married Elizabeth Bryan Allen in New York City, New York, New York, 14 Apr. 1928. Robert was divorced from Elizabeth Bryan Allen in Las Vegas, Clark, Nevada, 5 Dec. 1950. He married Elizabeth Grant in New York, 9 Dec. 1950. Robert died 27 Sept. 1981 in Canaan, Litchfield, Connecticut.
3	**Elizabeth Bryan Allen** was born in Louisville, Jefferson, Kentucky, 26 Dec. 1904. She died 28 June 1992 in Patterson, Putnam, New York.

Generation 3

4	**Henry Montgomery** was born in New York, May 1868. He married Mary Weed Barney 14 Dec. 1899. Henry died 25 June 1922 in Brooklyn, Kings, New York.
5	**Mary Weed Barney** was born in Bayonne, New Jersey, 30 Mar. 1875.
6	**Bryan Hunt Allen** married Rebecca Lowry Daniel.
7	**Rebecca Lowry Daniel** was born in Kentucky, 5 June 1886. Rebecca died 25 Aug. 1964 in Los Angeles Co., California.

Generation 4

8	**Archibald Montgomery** married Margaret Edminston.
9	**Margaret Edminston**
10	**Nathan Barney Jr.** was born in Wilkes-Barre, Pennsylvania, 25 Dec. 1819. He married Elizabeth Wotherspoon 24 Dec. 1856. He married Mary Ann Deverell in Noroton, Connecticut, 10 Nov. 1864. Nathan died 30 Mar. 1902 in Brooklyn, Kings, New York.
11	**Mary Ann Deverell** was born in Wallingford, Jamaica, British West Indies, 28 Oct. 1843. She died after 1923.

Generation 5

20	**Nathan Barney** was born in Hartford, Connecticut, 1776. He married Hannah Carey in Wilkes-Barre, Pennsylvania, 11 Nov. 1798. Nathan died 1860 in Missouri.
21	**Hannah Carey** died July 1863 in Wilkes-Barre, Pennsylvania.
22	**George Deverell** married Mary Ann Stephenson.
23	**Mary Ann Stephenson**

Generation 6

40	**Benjamin Barney** married Elizabeth Ackley in East Haddam, Connecticut, 16 Aug. 1764.
41	**Elizabeth Ackley** was born in East Haddam, Connecticut, 16 Mar. 1745. She died ca. 1831/2 in New Haven, Ohio.
42	**John Carey** married Susanna Mann.
43	**Susanna Mann**

Figure 1-3 continued on next page.

Generation 7	
80	**John Barney** was born in Taunton, Bristol, Massachusetts, before 1720. He married Sarah Luther in Dighton, Bristol, Massachusetts, 19 Sept. 1744.
81	**Sarah Luther**
82	**Nathaniel Ackley** was born in East Haddam, Connecticut, 7 Nov. 1711. He married Mary Williams ca. 1734.
83	**Mary Williams**
Generation 8	
160	**Jacob Barney** was born in Bristol, Massachusetts, 16 Jan. 1695. He married Mary Danforth before 11 Feb. 1716. Jacob died Dec. 1731 in Taunton, Bristol, Massachusetts.
161	**Mary Danforth** was born 5 Dec. 1698. She died 20 Aug. 1792 at 93 years of age.
162	**Consider Luther** was born in Swansea, Bristol, Massachusetts, 16 Apr. 1698. He married Margaret Jewett in Swansea, Bristol, Massachusetts, 23 Apr. 1719.
163	**Margaret Jewett** died 1760 or 1766.
164	**James Ackley** married Elizabeth [--?--].
165	**Elizabeth [--?--]**
166	**Charles Williams** married Mary Robinson.
167	**Mary Robinson**
Generation 9	
320	**John Barney** married Mary Throop.
321	**Mary Throop**
322	**Samuel Danforth** was born in Roxbury, Massachusetts, 10 Dec. 1666. He married Hannah Allen. Samuel died 14 Nov. 1727.
323	**Hannah Allen** was born 22 July 1669. She died 3 Dec. 1761.
324	**Samuel Luther** was born in Rehoboth, Bristol, Massachusetts, 25 Oct. 1663. He married Sarah [--?--]. Samuel died 23 July 1714 in Swansea, Bristol, Massachusetts.
325	**Sarah [--?--]**
328	**Samuel Ackley** married Bathiah [--?--]. Samuel died 27 Apr. 1745 in East Haddam, Connecticut.
329	**Bathiah [--?--]**
Generation 10	
644	**Samuel Danforth** was born in England, Sept. 1626. He married Mary Wilson 5 Nov. 1651. Samuel died 19 Nov. 1674 in Roxbury, Massachusetts.
645	**Mary Wilson** was born 12 Sept. 1633. She died 13 Sept. 1713.
646	**James Allen** was born in Hampshire, Massachusetts, 24 June 1632. He married Elizabeth Houchin 31 Aug. 1668. James died 22 Sept. 1710 in Boston, Suffolk, Massachusetts.
647	**Elizabeth Houchin** married Unknown Endicott. She died 5 Apr. 1673.
648	**Samuel Luther** was born in Taunton, Bristol, Massachusetts 1636. He married Mary Abell. Samuel died 20 Dec. 1716 in Swansea, Bristol, Massachusetts.
649	**Mary Abell** was born in Weymouth, Norfolk, Massachusetts, 11 Apr. 1642.
656	**Nicholas Ackley**

Figure 1-3

Generation 11	
1,288	**Nicholas Danforth** was born in Franlingham, Suffolk, England, 1 Mar. 1589. He married Elizabeth [--?--]. Nicholas died Apr. 1638 in Cambridge, Massachusetts.
1,289	**Elizabeth** [--?--] died 22 Feb. 1628/29 in England.
1,290	**John Wilson** was born in Windsor, England, 1588. He married Elizabeth Mansfield. John died 7 Aug. 1667.
1,291	**Elizabeth Mansfield** died 1659.
1,294	**Jeremy Houchin** was born ca. 1615. He married Esther [--?--]. Jeremy died Apr. 1670.
1,295	**Esther** [--?--] died 2 July 1698.
1,296	**John Luther** married Elizabeth Turner.
1,297	**Elizabeth Turner**
1,298	**Robert Abell** married Joanna [--?--].
1,299	**Joanna** [--?--]

Figure 1-3

I'M DREAMING OF A CELEBRITY COUSIN

Whenever I begin researching another celebrity, especially if I see the lineage heading to New England, I keep a look out for my own surnames. It was through my own *Mayflower* connection that I found a celebrity cousin that I was thrilled to find. Having grown up watching Bing Crosby in movies and on television, he will always remind me of white Christmases even though I no longer get to see them. He was quite proud of his membership in the Society of Mayflower Descendants. And it is through this ancestor, William Brewster, that he and I are connected as ninth cousins, four times removed. It may not be close, but I was happy all the same when I made the discovery.

when the Wright Brothers flew their first plane, or something else along this vein. If we can't be related to the person, then we sure want to be there when they did whatever made them famous. This is another popular family story.

When a colleague got interested in genealogy, her family shared a story with her about how her great-great-grandfather knew Jesse James. You can imagine the excitement of trying to find out how he knew Jesse and if he had taken part in any of Jesse's robberies.

Some stories such as this are easier to prove or disprove than an actual relation to a celebrity. If the family story tells you the exact person who was supposedly there, it makes it easier to compare through dates. Was your ancestor even alive when the event in question took place or the historical person was alive?

When the family story is more vague, as in "someone in the family" was there, then it gets a little harder. First you must try to identify which family

MY GRANDPA MET JESSE JAMES—OR DID HE?

My Uncle Teck told a story—to anyone who would listen—about how his father (my grandfather) once encountered the outlaw Jesse James hiding some bank-robbery loot in the Cookson Hills of Oklahoma and how that money had never been found. As a child I thought that was a wonderful tale—*my grandpa met Jesse James*. For a school theme assignment, I decided to write about how grandpa came to make the acquaintance of this notorious character. However, some basic biographical research at the local library crushed my theme topic and ripped apart the family lore. There were some glaring problems with Uncle Teck's story. Jesse James died in 1882 in St. Joseph, Missouri. Grandpa was born in 1873 in Georgia. He came to Oklahoma as a young man in 1892, which was 10 years after Jesse James died. Anyone with basic math skills can figure out that in 1882 my grandpa was only nine years old—unlikely to be wandering alone in the Cookson Hills thousands of miles from his family's Georgia home. When I told my uncle about what I learned at the library, he shrugged it off with, "Well, that's what Papa told me."

—Myra Vanderpool Gormley, C.G.

member it was. Sometimes it is easier to approach this type of story from the famous individual. Getting to know the event in question and the individuals who were present will give you a foundation upon which to work.

Other family stories in this vein are the ones where your ancestor was present during some famous event, such as the maiden voyage of the *Titanic*. Perhaps your family story talks about a relative who was on the *Titanic*, or was supposed to be. Some of these stories are easy enough to verify because so much information has been published about the event. In the case of the *Titanic*, the passenger list has been published in a number of books (see Figure 1-4 on page 20. Other major events may also have a list of those who were present, including battles in wars, major disasters, and epidemics. Finding the lists may depend on what the event is and when and where it took place.

For instance, if the family story is that your ancestor was present at the Appomattox Courthouse where Lee surrendered to Grant at the end of the Civil War, you may first need to identify which military units were there and then see if any of your ancestors were in those units. A search of the Internet may reveal this information, and there are many published books about the Civil War that will get you started on the trail of identifying the units involved.

As you can see from these different scenarios, genealogists use a lot of different records and resources. We must often rely on books or articles written on historical events. As you research your family history and legends, you will find yourself looking at census records, vital records, wills,

---

TITANIC RECORDS

The *Titanic* has long fascinated people, even while it was being built. People marveled at its size and grandeur, and then were shocked when the floating palace sank. The unsinkable ship was at the bottom of the Atlantic and the cost in human life was devastating.

Even today many are still fascinated, no doubt in part because of the movie with Leonardo DiCaprio and Kate Winslet. Of course because of the interest brought about by the movie, many books were either reprinted or rushed into production to jump aboard the latest craze.

There are many books and Web sites that offer a look at what happened and what could have gone differently. Some of the sites list the passengers and indicate those who survived and those who didn't. Even the Ellis Island On-Line Web site <www.ellisislandrecords.org/> has digitized the *Titanic*'s passenger manifest as it was hastily created aboard the *Carpathia* as the ship turned back to New York to disembark the wet and mentally anguished *Titanic* survivors.

Here are a few other sites you may want to check out:

- RMS Titanic, Inc.—www.titanic-online.com

- Titanic.com—www.titanic.com

- The Titanic Historical Society, Inc.—www.titanic1.org

- Titanic—The Unsinkable Ship and Halifax—http://titanic.gov.ns.ca

military records, and more. You will see these documents used throughout the book and some of the sources mentioned in the bibliography as well.

THE SCAMS

Just as there are scams in everything else, there are some scams associated with family history—and sometimes our own family traditions feed right into them. I mention them here so that you will be wary and avoid being taken in by scammers who claim that your family connections can make you wealthy.

One popular scam involves the "lost family fortune." First, the scammer explains that someone either has usurped your family fortune or has illegally acquired valuable land owned by one of your ancestors (for example, an oil company seized land upon which oil was discovered), and that this lost treasure can be yours. All you need to do is to supply the scammer with proof of your descent from a certain individual—and pay some type of a fee. Don't be fooled. The originators of these fantasies are simply preying on the human desire for gain without pain. While it is true that there are some unclaimed inheritances out there, no legitimate agency would require

Warning

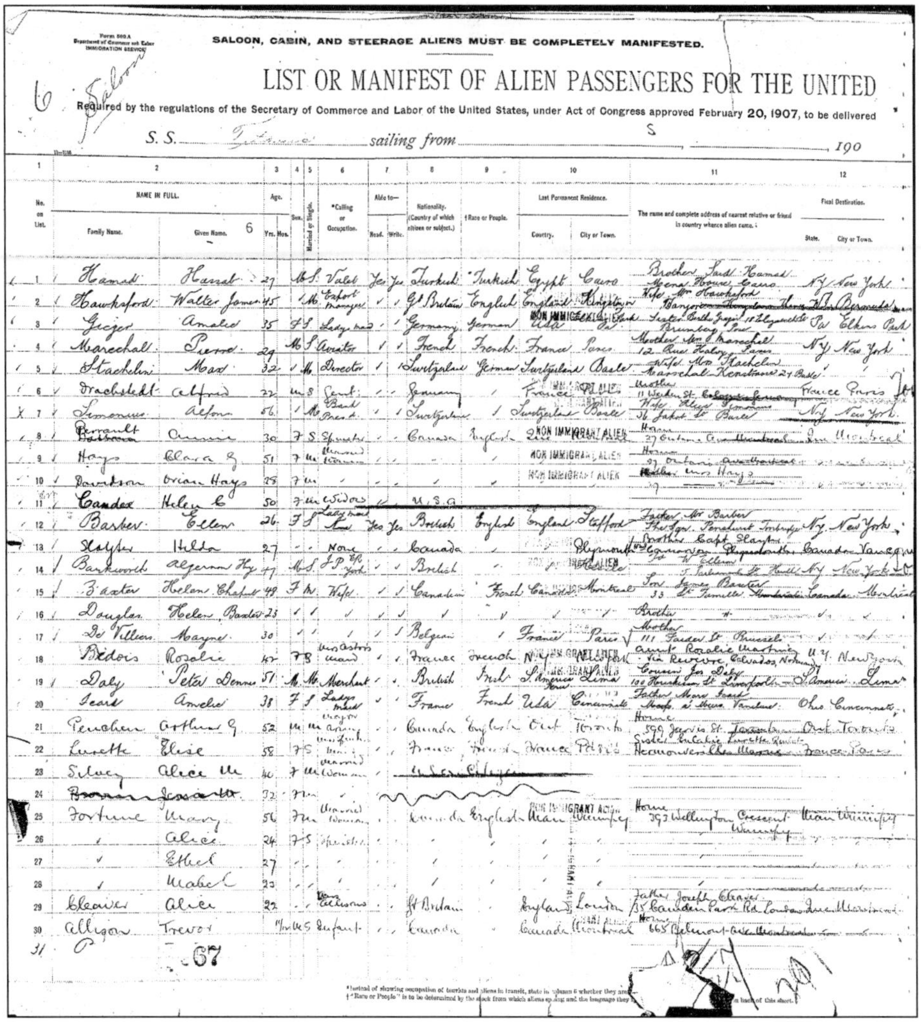
SALOON, CABIN, AND STEERAGE ALIENS MUST BE COMPLETELY MANIFESTED.

LIST OR MANIFEST OF ALIEN PASSENGERS FOR THE UNITED

Required by the regulations of the Secretary of Commerce and Labor of the United States, under Act of Congress approved February 20, 1907, to be delivered

S. S. ______ sailing from ______ 190

Figure 1-4
Passenger manifests of survivors from the *Titanic.*

an up-front fee to help you claim what is supposed to belong to you in the first place. Lawyers who help you collect on a legitimate claim will expect a portion of your inheritance as compensation for their work, but that would be a payment for services rendered; you shouldn't have to pay up front.

Another popular, but completely impossible, family legend involves descent from a Cherokee princess. The problem? The Cherokee Nation did not have any royalty; so while you may descend from a Cherokee, she couldn't have been a princess. Another Cherokee myth is that you descend from a Cherokee because you have Indian features. Because of Hollywood's concept of what Native Americans look like—which more closely resembles the distinct features of Plains Indians—many people are surprised to find the Cherokees have their own unique features.

Native American ancestry is commonly claimed in family legends, but these stories may be the least correct of all. So often researchers discover that their ancestry has no connection with any Native American tribe whatsoever. Of course, if your family claims Indian blood—or any other intri-

---

THE MEADORS OIL WELL SCAM

First a little background on the Meadors Oil Well. This story has been around for quite some time. In fact, back in 1989 I knew of another person who was trying to prove her connection to this Meadors line in the hopes of getting part of the inheritance. The confusion appears to trace to a letter dated 8 Feb. 1943 (though there is some belief that the letter was actually written in 1934) that talks about consolidating the royalty interests from Mr. James Meadors' accounts. The letter was addressed to a Mr. Wm. R. Meadors and was from Gulf Oil Corporation in Pittsburgh, Pennsylvania.

The confusion appears to be with this letter and the mention of Wm. R. Meadors. Research shows that James Meadors did not have an heir named William. And in fact, his widow and his children were alive and did receive the estate which has now been lawfully passed down to a living heir and two churches.

Many of the records for this research are found in the Dallas County, Texas, courthouse, including the deeds and affidavits showing the names of James' wife, then widow, and his children, including the married names for his daughters.

—Rhonda's Tips
Genealogy.com
9 September 1999

---

guing heritage—you will want to investigate. Just because the odds are against it does not mean that you should regard the story as false. See what you can find out. Perhaps in your case the family story is true.

IT STARTS WITH A STORY

You have now been introduced to some of the legends that are passed around in many different families. Of course, the rule of thumb with these stories is that there's usually a grain of truth mixed in with all the fiction. Your job? To sift through all the fiction until you uncover that one truth.

As I was describing these stories, I mentioned some of the things you need to do to verify them. The most important is to know your own lineage and become familiar with the history of the individual claimed as the famous relative. Clare Boothe Luce is a perfect example of this. While we saw the story of how her family supposedly changed the spelling of the Boothe surname to escape association with John Wilkes Booth, accounts of Clare's immediate family are also full of questionable information.

As I mentioned, there are times when the family will not appreciate your digging into the family history, for fear you will dig up unpleasant skeletons. In Clare's case, the family skeleton appears to be her parents' marital status.

CHEROKEE CONNECTIONS

In her book *Cherokee Connections* (Baltimore: Genealogical Pub. Co., 1998), Myra Vanderpool Gormley, CG, addresses some of the myths inherent in the research of Cherokee ancestry, real or imagined, and to the true looks of the Cherokees:

No Princesses

The Cherokees did not have royalty. So do not believe any Cherokee Princess legends. This is a term used by the English and colonial Americans, probably traceable in usage to stories pertaining to the famous daughter of a chief of the Powhatans known as Pocahontas. This inaccurate reference still appears in print in the works of historians, who ought to know better.

Tall, Athletic and Handsome

The Cherokees were a tall, athletic and handsome people. Their good looks, posture, and stamina were admired by the Europeans. Oval-headed and olive-colored, they did not have the high cheekbones and Roman noses of the Plains Indians. Both genders tattooed their faces, arms, and bodies, and wore silver arm bands, earrings, and nose ornaments. The men shaved their faces and heads, except for a small topknot. For war and ceremonies, the men also colored their faces with stripes and circles of red, black, ochre, and blue earthen pigments.

If they really did marry, no proof of that marriage has been found yet. In fact, her father was not divorced from a previous wife until Clare was ten years old; so either his marriage to Clare's mother never took place or it was an illegal marriage to begin with.

I mention Clare Boothe Luce because there are many different books about her and her second husband, Henry Luce. In many of these books, I have found misinformation about when Clare's parents married; some of the books give actual marriage and divorce dates for the couple. This type of problem is common and is not limited to published biographies; our own family stories are often full of misinformation.

DISSECTING THE STORY

If you can, get the story down on paper. It is often easier to see loopholes and problems in a story when you have it staring back at you. Take the written story and make a couple of photocopies of it. This way you will not mark up your original paper.

On one of the copies, highlight names, dates, and places that are included in the story. Next, make a timeline on another sheet of paper. Include information on your ancestor as well as that of the famous individual in question.

I know some people who divide the paper in half, listing their ancestor's events down the left side, and those of the famous individual down the right. This type of approach to analyzing the story only works when you are comparing one or two individuals to a historical event. **Creating the timeline often brings the loopholes of the story immediately to the forefront.**

UNCLE TUCK'S STORY VS. JESSE JAMES' FACTS		
Uncle Tuck's Story	Dates	Jesse James
Grandpa born in Georgia	1873	
	1882	Jesse James died in St. Joseph, Missouri
Grandpa came to Oklahoma as a young man	1892	

As you can deduce from the table above, it is highly unlikely that the family story placing Grandpa in Jesse James' gang is true. However, some stories aren't this obvious. In such cases, you may find that your ancestor was indeed living at the time of the historical person. Then it becomes necessary for you to locate your ancestor in records, determining where your ancestor was living when the event in question took place, or to see if your ancestor lived in any of the places where the historical figure lived. As you can imagine, this means determining the residences of the historical figure as well.

LET'S GET STARTED

You have been introduced to several types of family legends that are passed down from generation to generation. You may even recognize a story or two from what your family has shared over the years. Some stories have been passed down through the generations, while others seem to have appeared spontaneously. No one knows who started the tales in the latter group, or if there is any truth to them.

So how do you prove a family legend? Well, as I have mentioned before, you need to have knowledge of your own family history. If you are new to genealogical research, not to worry; the next chapter will introduce you to researching your own family history so that you can get started. The same methods you will apply in the research of your own family tree can also be applied to the research of the famous individual. Later in the book, however, you will see how historical accounts and records can both help and hinder your progress researching the famous, along with how to get around some of those obstacles.

So, let's get started.

TWO

You and Your Family Tree

Genealogy and family history involve the pursuit of a person's ancestry or lineage. While true genealogy is the researching of a blood lineage, family history often includes the research of adoptive lines and stories about the families—the broader picture, so to speak. Regardless of whether you are doing genealogical research or a family history, the search is where the fun will be found.

I liken the search for family history to the safe man's mystery. With each new record you find, you get clues in a grand mystery: the mystery of you. Each clue takes you farther along the path of the unknown. I have found that many people who are researching their family history also enjoy reading mysteries or solving puzzles; all present intriguing mental challenges. Those who like detective stories will be relieved to know, however, that no one will shoot bullets at you as you conduct your investigation into a family history mystery.

WHY DO YOU DO IT?

There are a number of reasons why people are searching their family history today. Some are researching for religious reasons. For example, members of the Church of Jesus Christ of Latter-day Saints believe that families can be together for time and all eternity. They research their family histories so that they can keep their families together forever.

Some get involved in researching their family tree because they need to answer questions about their medical history. Within the last fifteen years or so, the medical community has begun to realize the importance of knowing one's family medical history. Sometimes the birth of a child with health problems—or the potential for problems—is what sends people on this journey. People who have not yet had any such problems sometimes research their medical history just so they won't be surprised down the road.

Many people have told me that they got interested in family history because they had no connection with the past—their past. Families are now spread out like never before, moving from place to place as their jobs require—or to find employment in the first place. That pulling up of stakes can sometimes feel more like a cutting off at the roots. Families begin to feel a disconnection that somehow can't be filled just through phone calls and e-mail. For some, tracing their ancestry offers something to hold onto—a way to be sure that they still belong to a family.

I was actually introduced to genealogy twice. The first time didn't take. Of course, I was only about ten at the time. My grandmother had done the genealogy of her side of the family to join the Daughters of the American Revolution. I was aware of the fact she had to prove a family connection to get in, but wasn't interested in learning how she did it. The second time I was introduced to genealogy, I was intrigued. Admittedly I wasn't quite sure I would enjoy it, but being an analytical person, I should have known better. I was also thankful for the work my grandmother had done before. With a copy of the lineage she had compiled, I set about duplicating her research, looking in the same books and records she had used. That was my initial training. Back then there were few books on the subject; it truly was a baptism by fire.

It wasn't long before I knew I was completely hooked. Over the years, I have discovered that I love researching family trees—not just my own, but anyone's. I love picking up a trail and following it to see where it will lead. Although I continue to research my own heritage, when I research someone else's I often get the opportunity to delve into new records in places that my own ancestors have not taken me. The search stimulates something in me. I like getting a question and then deciding what records and resources will not only help me answer that question, but also will lead me on to the next generation.

Tracking a family history often requires you to examine a research question from many different angles. Each angle offers a different type of record or resource and many result in a different piece of the puzzle. Frequently, the research process uncovers different records that, when put together, reveal a whole new picture: a marriage, a death date, or the names of an ancestor's parents (and thus another generation on the family tree). Did I happen to mention I was hooked?

Once you become interested, where do you turn? How do you get started?

FAMILY HISTORY 101

Family history begins at home. It begins with you. While we soon will be talking about charts, forms, and genealogical programs, the best way to begin is to sit down and begin to write what you know about your family. It is a good idea to do this when you will not be interrupted. After all, seldom do we do our best thinking when the son's rock music is blaring from his room or when you know that you have to watch the clock in order to pick up the daughter from dance class. Pick a time when you can get lost in memories of your childhood and the family get-togethers that have taken place over the years.

Hidden Treasures

Get a notebook with some loose-leaf paper. I suggest the loose-leaf paper because it allows you to write now and organize later. Make a page for yourself and then for your parents and grandparents. Write down whatever you can remember about them, and don't forget yourself. You will also want to have some miscellaneous pages for odd memories that don't yet connect to anyone specific.

Under your name, write your birth date and birthplace. If you are married, record whom, when, and where you married. List the names and birth dates of any children. On the other pages, write as much as you can remember about your parents and grandparents. Don't worry if, when you get to your grandparents, your information is not as thorough; this is to be expected the farther back you go. I know some researchers who, when they began, didn't even know where their parents were born. Others, because of divorce or the early death of a parent, had no one to talk to and ask questions of. While they may not have had immediate family information, they still found it possible to research their family tree.

GETTING STARTED

If you want to save time and be more productive in your research, here are some books that may be of interest.

- Carmack, Sharon DeBartolo. *The Genealogy Sourcebook*. Chicago: Contemporary Books, 1997.

- Croom, Emily Anne. *The Genealogist's Companion & Sourcebook*. 2d edition. Cincinnati: Betterway Books, 2003.

- ———. *Unpuzzling Your Past: The Best-Selling Basic Guide to Genealogy*. 4th edition. Cincinnati: Betterway Books, 2001.

- Greenwood, Val D. *The Researcher's Guide to American Genealogy*. Baltimore: Genealogical Publishing Company, Inc., 2000.

- McClure, Rhonda R. *The Complete Idiot's Guide to Online Genealogy*. 2d edition. Indianapolis: Alpha Books, 2002.

- Rose, Christine and Kay Germain Ingalls. *The Complete Idiot's Guide to Genealogy*. Indianapolis: Alpha Books, 1997.

There are many other books mentioned in the bibliography at the end of the book that you will find as useful.

THE ADVENTURE BEGINS

Once you have written what you already know, you have taken the first step on this fascinating adventure. Of course, you may notice that while you are writing things down, questions come to mind. Not sure exactly when your mother was born? Well, in some instances that is because she doesn't want you to know just how old she is. (In my household, this tactic didn't work to my advantage. When my daughter was filling out her application for a passport, she almost made me five years older than I really am. Fortunately, I was there to set her straight—if not to protect my pride.)

Once you have written all you can, look at what you've got. The questions you can't answer and the blanks you can't fill are what will start you on the search—the search for records, that is. You will need documents to verify the dates and places you have written down. Start with your own birth certificate. Each record you check will not only prove something, but it should also bring you clues to individuals you don't know much about yet. With those clues will come more questions. Perhaps it is this ever expanding quest that appeals to so many family historians.

Start out by keeping your information as organized as possible. While you will begin with only a few papers, you may eventually accumulate enough material to take over the house. Make a photocopy of your birth certificate (to avoid losing your original), put the original away, and put the photocopy in a folder. Congratulations—you have taken the first step in tracing your family history.

Let's talk about organization now, because eventually you will have many photocopies and computer-generated pages. The goal of your research is to have a document or source to prove each date, place, and relationship. As you can imagine, that can easily and very quickly add up to a lot of papers. Using some organizational system from the beginning will save you a lot of headaches later.

While I have mentioned Sharon DeBartolo Carmack's book, *Organizing Your Family History Search,* as one possible resource, there is no hard and fast rule that you adhere to someone else's method. **The important thing is to come up with a system and then stick with it.** If you don't stick with the system, you soon will find that you have piles of records all over the place and you can never put your hand on the record you need. There is no need to add that type of frustration to a hobby that is supposed to be fun.

Printed Source

DON'T GET OVERWHELMED— ORGANIZE FROM THE BEGINNING

A book you may find useful is Sharon DeBartolo Carmack's *Organizing Your Family History Search* (Cincinnati: Betterway Books, 1999).

Important

A RECORDS PRIMER

Each record you get supplies you with specific information. For instance, your birth certificate tells about your birth, listing your name, your birth date, and place of birth. You knew all that, so why do you need the record? If you look at the document more closely, you will find that it tells much more. Believe it or not, your birth certificate is not all about you. (My children would be shocked to hear that.)

Your birth certificate tells you a little about your parents as well. Notice that it lists your father's name, and probably also his place of birth, and his age at the time of your birth. For your mother, it lists her maiden name, along with her place of birth and age. It may also show your father's occupa-

Figure 2-1
Birth certificate of Walt Disney's older brother Roy.

RETURN OF A BIRTH.

State of Illinois,
COOK COUNTY.

The Physician, Accoucheur or person in attendance should immediately return this Certificate, accurately filled out, to the County Clerk. Penalty, $10.00, if not so certified and returned within thirty days.

STATE BOARD OF HEALTH.

1. *Full Name of Child (if any). _Roy O. Disney_
2. Sex, _Boy_   Race or Color (if not of the white race),
3. Number of Child of this Mother, _Third_
4. Date of this Birth. _June 24th 1893_
5. †Place of Birth, No. _4_   Street _24th_   Ward.
6. Residence of Mother, " _Hermosa_   " _Illinois_   "
7.   Nationality: Place of Birth: Age of:
   a. Father, _Kennedy_   _Blue Vale_   _34_
   b. Mother, _Ohio_   _Norwalk_   _20_
8. Full Name of Mother, _Flora Disney_
9. Maiden Name of Mother, _Flora Call_
10. Full Name of Father, _Elias Disney_
11. Occupation of Father, _carpenter_
12. Name and address of other Attendants, if any,

Dated, _22nd_ _1893_   Returned by _James Bradley_   M. D.
        Residence, _Hermosa Ills_   Midwife.

* The given name of Child should be certified, if possible, when this Certificate is made, and should, in any case, be certified and registered within a year.
† City, number, street and ward; same in towns that have them; township or precinct.

Printed Source

BUT I LIVE SO FAR AWAY

Get a head start on your long-distance ancestors with Christine Crawford-Oppenheimer's *Long-Distance Genealogy* (Cincinnati: Betterway Books, 2000).

tion at the time. Most birth certificates also tell you how many children have been born to that mother, as does Figure 2-1 above.

You are probably sitting there saying to yourself that you already know all of this—and you may, since it is your birth certificate. But what about the birth of your parents or grandparents? How much do you really know about them? Beginning your genealogical research with yourself is like learning to ride a bike with training wheels. By checking records on events and people you are familiar with, you are practicing for a time when you will be searching for information on people you know precious little about.

Marriage and death records contain similar information. You will want to get copies of these records as well. Your parents may be able to give you some of them. Others you may need to request from the county courthouse or state department of health. Some vital records may be ordered online. At the very least, the Internet may be able to tell you what records are available for the locality from which you need them. We'll discuss how to use these records later on.

Decide how you want to keep track of the names you plan to research while you are still dealing with only a few of them. Fortunately, genealogists of today have the benefit of computers and the genealogy software that has been developed over the years to aid researchers in recording and publishing their information.

Those of us who began researching our family history before computers were invented (yes, there was such a time, though few of us like to admit to remembering it), recall the days when we had to create all our charts and fill out all our forms by hand. Now most researchers use one of the widely available genealogy software programs.

Family group sheets and pedigree charts are the most common forms for recording genealogical information. Figure 2-2 on page 29 is a Family Group Sheet

Supplies

Family Group Sheet of the ______ Family — Family Tree Magazine

VINCENT MINNELLI (Born- LESTER ANTHONY MINNELLI)
Full Name of Husband

VINCENT CHARLES MINNELLI
His Father

MINA LE BEAU
His Mother with Maiden Name

28 FEB 1903 CHICAGO, IL
Birth Date and Place

1945 (div. 1951)
Marriage Date and Place

25 JUL 1986 BEVERLY HILLS, CA
Death Date and Place

Burial

JUDY GARLAND (Born - FRANCES ETHEL GUMM)
Full Name of Wife

FRANCIS AVENT GUMM
Her Father

ETHEL MARIAN MILNE
Her Mother with Maiden Name

10 JUN 1922 GRAND RAPIDS, MINN.
Birth Date and Place

22 JUN 1969 LONDON, ENGLAND
Death Date and Place

Burial

Other Spouses	Marriage Date and Place
JUDY ALSO MARRIED	
1. DAVID ROSE	1. 1941
2. SIDNEY LUFT	2. 1952
3. MARK HERRON	3. 12 JUN 1964
4. MICKEY DEANS	4. 15 MAR 1969
VINCENT m2 LEE ANDERSON	m. after 1951

Children of This Marriage	Birth Date and Place	Death Date, Place and Burial	Marriage Date, Place and Spouse
LIZA MINNELLI	12 MAR 1946 LOS ANGELES, CA		m4 16 MAR 2002 to DAVID GEST

©FAMILY TREE MAGAZINE 2002

Figure 2-2
Filling out family group sheets by hand, as was this one of the family of Vincent Minnelli and Judy Garland, can be time consuming.

of the Vincent Minnelli family. While you will probably go straight to the computer for this (if you haven't already), I thought I would take a moment to talk about the printed forms.

When entering information about an individual, whether by computer or by hand on a blank form (as I have done in Figure 2-2), there are certain standards you will want to get in the habit of following. These guidelines are not intended to make family history a science; they are used so that everyone is on the same page, so to speak, when it comes to identifying individuals, whether born in this century or in the 1600s.

Of course, with computers, the recording phase of your research has been made much simpler. While you should still follow traditional guidelines

A FEW BASIC GUIDELINES FOR ENTERING GENEALOGICAL INFORMATION

Just like most hobbies, there are some guidelines when it comes to genealogy that help to eliminate potential misunderstanding or confusion when sharing your information with others or viewing it yourself at a later date.

- When recording handwritten names on either a family group sheet or a pedigree chart, you want to use mixed case for the given names and upper case for the surname. This leaves no question as to what the surname is.

- When recording a woman's name, in genealogy, you should record her maiden name. If this is not known, then the accepted format is to use the following characters [--?--] so that the name looks like: Mary [--?--].

- Dates are recorded as DD-MMM-YYYY on family group sheets and pedigree charts. This leaves no question as to what the day is and what the month is, which is not the case if you record dates as 6/6/92.

- Years are recorded using all four digits so that there is no question is 6/6/92 means 1692, 1892, or 1992.

- When recording place names, begin with the smallest jurisdiction to the largest jurisdiction: town, county or shire, state or province, country.

- It is best not to abbreviate any part of the place name. Not all researchers will be familiar with the common abbreviations of a postal system, especially if they live in another country.

when recording names, dates, and places, the computer at least saves you some time.

Internet Source

A LOOK AT VITAL RECORDS INFORMATION YOU CAN FIND ONLINE

VitalRec.com <www.vitalrec.com> and VitalChek.com <www.vitalchek.com> are useful sites for learning what's available when you need vital records.

FAMILY TREES, COMPUTER STYLE

There are many different genealogy programs available on the market today. The burning question asked by those interested in purchasing one is: *Which one is the best?* The answer that I always give stresses that the best genealogy program is the one that does what you want. When you are beginning though, you may not have an idea of what you want to do other than keep track of the individuals you are finding.

I have included a list of some of the more popular genealogy software packages along with addresses and Web site information. Some of them offer a free or trial version. If you are just beginning, trying one of these is a good way to get a feel for genealogy software without having to invest any money. If you are new to family history, you may not have any idea what to look for in a program. Even if you have been researching for a while, it isn't until you begin using a program that you begin to have some

GENEALOGY DATABASE SOFTWARE			
Name	**Contact Information**	**Web Site Address**	**Operating System**
Ancestral Quest	Incline Software, LC P.O. Box 95543 South Jordan, UT 84095-0543 (800) 825-8864	www.ancquest.com	Windows 3.1, Windows 95 or higher
Brother's Keeper	Brother's Keeper 6907 Childsdale Avenue Rockford, MI 49341 Fax (616) 866-3345	http://ourworld.compu serve.com/homepages/ Brothers_Keeper/	Windows 3.1, Windows 95 or higher
Cumberland Family Tree	Cumberland Family Software 385 Idaho Springs Road Clarksville, TN 37043	www.cf-software.com	Windows 95 or higher
Family Matters	MatterWare 3522 Sandy Ridge Trail Deland, FL 32724 (386) 736-8030	http://hometown.aol.com/ matterware/index.html	Windows 3.1, Windows 95 or higher
Family Origins	FormalSoft P.O. Box 495 Springville, UT 84663 (866) 467-6687	www.formalsoft.com	Windows 95 or higher
Family Tree Maker	Genealogy.com 39500 Stevenson Place Suite 204 Fremont, CA 94539-3103	www.familytreemaker.com	Windows 95 or higher
Legacy	Millennia Corporation P.O. Box 1800 Duvall, WA 98019 (425) 788-3774	www.legacyfamilytree.com	Windows 95 or higher
Personal Ancestral File	The Church of Jesus Christ of Latter-day Saints	www.familysearch.org	Windows 95 or higher
RootsMagic	FormalSoft P.O. Box 495 Springville, UT 84663 (866) 467-6687	www.rootsmagic.com	Windows 95 or higher
The Master Genealogist	Wholly Genes, Inc. 5144 Flowertuft Court Columbia, MD 21044 (877) 864-3264	www.whollygenes.com	Windows 3.x, Windows 95, 98, and Windows NT

ideas of what you want, and those ideas usually come to you when the program you are using doesn't do something the way you think it should.

The genealogy software offers a way to enter the names of individuals and link them together in family units. For most programs, you enter the names of a father, a mother, and then their children; for others, you enter the individual's name first and then the names of the parents. Once these names are linked through the genealogy program, you can print out a number of different reports and tree charts, including the two standard forms used the most

Notes

Figure 2-3
Genealogy software, such as RootsMagic, allows you to create many different reports, including a standard pedigree chart.

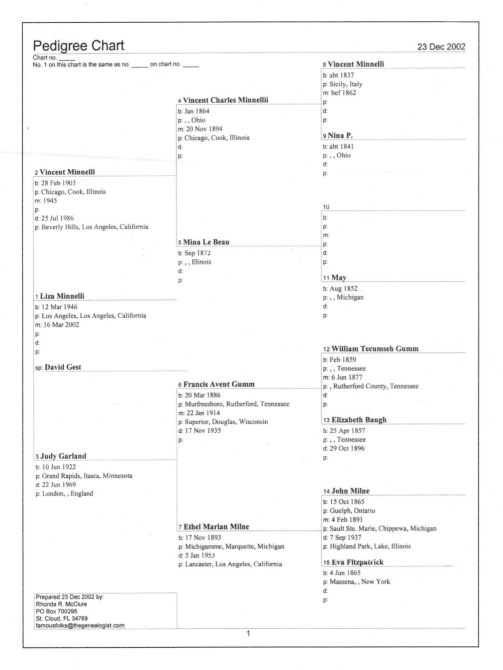

Pedigree Chart   23 Dec 2002

Chart no. _____
No. 1 on this chart is the same as no. _____ on chart no. _____

8 Vincent Minnelli
b: abt 1837
p: Sicily, Italy
m: bef 1862
p:
d:
p:

4 Vincent Charles Minnellii
b: Jan 1864
p: , , Ohio
m: 20 Nov 1894
p: Chicago, Cook, Illinois
d:
p:

9 Nina P.
b: abt 1841
p: , , Ohio
d:
p:

2 Vincent Minnelli
b: 28 Feb 1903
p: Chicago, Cook, Illinois
m: 1945
p:
d: 25 Jul 1986
p: Beverly Hills, Los Angeles, California

10
b:
p:
m:
p:
d:
p:

5 Mina Le Beau
b: Sep 1872
p: , , Illinois
d:
p:

11 May
b: Aug 1852
p: , , Michigan
d:
p:

1 Liza Minnelli
b: 12 Mar 1946
p: Los Angeles, Los Angeles, California
m: 16 Mar 2002
p:
d:
p:

sp: **David Gest**

12 William Tecumseh Gumm
b: Feb 1859
p: , , Tennessee
m: 6 Jun 1877
p: , Rutherford County, Tennessee
d:
p:

6 Francis Avent Gumm
b: 20 Mar 1886
p: Murfreesboro, Rutherford, Tennessee
m: 22 Jan 1914
p: Superior, Douglas, Wisconsin
d: 17 Nov 1935
p:

13 Elizabeth Baugh
b: 25 Apr 1857
p: , , Tennessee
d: 29 Oct 1896
p:

3 Judy Garland
b: 10 Jun 1922
p: Grand Rapids, Itasca, Minnesota
d: 22 Jun 1969
p: London, , England

14 John Milne
b: 15 Oct 1865
p: Guelph, Ontario
m: 4 Feb 1891
p: Sault Ste. Marie, Chippewa, Michigan
d: 7 Sep 1937
p: Highland Park, Lake, Illinois

7 Ethel Marian Milne
b: 17 Nov 1893
p: Michigamme, Marquette, Michigan
d: 5 Jan 1953
p: Lancaster, Los Angeles, California

15 Eva Fitzpatrick
b: 4 Jun 1865
p: Massena, , New York
d:
p:

Prepared 23 Dec 2002 by:
Rhonda R. McClure
PO Box 700295
St. Cloud, FL 34769
famousfolks@thegenealogist.com

1

by genealogists: the family group sheet and the pedigree chart. Figure 2-3 above is a pedigree chart of Vincent Minnelli and Judy Garland.

It is much easier to record all that information in a computer file than in a handwritten chart, especially if you later discover that your original information is incorrect. In the computer, you can make individual corrections and then simply reprint the entire form as needed, whereas a form you've filled in by hand may need to be completely recopied. If you choose to use handwritten forms, fill them in with pencil rather than ink, so that should you discover alternate or conflicting information later, you can simply erase the erroneous data and add the correction.

Although I still use blank forms occasionally—usually when I am somewhere that does not allow me to take my notebook computer—most of the time I enter the information I find directly into my genealogy program. I do this for two reasons. First, it helps me avoid unnecessary duplication. When using standard forms, I find I must recopy a lot of information as I fill out pedigree charts and family groups sheets, but the computer will automatically transfer information from one type of form to another. Second, I make it a habit to cite my sources as I enter the information. Sources may include birth certificates, marriage records, tombstones, letters, e-mail messages, or Web sites. Citing sources at the time you enter the information will save many headaches later on, especially if you are relying on secondary sources—perhaps something you found in a book or on the Internet—rather than on primary documents. In Figure 2-4 on page 34, I document immediately where I found Roy O. Disney's birth certificate.

KNOW WHERE YOU'RE GOING BY KNOWING WHERE YOU'VE BEEN

Many beginning genealogists often do not keep track of where they are getting the information they are recording. By not citing a source, a genealogist runs the risk, when faced with conflicting data, of not being able to evaluate which one is the more reliable. The genealogist is also likely to repeat past research because she doesn't remember that a particular source or record has already been searched.

It is a good idea to cite a source as thoroughly as possible so that others using the research later will be able to return to the records used to see if they also agree with the conclusions. There are two useful books that will supply examples of all possible sources that a genealogist might use.

- Croom, Emily Anne. *The Sleuth Book for Genealogists: Strategies for More Successful Family History Research.* Cincinnati: Betterway Publishing, 2000.

- Mills, Elizabeth Shown. *Evidence! Citation & Analysis for the Family Historian.* Baltimore: Genealogical Publishing Company, Inc., 2000.

MOVING WITH THE SPEED OF THE INTERNET

Genealogists have flocked to the Internet like ducks to water. I find it amazing that those who spend so much time looking into the past have welcomed the future with open arms—at least when it comes to researching their family trees.

While the Internet is really not new, having been used by the military and universities for years before the rest of the world discovered it, it has become one of the major tools on which genealogists rely. Every night genealogists can be found sitting at their computers in search of other researchers or information about their families.

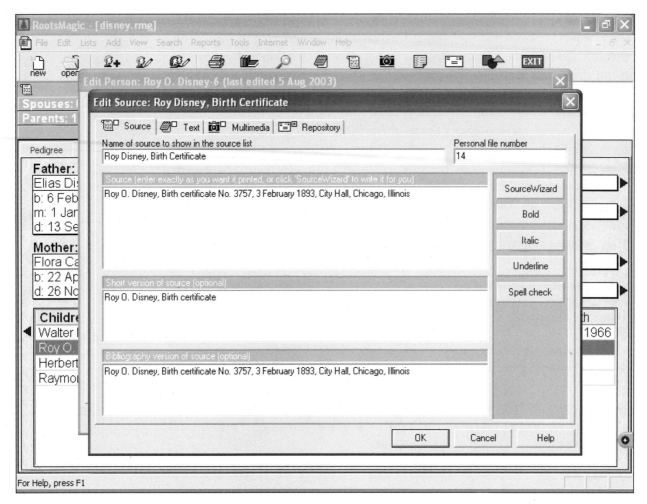

Figure 2-4
Source citations are important. They remind you where you found a particular date or information about a certain event.

Internet Source

Once you have gone back a couple of generations, you too will want to surf the Internet for more information about your ancestors. Genealogical searches on the Internet will probably be most successful if you look for people who lived during the first part of the twentieth century or earlier. Data on later generations is limited due to privacy issues as well as a lack of records that are allowed to be abstracted or transcribed.

The Internet offers many resources, from digitized records and compiled family histories to indexes and other databases. Finding members of your family listed in such records depends on at least two things. First and most important is how much you already know about the individuals for whom you are looking. For instance, if you are looking for a *John Stanley* but you know nothing other than his name, it will be difficult to ascertain whether you have found the right person as you begin to search for him in various databases of compiled pedigrees. If, however, you know John Stanley's birth date and spouse's name, then you can easily determine if there is previous research available on him. When you are searching for a common name, the more

COMPILED PEDIGREE DATABASES	
Ancestral File	www.familysearch.org
Ancestry's World Tree	www.ancestry.com/trees/awt/main.htm
Pedigree Resource File	www.familysearch.org
World Family Tree	www.genealogy.com
WorldConnect	http://searches.rootsweb.com
Some of these compiled pedigree databases require that you pay a subscription fee or buy CD-ROMs, while others are available free of charge.	

details you can provide, the better. The second factor is the availability of previous research. For whatever reason, some localities and eras have been more heavily researched than others. People investigating those areas or periods will have better luck than someone researching an obscure and previously ignored county or year.

RESEARCHER BEWARE

Let me take a moment to talk about the Internet as a resource. I am the first to admit that much of what I do, especially when it comes to celebrity research, is possible because of the Internet. Unlike the library or county courthouse, the Internet is always open and is available to me regardless of how I am dressed or what I plan to do there. The Internet offers information about so many different subjects that I can search for historical as well as contemporary information. The Internet, however, is not the only research tool I use, nor should it be the only one you use.

For every good, accurate piece of information you find through the Internet, you will, unfortunately, find two or more inaccurate pieces of information. The family histories published on the Internet are not always verified using good genealogical research practices. Sometimes this is due to the inexperience of those sharing the information, who are just so excited to find what they think is their family tree, that they turn around and share it on their Web site before they have bothered to check it out in original records such as birth records, wills, and censuses. Other times errors result from mistaken assumptions that people make when working with records. Occasionally, it is sad to say, errors occur when people intentionally post misinformation in order to track how their data is used by others.

I often use the Internet to jump-start my research. I look in the compiled pedigree databases to see if anyone has already researched the line I am about to begin work on. If I find a line, then I print that line out, and begin the real research. I turn to library catalogs at some of the repositories I use most often (and which I will discuss later) to see what resources I can access that might prove, or in some cases disprove, the information shared by the other researcher.

For More Info

WORLD'S COLLIDE

For a look at how to incorporate both the computer and traditional research into your hobby, see my book *The Genealogist's Computer Companion* (Cincinnati: Betterway Books, 2001).

Warning

With the recent push to make digitized records available through online subscription services, I have been able to do some of my preliminary records searching online before making any trips to libraries. Digitized records offer me the chance to view the record as though I had gone to a library and put a roll of microfilm on the reader. For all intents and purposes, either method is just like looking at the original record. The growing availability of online digitized records is just one of the advantages the Internet offers genealogists.

MINING THE FAMILY FOR FAMILY HISTORY GOLD

While the Internet and records repositories are important resources to utilize when researching your family tree, don't overlook your own family resources. By all means, venture onto the Internet and write away to county clerks for birth and marriage certificates, but also write, phone, or visit your own relatives. I believe you will be surprised by the information they may be able to supply you with. I will warn you, though, that if word gets out that you have taken up the family history challenge, you may suddenly begin to get packages from the family full of records and pictures.

When I first got involved in my own family history research, I asked my grandmother for a copy of the lineage she had compiled when I was much younger. I know she was thrilled to think that someone else in the family would be continuing the search. After she passed away, and my grandfather began to go through everything in the house, I began to get boxes in the mail. You guessed it: they were full of pictures, letters, diaries, documents, and more. To this day I am thankful for this bounty, as I doubt I could have had such a fine collection of family photographs without his sending them to me, and I shudder to think what might have happened to them all if he hadn't sent them. Of course, it has taken years for my postman to speak to me again.

Some of the documents that my grandfather shared saved me from having to write away for them. He had marriage certificates and birth certificates. There were obituaries from newspapers and deeds for cemetery plots. He even took the time to identify as many people as possible in the photos he sent.

I will say that not all family members will react to your news about searching for the family history with the same amount of enthusiasm. In fact, some may try to dissuade you, especially if there is a skeleton or two hanging around on the family tree. Tread softly with these relatives. See if they will at least answer some questions for you. If you ask them what they remember about events rather than asking pointed questions like, "What is Aunt Pearl's birth date?" they may be more willing to share stories with you, and from the stories you can begin to glean the facts you need. Just like the family stories that you read about earlier, these remembrances will contain both fact and fiction—but even fictionalized stories are better than nothing at all.

When writing to relatives who are more receptive, include some family group sheets. Ask if they can fill in any of the blanks for their immediate family or other generations, and if all the dates and places you have included are correct. I often send a pedigree chart showing the recipient as Person

Definitions

ABSTRACT VS. TRANSCRIBE

Abstract means you summarize the important details of the document. Transcribe means to record word-for-word the entire document, including any typos, grammatical errors, or other spelling errors.

One as well. I know someone who intentionally alters the recipient's age before sending a pedigree chart to a relative, which almost guarantees a response—especially if the recipient is a woman. Fortunately, I haven't had to resort to this extreme when corresponding with relatives.

KEEPING TRACK OF WHO YOU CONTACT

It is a good idea to keep a log of whom you have contacted through e-mail, a bulletin board, or more traditional methods such as regular mail. This allows you to know if you are still waiting on a cousin or repository, such as a court-house, to respond to you with either answers to questions or documents you requested. A good log should include enough information so that you can easily identify what you may still be waiting for, such as

- Name of individual or repository
- Address of individual or repository
- Date letter or other correspondence sent or posted electronically
- Brief description of information requested
- Indication if money was sent
- Date follow-up sent
- Response received
- Whether or not the response was helpful

Sometimes you will find you get more information with the personal touch: a visit with the individual. This is often true of the elderly. Some are not comfortable using e-mail, or have a hard time hearing over the phone. Arthritis may make it difficult for them to fill out forms. But when you ask them to tell you about their growing up years, or where they were when Kennedy was shot, the flood gates open and you find you have more information than you know what to do with.

Oral History

A number of books listed in the bibliography suggest questions for you to ask your relatives. Consider using a tape recorder as you interview them, but be sure to get their permission first. I know some people who now use video cameras to record their older relatives. This is certainly an option, if you can get permission from the person you are interviewing and you can get them to forget about the camera and concentrate on the stories you hope they will share.

JUST THE FACTS, MA'AM

While talking with your relatives, you may be tempted to ask for just the facts. Genealogists, while delving into a past that has sometimes not been touched for centuries, are some of the most impatient people I know. We want it all and we want it right now! I can say that, because I know I am in that category. As a result, we sometimes rush past the stories to get the names, dates, and places. But really, family history is much more—the stories of your older relatives are a glimpse into a time that no longer exists.

You may be inclined to stop a rambling story because you feel it has gotten too far off the path of where you wanted it to go. However, if you pay attention to the story and stop worrying about your personal agenda, usually you will find that you get a lot more than you hoped for.

As your family member shares their story, try not to get too caught up in writing down the facts. This is difficult, especially when you are not allowed to use a tape recorder, because you undoubtedly will fear missing something important. However, in your zeal to get it all written down, you may appear uninterested in the story itself and your relative may clam up. Smile and nod in agreement or commiserate as the story is shared. This lets your relative know you are paying attention and have feelings of your own about what they are sharing.

Remember that it is easier for people to remember events and how they felt at that time than it is for them to recall specific facts. Rather than putting relatives on the spot as though they are being interrogated by asking them to tell you when Uncle Dino was born and where, ask them about a birthday party or a family reunion. Casually slip in a question asking how old Uncle Dino was when he was at the reunion. You will be surprised how many times you will get the information you were seeking all along.

Sometimes I find it is interesting just to hear what life was like for my older relatives. My children are sometimes surprised when they hear about growing up without personal computers in our homes. They marvel that we had only three channels on the television. I find it fascinating to read stories of those who emigrated to this country and came through Ellis Island. I am amazed at how people set up new communities in the wilderness. If we don't talk to those who still remember what life was like for past generations and somehow record their stories, that information soon will be lost.

ONWARD ON THE TRAIL

As I have already mentioned, your family history research may reveal a less-than-savory character. Your reaction to the discovery of such an ancestor will depend on what the individual did and how many generations separate you from him or her.

The good news about these colorful characters is that they often generate lots of records. While they may have tried to avoid the census taker as well as the law, the law probably caught up with them eventually, and the proceedings are probably well documented. You may find more information about a rogue relation than you could have imagined.

THREE

Finding the Unexpected: Skeletons in the Closet

Most of our ancestors were far from perfect. Perhaps we look back to the past through rose-colored glasses and even have a psychological need to believe our ancestors were perfect, or nearly so. Or, are we somewhat like children, placing them on pedestals in the same way we do celebrities or the sports heroes of our youth? Some of us continue to revere those people on pedestals even though we are no longer young. No one likes to think less of a person, and likewise, no one likes to think less of an ancestor.

The lives our ancestors led were sometimes as difficult, if not more so, than the lives we lead today. We have many modern conveniences and labor-saving devices, but we also have a lot of stress. Our ancestors had different types of problems, but their lives were not without stress and the crises that truly test all mankind. Think of our ancestors who were farmers. They were at the mercy of Mother Nature, and were often on the brink of ruin—just one rainstorm, drought, or insect invasion away from a failed crop. I cannot imagine working so hard for the entire planting season, only to watch it all taken away by what must surely have felt like a cruel joke played by Mother Nature.

Of course, for all of the hard working farmers you find, you are also likely to discover a black sheep, skeleton, or scoundrel lurking back there in the past. Even on illustrious family trees one can find a few less-than-perfect progenitors. Some researchers accept their black sheep more readily than others, just as some families more readily accept their living black sheep. Some researchers delight in uncovering their ancestors, taking pride in those who worked hard and appear to have accomplished what they wanted to in life. By the same token, those same researchers take a little wicked delight in knowing that their past holds a colorful character or two to spice things up. Much depends, of course, on the black sheep's offense. Some sins of the past, such as having a child out of wedlock or being accused of witchcraft, no longer have the moral stigma they once did. Others now carry a stigma that didn't exist when our ancestors were alive, sometimes tarnishing the finish of an otherwise respectable, hard-working ancestor. (Slaveholding immediately comes to mind here.)

Warning

39

How you or your family react to the uncovering of a skeleton will depend on how close in time and kinship you are to that black sheep and just what he or she did. Discovering that your third great-grandparents had their first child a little early will probably not affect you as much as, say, finding out that your parents had their first child a little early—especially if you were that first child. Regardless of how much time has elapsed, some family members may never accept a skeleton graciously, so you may have to accept the idea that there are certain aspects of your research you won't be able to share with them. More about what to do with the skeletons after you have uncovered them is addressed in chapter eleven.

While the family stories may have alluded to someone who is simply not talked about, or you have heard whispering about Aunt Rhody or Great-grandpa Jesse, more often than not your skeleton will just pop out of the closet unexpectedly. Even if they have no legends or suppositions on which to found their fears, some family members may be concerned that your genealogical research will uncover the worst: a skeleton. As a result of their fears, they may not be thrilled with your newfound hobby and might even try to discourage you from digging around in the past. Other relatives may have more reason to fear. They may have grown up hearing about the black sheep, or may even have been present when the crime was committed. To them it is better that the offender stay in the shadows, hopefully to be forgotten. Indeed, I know of some families in which those "in the know" supplied totally false, misleading information to the researcher, in the hope that the skeleton would never see the light of day.

Regardless of which scenario, it is not unusual to get little or no help from the family when it comes to identifying black sheep in advance—unless, of course, he or she entitles the family to wear a badge of distinction. Many families might consider it an honor to be descended from an accused witch of Salem, Massachusetts, or from a man who rode with the outlaw folk hero Jesse James. For whatever reason, some skeletons are no longer considered shameful, while others may forever be relegated to a dark closet because the family refuses to acknowledge them.

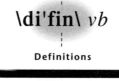

\di'fin\ vb

Definitions

BLACK SHEEP

A *black sheep* is an individual in the family who has done something illegal or scandalous thus "blackening" the good name of the family.

ANCESTORS WERE HUMAN, TOO

History cannot be altered. It can be forgotten (and as some will say, then repeated), but whether you seek it out or ignore it, you cannot change it. There are those who would like to see history rewritten. There are those who set out to tear down idols by ignoring the good in them and pointing out the bad. In truth, all of us are mixtures of both bad and good, and we all make decisions based on our own unique situations.

There is an episode in the original *Star Trek* series in which the transporter malfunctions while beaming Captain Kirk back aboard the *Enterprise*. Unbeknownst to the crew, the captain has been split into two people: one with all of his good qualities—honesty, integrity, compassion, and love—and the other with all of his bad qualities—anger, hate, and a need to fight and kill.

THOMAS JEFFERSON AND SALLY HEMINGS

Thomas Jefferson, best known as the third U.S. President and the writer of the Declaration of Independence, has once again found his personal life a matter of public discussion. In 1802 allegations were published in the newspaper in Richmond, Virginia, that he was the father of the children of one of his slaves, a Sally Hemings. Later on in history, this rumor was dismissed as a plot to ruin his reputation. Now two hundred years later, modern medical technology has once again put his personal life into the public eye. DNA testing done in the late 1990s seems to support his relationship with Sally Hemings and the subsequent birth of her children. While the DNA testing has only identified descendants of son Eston Hemings, one of the sons of Sally, as sharing the Jefferson DNA, the genealogical research and subsequent articles that have been published, such as Helen F.M. Leary's "Sally Heming's Children: A Genealogical Analysis of the Evidence" (*National Genealogical Society Quarterly*, 89, September, 2001, 166-207), show that it is believed that all of Sally's children were fathered by Thomas. The controversy continues to rage as supporters and detractors of various theories continue to try to find proof to support their side.

The episode goes on to demonstrate that separately, neither half functions as well as the whole. While Kirk's story is obviously a fictional one, real people sometimes experience similar personality splits. There are times when one of our sides seems to get the upper hand; and unfortunately, there are instances when a person's evil side wins out and the person becomes a pariah.

Most people, however, are able to keep the two halves together and keep them talking. In this regard, our ancestors were much like us. They had good days and bad days. They made good decisions, and—just as we do today—they made a few bad ones. The problem that often arises when we consider the lives of our ancestors is that we tend to apply our modern way of thinking to their eighteenth-century decisions. I suspect that our forebears would be as appalled to have to claim some of us as descendants as we are to claim them as ancestors. One of my colleagues often jokes about sawing off an offending limb of cousins; no doubt some of our ancestors have been sharpening their saws for some time now.

BUTCHER, BAKER, LAWYER, POLITICIAN

For every upstanding lawyer or politician one finds on a family tree, I suspect you can find an equal number of people who elected to take the easy road. In the movie, *The Hunt for Red October*, there is a line by an advisor to the U.S. President. He describes himself as a politician and qualifies that by saying "when I'm not kissing babies, I'm stealing their lollipops." That line has stayed with me for years now. While it is his way of saying that he keeps his options open, I have often felt that it was a classic description of so many of today's politicians. I suspect it applies equally well to many politicians of the past. And yet, how many families have encouraged their children to enter politics? At what point does a politician go from being victor to villain? When do we begin to consider them as potential skeletons? For some families, all too soon, but for others—perhaps because of the number of years that separate us from them and our lack of understanding of what they did or didn't do while in office—we continue to claim them proudly on the family tree.

Sometimes the good things that made the politician famous and ensured his place in history can color our entire attitude toward him, even if in their daily lives they were doing things that our less notable ancestors are being condemned for. Take Edward Rutledge, for instance.

Edward Rutledge was a member of the Second Continental Congress— yes, the body responsible for the Declaration of Independence of the United States of America. Rutledge was a delegate from the state of South Carolina and is known today as the youngest signer of the Declaration (he was 26). He was also a slave owner. However, unlike many run-of-the-mill slave owners (who we will discuss later), Rutledge remains on a patriot's pedestal. In fact, it is said that actress Goldie Hawn, whose father's family has long claimed descent from Edward, gave her son the middle name of Rutledge because she is so proud of the relationship. Of course, as I showed in chapter one, Goldie is not a descendant. At the best it might be that she and Edward were cousins, though current research has not found any link between the two Rutledge lines.

SLAVE OWNERS

Whether you are Anglo-Saxon or African American, it is possible that your research in the United States will lead you to a slave owner, often for different reasons, though there are some slave owners who were themselves African American. Slave owners were a product of their time, and while we are today uncomfortable or dismayed, these ancestors exist and must be dealt with on the family tree. It is because of some of the actions of the white slave owners that we now find black and white descendants, though in some cases neither side of the family is willing to accept it.

Why is it then that if the average candlestick maker owned slaves we think less of him, but Edward Rutledge's slave owning is overlooked? It's all in perception. Dig deep enough into anyone's life and I suspect you will find a scandal or two. Some aren't nearly as horrendous in today's eyes as they were at the time, but others are no longer acceptable. Our ancestors who followed the customs of their time are condemned to be seen as less human because we, their descendants, apply today's morality to their time.

GUESS WHO I FOUND ON THE FAMILY TREE?

Some family skeletons are so sensational that even the most upright members won't be able to resist claiming a connection with the rascals. These are the thrilling ones—and the ones about whom you can probably find a wealth of information. Later on we will look at some of those black sheep who are not nearly as glamorous, but are part of our heritage nonetheless.

A Witch, a Witch! Burn Her!

Many people with roots in early New England may uncover a witch or two in their ancestry, but those with a connection to anyone accused in the famous Salem witch trials of 1692 are somehow looked upon as special. The discovery of a witch on the family tree doesn't upset most people today, but that is probably because we recognize that so many accusations of the early colonial period were the result of ignorance and misunderstanding on the part of the accusers, not because the accused were truly evil. One has to wonder about Salem in 1692, and why twenty-one people would lose their lives: nineteen executed by hanging, one dying in prison, and the other being pressed to death for neither confessing to nor denying the accusation. There are many other incidents of people having been hanged or burned at the stake (as was common in Europe) for witchcraft, and yet the Salem witch trials of 1692 are probably the best-known among American genealogists. Having New England ancestry, I have been intrigued by these witches for years and have always been excited to discover another accused witch or accuser on my family tree. (In Andover, where my witches hail from, both witch and accuser might be in the same family.)

PRESSED TO DEATH

Poor Giles Corey refused to answer one way or the other if he was a witch when he was accused in Salem, Massachusetts, in 1692. One has to wonder if he had seen the trend—deny, you die, admit, you live—and couldn't bring himself to lie and say he was a witch. Instead he chose to say nothing at all. As a result, in an effort to force him to answer the question he was laid out with a large board placed on top of him and those present began to add rocks to the board. Eventually the load became so heavy that Giles' body was crushed under the weight of it, and he was killed, though he never did answer their question.

One has to wonder at the lack of common sense that was rampant in Salem Village at this time. Reviewing the history of the event, you soon discover that the accused could be saved simply by admitting to being a witch. If they denied the accusation, they were hanged. Poor Rebecca Nurse considered excommunication from the church for witchcraft to be a punishment worse than death; she was hanged because she was too honest to "confess." On the flip side, Tituba, the slave, admitted to being a witch and survived. Giles Corey perhaps thought he had a handle on the situation by choosing to say neither yes nor no, but that strategy didn't work out too well for him, as explained in "Pressed to Death" on page 43.

ACCUSER JUST AS BLACK A SHEEP?

I often joke when talking about my family history that I have traced the families to include seven accused witches. I do not really see them as black sheep and marvel at those that managed to survive until the hysteria had passed. I also admit to being an "equal opportunity" descendant in that I can trace my family to almost an equal number of accusers as well. Most of my witches were from Andover—they borrowed the girls from Salem to root out the evil in Andover— but in Andover the accusers were often part of the same family as those they were accusing. I suspect that made for interesting family gatherings when the trials were over and the accused survived.

A well-known and often repeated story that came out of the Salem witch trials is that of the threat or oath issued by Sarah Good to the Reverend Noyes at her hanging. When he tried to get her to confess, she responded, "I am no more a witch than you are a wizard, and if you take away my life God will give you blood to drink." That is exactly what happened to the good Reverend Noyes. Twenty-five years later, despite having tried to make restitution to the families he hurt during the great delusion, Noyes died bleeding from his mouth, the result of an internal hemorrhage. It was probably just as well that Sarah Good had already been hanged, or the people of Massachusetts might have been even more convinced that she was a witch— and who knows what that might have sparked.

He's a Thief

Few people would expect many records to exist or be available for research on the history of a thief. This is a major misconception. While digging around in some convict dockets—records that detail the admission of criminals to a prison—I discovered that larceny was one of the more common offenses. While I am sure that some of those who were arrested were stealing for the sake of stealing, I suspect that many of them were forced to steal because they were hungry, or because they were trying to get something to sell in order to provide for their families. For the latter, theft probably was a last resort. But even if you find a "convict" with questionable motives in your ancestry, you need not feel ashamed. Australians, for instance, are so proud of their criminal origins that they have established a lineage society; anyone wishing to join must first prove descent from one of the convicts who first colonized the continent.

Of course, if you're not Australian, it may not be as easy to stomach the idea of a thief hanging on your family tree—unless, perhaps, he was riding with the James boys, or the Sundance Kid, or the Wild Bunch, or another

CAROLE'S CURSE

Carole Lombard, actress in her own right and love of Clark Gable's life, was born Jane Alice Peters, 6 October 1908 in Fort Wayne, Indiana. While born in the Midwest, she has a connection to Salem. Her seventh great-grand uncle was none other than the Reverend Nicholas Noyes—the man who appears to have been cursed by Sarah Good at the time of Good's hanging.

© *ZUMA Movie Stills*

CONVICT SHIPS

After America had won its independence, England had to find somewhere else to ship its convicts—as it had used the American colonies as a sort of punishment. Enter Australia. The first convict ship arrived in 26 January 1788 under Captain Arthur Phillip, who landed at New South Wales. Of the 1,000 people aboard ship, 717 were convicts. They were all to establish a new colony. While England had sent convicts to America, it had never set about creating a colony that would serve as the jail. Convict ships would continue to travel to Australia until the mid-1800s.

Unlike most people, present-day Australians often take great pride in connecting their lineage to one of these early convicts. There are lineage societies based on these first arrivals, with the applicant having to show a direct descent from an accepted convict, most of them subsets of the major genealogical societies in Australia.

A BLACK SHEEP, WHITENED

Let's say that your great-great-uncle Remus Starr, a fellow lacking in character, was hanged for horse stealing and train robbery in Montana in 1889. A cousin has supplied you with the only known photograph of Remus, showing him standing on the gallows. On the back of the picture are the words:

> Remus Starr: Horse thief, sent to Montana Territorial Prison, 1885. Escaped 1887, robbed the Montana flyer six times. Caught by Pinkerton Detectives, convicted and hanged, 1889.

Pretty grim situation, right? But let's revise things a bit. We simply crop the picture, scan in an enlargement and edit it with image processing software so that all that is seen is a head shot. Next, we write the text:

> Remus Starr was a famous cowboy in the Montana Territory. His business empire grew to include acquisition of valuable equestrian assets and intimate dealings with the Montana railroad. Beginning in 1885, he devoted several years of his life to service at a government facility, finally taking leave to resume his dealings with the railroad. In 1887, he was a key player in a vital investigation run by the renowned Pinkerton Detective Agency. In 1889, Uncle Remus passed away during an important civic function held in his honor when the platform upon which he was standing collapsed.

—Anonymous

notorious outlaw band. Some famous gangs have become glamorous folk heroes, their actual dastardly deeds having been buried in legend with the passing of time.

I can't help but wonder about the term *gang*. In the time of the Wild West, it might have described a bunch of swarthy men traveling on horseback with six-shooters. Today it connotes a group of vicious individuals who deal in drugs and think nothing of shooting at someone. What was it about those earlier gangs that makes them attractive to us, while we regard members of today's gangs as hoodlums? I doubt that you would want to tell the world that your son or cousin is in a street gang, but many people who have found a tie to Al Capone or a mafia family—some of the biggest gangs out there—seem thrilled by the connection.

When did being bad become romantic? Just as women tend to faint over the actors with the darkest reputations, a lot of people go gaga over their reprobate relatives. No wonder we get confused when it comes to deciding how to handle skeletons in a family history. The same person who is ashamed to acknowledge a relationship to someone who was briefly incarcerated for stealing to put food on his family's table may love to brag about a connection to a ruthless gunfighter.

When you stop to think about it, there shouldn't be anything attractive about hoodlums who robbed and killed, and yet we are drawn, like moths to a flame, to these colorful characters of the past. Perhaps because we've read so many exciting, fictionalized tales about figures like the gunmen of the Old West and the early mafia families, we have become desensitized to what they really did. If we were to read an account of the crimes committed by Jesse James, but without his famous name attached, we probably would find it repulsive. Moreover, it is likely that we would rather identify with the victim than with the perpetrator. Instead of trying to claim a connection with a common criminal, we might try to push that skeleton back into the closet. When the gunslinger is famous, however, we tend to make excuses for him as we proudly proclaim that we're related. It is interesting to consider what this tells us about human behavior.

Murderers

When a robbery goes bad, the robber may end up killing someone, but there are many other instances of individuals killing just to kill or crimes of passion, as in Figure 3-1 below. While I was researching the ancestry of the Bordens of Massachusetts, it wasn't long before I was hot on the trail of Lizzie Borden—yes, the one who supposedly killed her father and stepmother by whacking them with an axe.

To this day, people still question whether she did it (including me). Of course, Lizzie is just one of many murder suspects who have become famous. Many more were executed into obscurity, leaving little behind to help us understand why they did what they did. Unless we find a record offering some insight, we may forever wonder.

> **FROM THE MOUTHS OF BABES . . .**
>
> Lizzie Borden took an axe
> And gave her mother forty whacks.
> And when she saw what she had done,
> She gave her father forty-one.

> Robert Hall -
> He was an Actor. and killed Lillian Rivers his mistress, in a fit of jealousy.
>
> **You never know where you will find birth names of actors and actresses.**
>
> No. 27   Date, May 8 - 1888.
> Name, Robert G. Hall.
> Age, 35 Years. Weight, 145 Lbs. Color, White
> Time,
> Murder of Sophia E. Smith alias Lillian E. Rivers
> Sheriff, Krumbhaar

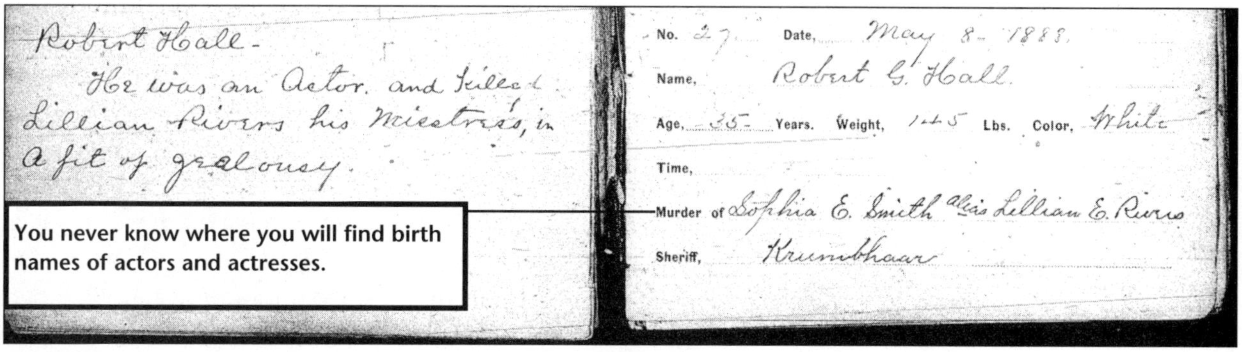

Figure 3-1
Entry in execution book from Philadelphia County, Pennsylvania. (FHL #975748, item 3.)

In the mid-1990s, many of us were glued to our television sets as we watched the murder trial of O.J. Simpson, who was accused of murdering his ex-wife and her boyfriend. Lizzie Borden was very much the O.J. Simpson of her day (see Figure 3-2 on page 48). A look at *The New York Times* and local Fall River papers for late 1892 will tell you that Lizzie couldn't even roll over in bed without someone reporting it. And while the journalists were relentless in their coverage of the investigation and the trial, the towns-

Figure 3-2
Arrest of Lizzie Borden as reported in *The New York Times*, 12 August 1892.

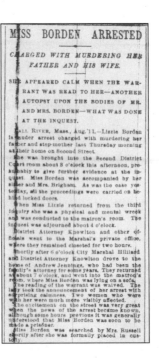

For More Info

A FASCINATION WITH LIZZIE BORDEN

If you find you can't get enough of the Lizzie Borden story, you may want to visit the Lizzie Borden Bed & Breakfast Museum site <www.lizzie-borden.com>. This is a museum that allows you to not only touch the artifacts, but sleep on them.

people of Fall River kept waiting for a time when Fall River and Lizzie Borden would no longer be synonymous.

Even now, more than a hundred years after that terrible event, some inhabitants of Fall River would like to forget the incident, but it refuses to die. If you really are interested, you can not only visit the house in which the murders took place, but you can also stay in it, as it is now a bed-and-breakfast. Libraries are full of books on the subject. Since Lizzie was acquitted, there are many theories about whether she did it, and if so, why; and if not, then who really did.

While Lizzie never had any children, making it impossible to descend from her, it is still possible to claim her as a cousin. Perhaps because her trial and subsequent acquittal attracted enough attention to make her famous, Lizzie has become an acceptable murderer to have on the family tree.

If I stumbled upon a murderer in my ancestry, I would respond by trying to uncover as much as I could about that individual and the circumstances of the crime. I would probably look for a way to justify the action, both in my own mind as well as in the history I was setting down for posterity. Perhaps my ancestor lived on the western frontier, when things were rough and tough and guns were a way of life, and shooting sometimes was necessary for self-preservation. We may never discover what motivated our ancestors, or we may decide that their motives were less than pure; but we should always remember that even if we cannot excuse what they did, *we* are not responsible for their actions. Our ancestors made the choices they did based on their own situations. We don't have to condone their behavior, but we don't have to feel marked by it either.

LIZZIE'S LINEAGE

Lizzie Borden's lineage traces back to the early established—Gary Boyd Roberts calls them the "founding families"—of Portsmouth, Rhode Island. That means the potential to have Lizzie as a cousin increases dramatically. Among those identified as cousins of hers are Sir Winston Churchill, Jennie Jerome (known better as Lady Randolph Churchill), Tennessee Williams, Canadian Prime Minister Sir Robert Laird Borden, Lana Turner, and Willie Nelson.

Child Murderers

Encountering someone on the family tree who murdered an adult is difficult enough, but uncovering someone who murdered a child can be particularly shocking. I suspect that few family members would be willing to look for a good side to such a story. In the case of, say, a woman who has killed her own child, you probably will discover that the family wants to hear absolutely nothing about it, and certainly doesn't want you to talk about it. I have seen family histories published two hundred years or more after the event that refuse to acknowledge such a crime.

Recently, we have seen a rash of stories reported in the news about mothers killing their children. Everyone is shocked and outraged. If tarring and feathering were still allowed, I suspect that a few of these women would be covered in both. But is our gut reaction to these cases more justifiable than Salem's response to its alleged witches? Often, we are too quick to judge someone before we know all the facts. What amazes me is that we in the twenty-first century purport to have an enlightened consciousness, yet just as the residents of Salem Village hanged first and asked questions later, we too can be guilty of rushing to judgment in some circumstances.

While it may seem that the murder of children has become more common in recent years, in reality we just hear more about a few horrible incidences, thanks to television and other modern media. I have found, however, that child murder is not new in this generation, as evidenced by Figure 3-3 on page 50. It is sad, but true, that our ancestors did not always enjoy good mental health; moreover, they lacked the medicines and the understanding of psychiatry that we have today. Unfortunately, it is possible that while searching through newspapers of the past, you may uncover an article revealing that someone in your family or community killed one or more of her children.

Even though horror is a natural reaction to such a discovery, we should try to have some compassion for the woman. How misunderstood must she have been? Although supposedly the more sheltered segment of soci-

Figure 3-3
Newspapers are a great source of information.
© 2000–2002 MyFamily .com, Inc. Screen shot from Ancestry.com. Used with permission.

Figure 3-3
Newspapers are a great source of information.
© 2000–2002 MyFamily .com, Inc. Screen shot from Ancestry.com. Used with permission.

ety, women of the past were seldom given an opportunity to voice their thoughts and concerns, and therefore they often had no outlet for their anxieties. Not everyone takes to motherhood as easily as some, and the physical and emotional stress of child rearing can become overwhelming. Even today, with what doctors now recognize as the "baby blues" and more serious forms of postpartum depression, women are often misdiagnosed—or are simply too ashamed to seek treatment in the first place.

Traitors and Assassins

This is an interesting group of black sheep. A traitor can be considered a criminal or a hero, depending on whose side he is on. The heroes of the American Revolution are perfect examples. If those fighting for American independence had not succeeded, they would have been tried as traitors to the English crown, and some of our ancestors would have been hanged.

SPIES FROM THE PAST

Liza Minnelli, actress and singer in her own right, is the daughter of director Vincent Minnelli and actress Judy Garland. Through her mother's lineage, Liza has an English spy from the American Revolution. Her fifth great-grandfather was Peter Fitzpatrick, a spy for the British during the war. He was captured in September 1781 and held prisoner for two years in Albany, New York. After his release, he eventually settled in Canada and in 1786 submitted a claim to the English government for his service during the War.

The same can be said of spies. Those who spy for the good of their country are considered heroes; but even though their actions may be no different, those who spy for another country or for the enemy are condemned as traitors. Our estimation of a traitorous individual depends upon our perception of the nobility of the cause for which he or she fought.

The American Civil War brought this out all too clearly—the war that pitted brother against brother. Many of us will find we have connections to both sides. So who becomes the hero and who is the traitor? Does the fact that the Union won force the Confederates into the role of traitors? I find that with my own research, I feel sadness at the huge losses my families on both sides endured in lives, lands, and livelihood.

In his biography *Henry and Clare, An Intimate Portrait of the Luces*, Ralph G. Martin attributes a story to Clare Boothe Luce as to the spelling of her maiden name and how the "e" was added to the surname to separate her lineage from that of John Wilkes Booth after he assassinated President Lincoln. It makes for a good story, though there has not been any indication to date that Clare's family is related to John's family, but apparently the name was enough to make it an embarrassment to the family.

\di'fin\ *vb*

Definitions

SPELLING VARIATIONS

Spelling doesn't always count. *Idem sonans* is the legal term that applies to names which are in essence the same, though there may be slight spelling variations.

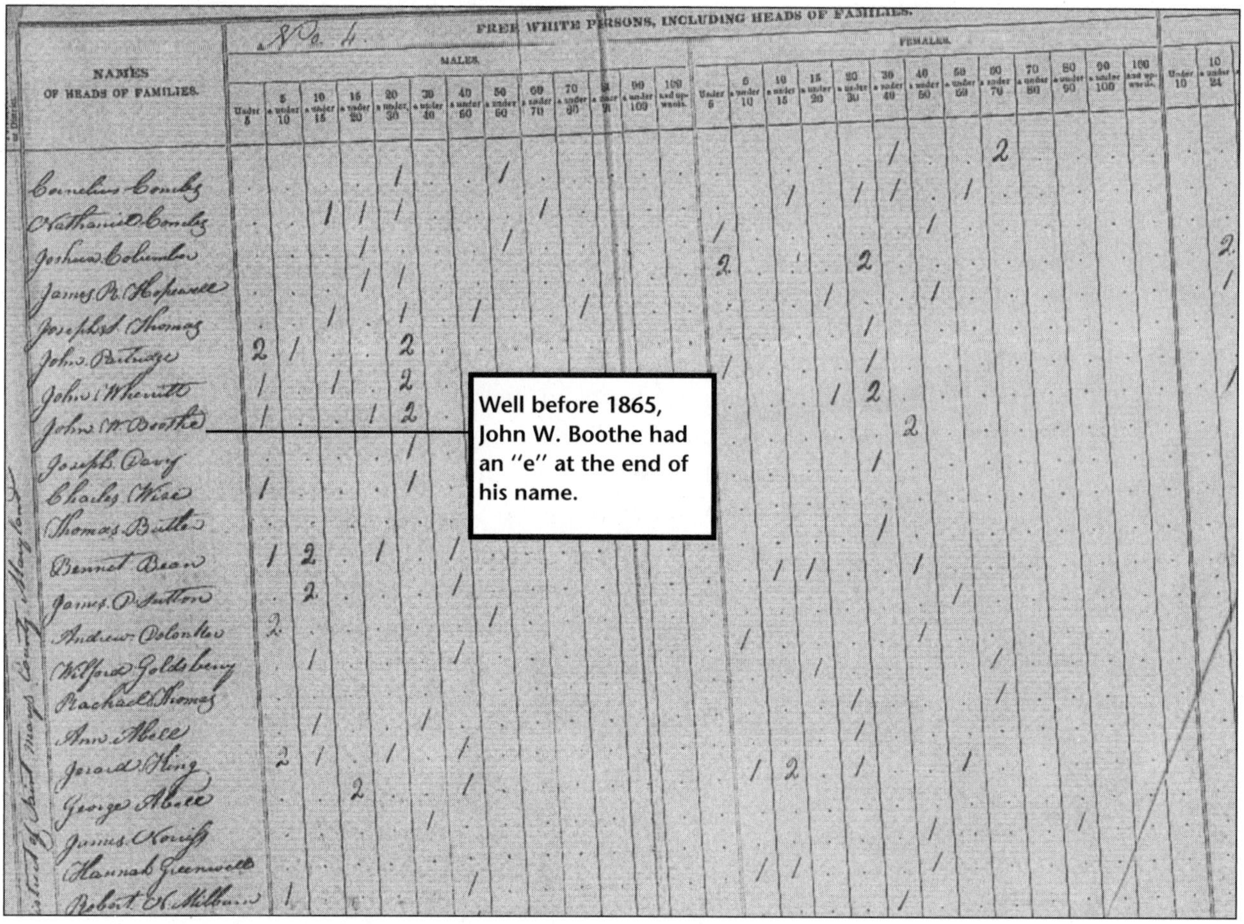

> Well before 1865, John W. Boothe had an "e" at the end of his name.

Figure 3-4

Enumeration of John W. Boothe. (1840 Census, St. Mary's County, Maryland, M704, roll 170, page 140.)

Although it makes a good story, Clare Boothe Luce's assertion doesn't hold up. As I researched the family, it became clear that the spelling of Booth was not suddenly altered after 1865, but was often spelled with the "e" as far back as the 1840s, proven by Figure 3-4 on page 51. Variations in the spelling of a surname were very common in the past, and thus cannot legally be used to prove a relationship—or to disprove one, either.

If your ancestor was a spy for the winning side, it is likely that your family has shared the story, and it may provide you with clues to research. Unless your ancestor's case became famous, your search may require a great deal of diligence. Information about espionage operations might be buried in military files. Searching through these and other sources might bring you a fuller understanding of the circumstances and your ancestor's involvement. Too often we see just one side of the story, as it is shown to us by the author or biographer. Historians may extol or condemn as they feel appropriate, based on the evidence they have found; but unless their research has been thorough, their interpretations may not necessarily reflect the whole truth. Likewise, if we cease searching records before verifying the information just because we like what we have already found, we may be guilty of misrepresenting historical facts. A good researcher won't stop searching as long as there are still records to check, regardless of how those records may affect the researcher's conclusions.

Was She Really a Landlady or a Dressmaker?

Females who had to support themselves in earlier times were often forced to turn to prostitution. By and large, society prevented women from obtaining the kind of education that would allow them to hold jobs outside of the home. Census records show that the woman of the house often was illiterate, and that while the boys in some homes attended school, girls of the same age did not. There was little that an uneducated woman could do to support her family should her husband die; of course, she could look for another husband, but that wasn't always an option. Sometimes girls turned to prostitution to support themselves after running away to escape an unhappy home life. The discovery of a prostitute on the family tree can be unsettling, especially if we suspect that the cruelty of other ancestors might have forced the girl to leave home. Such a revelation can stir up emotions that perhaps we haven't had to deal with before. In order to come to terms with our feelings toward an ancestor with an ignoble profession, we must remember that that person probably didn't have the same options that are available today (see Figure 3-5 on page 53).

NOT NEARLY AS GLAMOROUS

Up to this point we have looked at some of the more glamorous skeletons that you might find hiding in the family tree. I must admit that when my research uncovers any reprobate relations, I tend to get a little excited. I

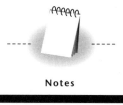

Figure 3-5
Bessie Earp, "sporting" woman in Wichita. (1875 State Census, Sedgewick County, Kansas, FHL #570217.)

know there will be a lot more recorded about the people involved in a scandal than about a nice, quiet, law-abiding farmer, and it is through the records that I find clues to more of my heritage. Of course, as we have discussed before, most of our ancestors were just simple, hard-working folks trying to carve out lives in what was often a hostile and unforgiving environment. Through it all our ancestors were making decisions, for which later generations have sometimes judged them harshly.

I have already mentioned slaveholding—a common occupation of the past that carries one of the greatest stigmas today. To discover that you have a slave owner on your family tree causes many people to examine their own feelings and prejudices. To be honest, I was thrilled and relieved when I determined that the maternal side of my family came mostly from New England, because then I wouldn't have to deal with the slavery problem. My father's side, however, has surprised me at many points along the research trail, and as I saw families from that line begin to head south, I knew it was probably just a matter of time before I had to come to terms with slaveholding forebears. I did indeed uncover some slave owners on my family tree, which was disappointing; but I have to remind myself that there is

Notes

IT ISN'T ALL ILLEGAL

Prostitution isn't illegal everywhere. In Nevada, each county individually decides whether or not to allow legalized prostitution, and all but two counties have elected to do so.

nothing I can do about it. Slavery is wrong—many people even in the 1700s felt this way—but it was a fact of life for many southern families. By the time of the Civil War, the economy of the South was so tied to slavery that many people truly believed they would not be able to keep their farms and plantations without it. Generations grew up thinking of slavery not just as a necessary evil, but as a normal part of life. I may find more slave owners on my family tree before I am finished, but I should not be embarrassed by them. Perhaps I can try to find some indication that my ancestors were kind to their slaves. Of course, you know what they say: *be careful what you wish for*. It is always possible that my research will determine the opposite. I think I will deal with that one when it comes up.

IF THESE WALLS COULD TALK

Some of the less sensational skeletons you might find in your family's closet are those mundane problems that arise in many homes between a husband and wife. Today, walls do talk; we hear their chatter on a number of talk shows devoted to the most dysfunctional of families, who apparently take pride in their dysfunction. In the past such talk was hushed up, or remained behind closed doors. Today there are still some subjects that carry with them a taboo—they simply aren't talked about even if you know what is going on. And if the subject does come up, you may not get the whole story.

Reminder

First let me say that you may not find many records on some domestic issues. Perhaps you are lucky enough to possess a diary kept by some family member who alluded to a domestic problem, thinking the diary would never see the light of day. More often than not, however, you will have to pick up clues from things like the marital status column in the census or on the death record. For me, the first clue to my great-grandparents' divorce should have been my grandmother's wedding invitation, which listed her older brother and his wife rather than her parents as those who were proud to announce the impending wedding. But then so often, we see only what we want to see.

Divorce, Adultery, and Domestic Violence

In today's society we have no-fault divorce. Legally speaking, it's no one's fault when a couple just doesn't get along and wants to end their marriage. In the past, however, divorce generally wasn't that easy. Usually someone had to point the finger at the other party and show that there was an extenuating circumstance, as in Figure 3-6 on page 56. By far the most common reasons given for requesting a divorce were adultery and domestic abuse. In each case, if you can find the divorce records, you may discover just how bad the abuse was, or with whom the defendant committed the adultery.

Today divorce is nothing. It happens all the time, but in the past that was not always the case. It was an embarrassment to the family if someone got divorced. Being a widow was much more acceptable. I wonder sometimes how many young widows in the census were actually divorced. Even if you

FROM COMMITMENT TO DIVORCE

It is impossible to live in the state of Florida and not know who Henry M. Flagler was. There is a county named after him. Numerous streets and schools bear his name, as does a college. Take a visit to Saint Augustine, Florida, and hop aboard one of the tourism trolleys, and you will learn a lot about Henry Flagler, including how he managed to divorce his second wife.

There is some question about whether Henry's second wife Ida Alice Shourds, eighteen years his junior, really needed to be institutionalized. While various biographies written about Henry discuss how on the day she was committed in New York she had been raving about the fact she was going to marry the Russian Tsar, there are some that believe Henry had her committed for other reasons, such as the possibility he was unhappy in his marriage. If he committed her so he could divorce and marry again, he had to wait for some time, as the laws in Florida at the time would not permit him to divorce her. While she was committed on 23 March 1897, Florida did not pass a law declaring incurable insanity as grounds for divorce until 1901. There are those who believe he was involved in getting this law passed, and it appears he wasted no time after the law was passed, as he married again on 24 Aug. 1901, at the age of seventy-one, to his third wife, the lovely and young Mary Lily Kenan, who was a North Carolina belle and all of thirty-four years old.

don't suspect a divorce, it wouldn't hurt to go through the court records discussed in the next chapter for whatever county you are researching in. Better to rule out all the records than to be wondering if there was something you missed in the courthouse or library.

You never know when your skeleton will appear. Imagine searching through deed books for various land records showing your ancestors either buying or selling land, and instead coming across a document that starts out: "I Resolved Chace of Dartmouth in the County of Bristol, Mariner of lawful age testify & say. . . ." This is not the normal wording of a deed record. Further reading of the document shows that Resolved Chace (yes, a man) is testifying that one John F. Stebing committed adultery, and that Stebing subsequently contracted a venereal disease. Further on in the document you learn that this entry has been made at the request of Julia Ann Stebing, "to be Preserved in Perpetual Remembrance of the Thing." I guess she wasn't too happy with her husband's extracurricular activities. Of course, when the researcher began her search that morning in the Family History Library, she never expected to find a document like that—although I suspect she was happy to be descended from Resolved Chace rather than from John F. Stebing. (See Figure 3-7 on page 57).

While adultery is certainly colorful, it is embarrassing and therefore seldom discussed. Domestic violence is more than embarrassing. I know that

Figure 3-6
Divorce records often supplied intimate details about what was happening at home. (New Haven County, Connecticut, FHL #1672890.)

To the Sheriff of the County of New Haven ~~or Middlesex; the~~
deputy ~~of either~~, or either constable of the town of New
Haven ~~or Middletown~~, in said respective counties- GREETING:

By authority of the State of Connecticut you are hereby
commanded to summon and notify Gurdon J. Fox, of the town
of New Haven, in said New Haven County, to appear before
the Superior Court to be holden at New Haven, within and
for the County of New Haven on the first Tuesday of February 1894, then and there to answer to Louma A. Fox, of said
town of New Haven, in a civil action wherein the plaintiff
complains and says:

1. On August 8, 1889, the plaintiff and defendant went
through the form of a marriage ceremony performed by Rev.
Herbert M. Denslow of Grace Church, New Haven.

2. At the time of said supposed marriage and for a long
period previous thereto, the defendant had been subject to
fits of insanity, all of which were unknown, at the time of
said supposed marriage, to the plaintiff.

3. Immediately after said supposed marriage, the defendant became violently insane and within a short time
was removed by the authorities of the town of New Haven
to the Connecticut Hospital for the Insane, at Middletown,
where he has been ever since, and now is, confined, and
is incurably insane.

4. The plaintiff and defendant never lived together after said supposed marriage except for a period of less than
a week, on account of the insanity of the defendant. And
the plaintiff has never received any support from the defendant since said supposed marriage.

I feel bad when I find that someone has had to sue for divorce on those grounds, perhaps because so often it was the women who were being abused. I am saddened to think of the many women who were not strong enough to sue for divorce, concerned that they would lose their children. Unless you find a divorce record, you may never find any other indication of domestic abuse in the family. Today, kids go on talk shows and describe their unhappy home lives as a form of therapy, but in the past this topic was one of the biggest taboos out there. Women just didn't admit to being abused—and given the fashions of the day, it was possible for a woman's entire body to be black and blue without anyone being the wiser.

Suicide and Abortion: The Silent Deaths

Ranking high on the list of subjects that aren't talked about is suicide. The strange thing is that while the family may choose not to talk about it, the

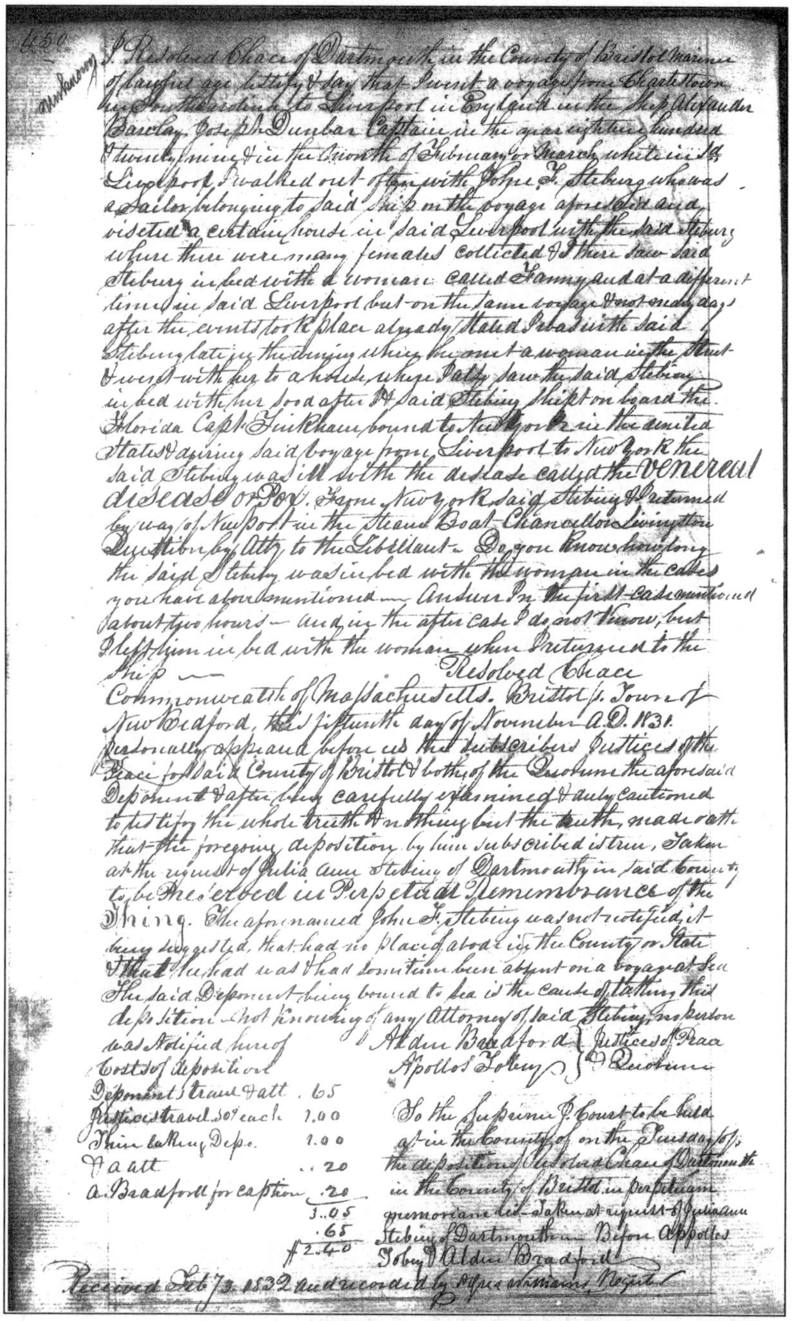

Figure 3-7
The testimony of Resolved Chace was a surprise entry in this deed book in Bristol County, Massachusetts. (FHL #572452.)

suicide is often mentioned in the newspaper and, of course, on the death certificate. This is another of those surprises you may find in historical records. Everyone dies eventually, and most deaths are recorded, so finding a death record is expected; what is not usually expected is finding that your ancestor did not die of natural causes. Suicide is hard to take. Even seeing that your ancestor was murdered is usually easier to handle, because, after all, your ancestor was the victim. When people hear *suicide*, they think the person was nuts. When the family hears the word *suicide*, they want to keep it quiet.

Of course, when documenting an ancestor who killed himself, all you need to do is to record the death date and place. If the suicide took place a long time ago, you can decide whether or not to include that information. If it was a more recent death, it is possible that family members are feeling a little tender about the issue, so you may want to omit this information before publishing your research to avoid inflicting more pain.

A close second to suicide on the list of sensitive family history issues is abortion. Even though abortion is legal today, it is seldom something that folks talk about. It is a controversial subject to say the least. Everyone has an opinion on the right and wrong of abortion. In the early 1900s, when the procedure was illegal, abortions were done in secret, usually at great risk to the woman having the abortion. Even in the 1800s it was illegal in some places, though there are a few records you can find, usually in the county court (see Figure 3-8 below).

Figure 3-8
Abortion wasn't legal in 1887, at least not in Kanawha County, West Virginia. (FHL #0249711.)

![Circuit court record reading: 1887-3 Circuit Court Kanawha Co State vs Finnegan, Samuel Felony - Abortion Indictment, 3 Bills of Exceptions, 3 Summons. Guilty]

ADOPTION ASSISTANCE

For a guide to researching in adoption situations, you may want to read Deborah L. Martin's *An Annotated Guide to Adoption Research* (Washington, D.C.: Child Welfare League of America, 1999).

Did You Know You Were Adopted?

Adoption is another of those taboo subjects of the past. The fact that most adopted children were illegitimate is what made this a sensitive subject. Today many single women are raising children on their own. We frequently hear stories of teenage girls giving birth and keeping the child, but in the past, this was unheard of. Often, the pregnant girl was sent to a special home for unwed mothers, where she would stay until the birth of the baby. Afterward, she would return home. Everyone knew what had happened but no one talked about it.

Many children in generations past grew up without a clue that they were adopted. This was the case with one of my friends. I remember her telling me that she never felt like she truly belonged in the family she grew up in. This was not to say that the family was mean to her or that she was treated differently from the other children; what she meant was that she didn't feel a real connection with them.

ABORTION IN THE NINETEENTH CENTURY

Abortion is a touchy subject for most. It is hardly a new subject, as evidenced by this article from GenealogyMagazine.com, and used with permission.

Abortion in the Nineteenth Century

By James Pylant

Several years ago, having been hired to continue the work of a late family genealogist, we came upon an usually candid biographical note. The late family historian wrote of an aunt, who in 1894, "went into the local hospital for nurses training after high school & promptly got pregnant. Had abortion at home."

By this young woman's generation, such homemade remedies were not uncommonly known. Although illegal, methods for inducing abortion were found in home medical guides as early as 1810. Dr. Thomas P. Lowry estimates that by 1870, there was one abortion for every five live births. This was a significant increase from the 1840s, when there was one abortion for every thirty live births.[1]

Historians believe that mid-eighteenth century Southerners had a more conservative attitude on the subject than that of Northerners. In Philadelphia, for instance, an abortion was somewhat easily available for about $100.[2]

Notes

1. Thomas P. Lowry, M.D., *The Story the Soldiers Wouldn't Tell: Sex in the Civil War* (Mechanicsburg, Pennsylvania: Stackpole Books, 1994), 95-97.

2. Catherine Clinton, *The Plantation Mistress: Woman's World in the Old South* (New York: Pantheon Books, 1982), 291.

For more information about the history of abortion, see:

*   Keller, Allan. *Scandalous Lady: The Life and Times of Madame Restell: New York's Most Notorious Abortionist.* New York: Atheneum, 1981.

*   Mohr, James C. *Abortion in America: The Origins and Evolution of National Policy, 1800–1900.* New York: Oxford University Press on Demand, 1978.

*   Reagan, Leslie J. *When Abortion Was a Crime: Women, Medicine, and Law in the United States, 1867–1973.* Berkeley: University of California Press, 1998.

It wasn't until she found out that she was adopted that the pieces began to fit. After researching her biological family, she eventually got the opportunity to meet some of them. She said that there was just something there that told her this was her family.

Most states have laws that involve sealing the records of adoptees. In such cases, an amended birth certificate is substituted for the original. The

See Also

problem for researchers is that you usually can't tell whether a certificate is original or amended, so it is sometimes difficult to know whether a person has been adopted—especially if the family doesn't talk about it. Some states have begun to revise their adoption laws, as more adoptees and birth mothers fight for the right to get together. **Chapter seven includes a list of good Web sites for adoption help and information, as there are quite a few celebrities who have been adopted.**

DON'T LET THAT STOP YOU

No one has a perfect family. As you begin to research your family history you will find that the majority of your ancestors were just hard-working, good people who got up each day, went to work, came home and spent time with the family, and then did it all over again the next day. The skeletons are few and many family "secrets" may not be considered taboo anymore. I think you will know what might upset the rest of the family as you conduct your research, so in chapter eleven we'll talk about how to deal with those secrets and skeletons and what to do with the family member who really may not appreciate what you are finding.

As you will see in the next chapter, while others are scrounging to find their respectable ancestors in traditional records, you may have good luck locating references to your black sheep in documents most people never think of searching. These records not only contain details of the crime or event in question, but may also include a great deal of information about the individuals involved.

FOUR

Locating Black Sheep

W henever I find even the hint of a skeleton, I like to pursue the trail, partly out of curiosity to see what the scandal was, and if we would today consider it to be so terrible. I have also found that I can learn a lot about the individual and sometimes the family as well. Since skeletons often have the most paperwork, I think they make the best ancestors or collateral relatives. Our upstanding hardworking ancestors put their shoulders to the wheel and just worked hard all their lives, leaving very little proof of their existence in the form of records. On the other hand, skeletons are often written up in any number of different records, some extolling their activities, others reporting what happened to them.

Genealogists spend a great deal of time digging in vital records, census records, probate records, land records, and many other published resources. Of these records, few indicate if the individual was a scoundrel. Vital records are designed to record the birth, marriage, or death of an individual. They do not include information about other activities. Probate records are designed to disperse an estate, though if the county in question doesn't have a separate guardianship court, you may also find commitment papers or guardianship requests included with these records as well. Again, the purpose of the record is to show estate dispersement and does not include information about the occupations of the family members, though you can often find indication of where a person was living at the time of the probating of the estate. Census records and published resources can hold more clues, as does Figure 4-1 on page 62. There are also many additional records that may have more information about just what your ancestor did and what happened to him or her.

\di'fin\ *vb*

Definitions

COLLATERAL RELATIVE

A *collateral relative* is a person you are related to but from whom you do not directly descend. Basically, any cousin, aunt, or uncle would be a collateral relative. Every sibling of your direct line ancestor is a collateral relative, as are those who descend from the siblings.

A VARIETY OF RECORDS

Genealogists like to stay with the tried and true. This is understandable. We are comfortable with the records we know, and we're familiar with what

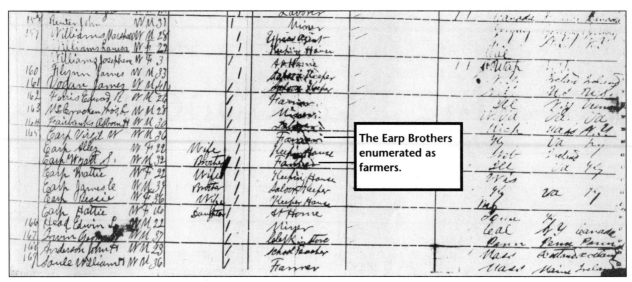

The Earp Brothers enumerated as farmers.

Figure 4-1
Virgil and Wyatt Earp as farmers? According to the 1880 census they were. (1880 Federal Census, Pina Co., Arizona, Tombstone, T9, roll 36, page 163C.)

Research Tip

they will tell us. We also know how to access them or request them. **When searching for a skeleton, however, it becomes necessary to branch out to a variety of different records, some specific to those who have gone outside the law.** Others should be on our list of regular stops in all of our research, but perhaps they haven't been familiar resources up to this point.

Let's first look at some of the records you are familiar with but may not have thought about when searching for your "black sheep." Then, we will look at those records that are unique to someone who has had a run-in with the local law. And remember, just because your ancestor was on the other side of the law does not always make him a "black sheep." After all, those who fought in the American Revolution for the American colonies were actually traitors to the English crown. Had things gone differently, they would have been labeled as such instead of as heroes.

FAMILY HISTORIES

We frequently use a published family history as a resource. After all, why re-create the wheel if you do not need to? Though it is always best when possible to verify information found in any published source with original documents, having found the information in a published family history at least gives you a road map to follow when starting out.

Family histories are a wonderful resource because you can find many generations of a family or lineage in one source. The better family histories, such as the award-winning two-volume *The New England Descendants of the Immigrant Ralph Farnum of Rochester, Kent County, England and Ipswich, Massachusetts* by Russell C. Farnham, CG, (Portsmouth: Peter Randall Publishing, 1999), offer not only detailed family history but exceptional source citations, allowing other researchers to follow the trail, find the original records, and make their own interpretations of those records.

I mention this book specifically because the Farnum family was heavily involved in the witchcraft hysteria that took hold in Massachusetts, specifically around Salem Village, in 1692. In his research, the author had a choice. He could have glossed over the entire affair, as the Farnum family was heavily involved in accusing individuals of witchcraft. Instead, he chose to include the information in great detail. As a result, readers of the Farnum family history know exactly what happened to the Farnums and those they accused. There is even some information about the relationships among these families before the accusations began to fly in 1692, giving the researcher possible motives for the accusations.

Of course, when it comes to published family histories, such a wealth of detail isn't always the case. **Sometimes the individual is listed with the simplest of information—name, dates of birth and death, and marriage if appropriate—without any reference to any shameful or unforgiving acts in which the individual was involved.** Researchers may meticulously go through a family history and never even know the family is hiding something about one of those included. Using history can be helpful in such instances. Someone dying in Massachusetts in 1692, for instance, would be a flag for research into the witchcraft records of the time.

Warning

MISSING MISSTEPS

If you come across a child in a family history, and it says something about "letting the mantle of charity cover her history," then you have a pretty good idea that she did something she wasn't supposed to. You may find that the individual is referred to as "flamboyant" or that he was a "free spirit." Any time you find someone mentioned and it doesn't really tell you anything specific, it is a good indication that there is more to that person than has been recorded in the family history.

Other times knowing the general history of the region, state, or county may shed light on the family's past. There were certain places in which gunslingers, for instance, were known to gravitate toward. Finding that your ancestor died in such a place may indicate that further research in the records of the area, especially those intended to report news or other goings-on, is warranted.

While a family history is intended to record the information discovered on a family, they do not always include *everything* about a family, especially if there are "black sheep." Do not assume that your family is boring because you have not found anything to the contrary in a family history. I have found that most families have a couple of colorful characters.

COUNTY HISTORIES

County histories are another published resource that genealogists use, though not always as efficiently as possible. Unfortunately, many of those published in the late 1800s, often referred to as "mug books," were not indexed. While they generally include some biographical dictionary of the more upstanding individuals of the towns, those mentioned in the rest of the volume—and there are many—are seldom easily located without reading through the entire book.

MUG BOOKS

A "mug book" is the nickname for county histories published in the late 1800s and the early 1900s. They usually included a biographical dictionary of sorts that included write-ups and photos of some of the more prominent residents in the town or county. These individuals always had complete genealogical information going back at least two or three generations, and black sheep of the family need not apply. Mug books are, however, useful if you can find a family member written up. The clues help point you toward the next step. Use "mug books" with care because they are often wrong when it comes to the genealogy, usually because those highlighted in the biographical dictionary paid for the honor of being included.

While many county histories have been indexed through the volunteer efforts of local genealogical societies, there are times when it becomes necessary to just jump into the body of the book. Those highlighted in the biographical dictionary section usually paid a fee for their inclusion, so, as mentioned, seldom are the less-than-upstanding individuals included. However, if there was a major historically relevant event in the town or county, it is often mentioned in the body of the book, where you will find the details about the individual towns.

Most county histories are set up in a similar way. They detail the founding of the county, and give historical information about some of the county's early settlers and how the towns were founded. Often they go from describing the county as a whole to looking at the history of each individual town. In the town sections you will find lists of those elected to various offices, and given the state of politics most of the time, that list could include your skeleton. And while you would think that being elected to an office should automatically guarantee the person a place in the dictionary section, it doesn't always. There are many low level positions listed in the town history section that do not guarantee that the person was considered to be a mover and shaker.

The town sections will also indicate when various churches and other societies and groups were established. They may include information about when the jail was set up, and if there was something of importance that took place in the town, for example a particularly heinous crime, they may record it. Of course, since this section of the book is not indexed you would not find it unless you were looking for it.

LOOK UP LISTS

While your ancestor may not be written up in the biography section of a county history, he may show up in one of the many lists that are often included. There are lists of men and women for many different organizations, including early church members, fraternal organizations, and early government positions that were filled, including clerks, police, sheriff, teachers, and more. Sometimes the county history isn't indexed, but you may find in a library catalog that a genealogical society or fellow genealogist has created an index. You may also find indexes to the older county histories have been published online through the volunteer projects, such as USGenWeb.org <www.usgenweb.org/>.

Most genealogists I know concentrate on the biographical dictionary section of county histories. Such a section is often alphabetically arranged, making it easy to search. Usually the name of the highlighted individual is in bold print, jumping off the page as you search, making it all the easier to quickly scan the section. As most of my ancestors were not the movers and shakers of the communities in which they lived, I know that I will seldom discover them highlighted in this section. However, if I take the time to go through the town histories I've targeted, I can sometimes pick up a tidbit or two. At the very least, I can usually establish when the family came to the community or left.

The next time you find yourself looking at a county history, go beyond the biographical dictionary. Look at the names listed elsewhere. When the county history is divided by townships it is not as overwhelming to work through the book looking for information about your ancestors.

Tip

CENSUS RECORDS

While census records are one of the record types we use frequently, we do not always take the time to read the census page and see what it really says. Often when we copy the page, we concentrate more on the age of the individuals listed, the places of birth, or years of immigration than we do anything else. We tend to assume we know what occupation will be listed for an ancestor. However, sometimes, as seen in the 1880 census of Tombstone, Arizona, the occupation listed is not at all what you would expect (see Figure 4-1 on page 62). While Wyatt Earp was many things, I have never heard him referred to as a farmer—gambler, gunslinger, lawman, miner, yes, but not a farmer. And yet there he's listed as a farmer, living in his brother, Virgil's, household. Of course he is also listed as single though Mattie Earp, accepted as his second wife, probably through common law

For More Info

CENSUS ASSISTANCE

For more information about census records, check out Kathleen W. Hinckley's *Your Guide to the Federal Census* (Cincinnati: Betterway Books, 2002).

marriage, is listed right below him with the relationship of "wife."

There are times, though, when the census is quite plain about the occupation or residence of an ancestor, and we discover the fact that our ancestor was a bit of a rebel. With census indexes, we are often led right to the page where our ancestor has been enumerated. This is helpful because we tend to ignore the sections of the census that enumerate those in hospitals, jails, asylums, and other "unacceptable" residences (see Figures 4-2 and 4-3 below). We are convinced that our ancestor could never be among them. Of course, we can be mistaken. It isn't until we pay attention to where the person is living that we may discover we have uncovered a skeleton.

Sometimes it isn't where the person is living that identifies him as a skele-

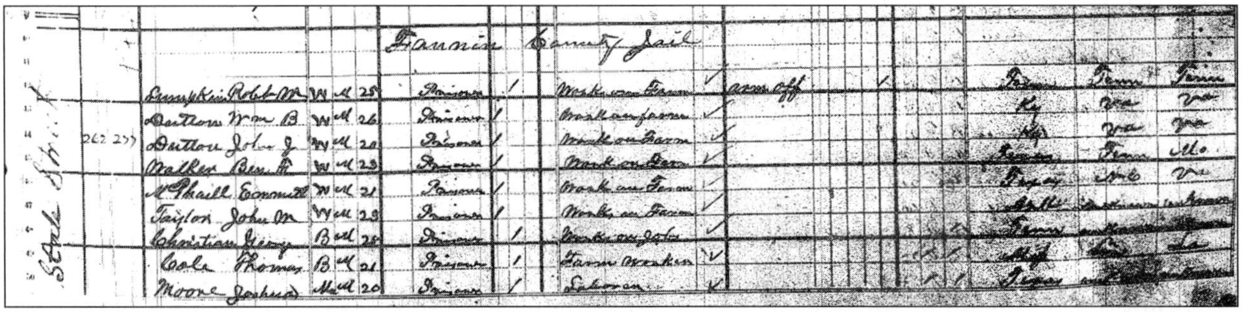

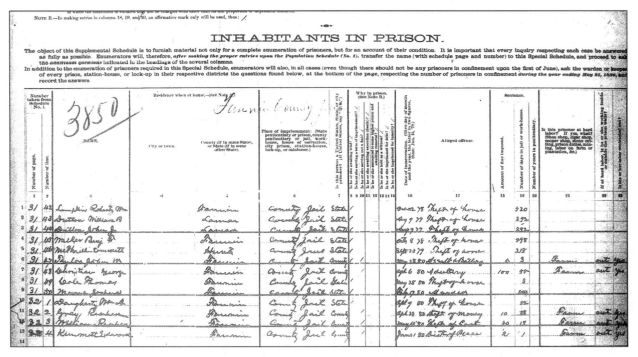

Figure 4-2
Fannin County Jail, as enumerated in 1880 Federal Census population schedule. (Fannin County, Texas, Bonham, T9, roll 1302, page 318C.)

NOTE B.—In making entries in columns 18, 19, and 20, an affirmative mark only will be used, thus: /

INHABITANTS IN PRISON.

The object of this Supplemental Schedule is to furnish material not only for a complete enumeration of prisoners, but for an account of their condition. It is important that every inquiry respecting each case be answered as fully as possible. Enumerators will, therefore, *after making the proper entries upon the Population Schedule (No. 1)*, transfer the name (with schedule page and number) to this Special Schedule, and proceed to ask the *additional questions* indicated in the headings of the several columns.

In addition to the enumeration of prisoners required in this Special Schedule, enumerators will also, in all cases (even though there should not be any prisoners in confinement upon the first of June), ask the warden or keeper of every prison, station-house, or lock-up in their respective districts the questions found below, at the bottom of the page, respecting the number of prisoners in confinement *during the year ending May 31, 1880*, and record the answers.

Figure 4-3
Fannin County Jail, as enumerated in the 1880 DDD Schedules or "Defective Schedules," offers more insight into the inhabitants of the jail than the 1880 population schedule did. (FHL #1421043.)

ton, but rather the occupation. There are times we may need to reexamine the occupation listed. We may find a woman running a boarding house only to discover that the house was a brothel instead. The 1900 census for St. Paul, Minnesota, lists Nina Clifford as a "landlady" (Figure 4-4 on page 68), but look a little closer at those who are living in her home. In addition to an impressive number of servants, including a cook, a housekeeper, three chambermaids, a musician, and a porter, there are nine inhabitants of the house listed as boarders, and for occupation, they are all listed as prostitutes. The house at 147 Washington Street, right in the "red light" district of St. Paul, was a well-known brothel in its day, and Nina Clifford has been referred to as St. Paul's most notable madam.

Printed Source

1880 "DEFECTIVE" SCHEDULES

The 1880 Defective census schedules were used when individuals in the general population schedules were listed as deaf, dumb, blind, and in prison. To find out more see Sharon DeBartolo Carmack's *A Genealogist's Guide to Discovering Your Female Ancestors* (Cincinnati: Betterway Books, 1998).

THE OLDEST PROFESSION

While I have found many "working girls" were willing to state their profession outright when it came to the census, you may discover that prostitutes were also listed in other ways. We have already seen that Nina Clifford was listed as a "landlady" when she was actually a madam. You may also find, as we did with Bessie Earp, that they are listed as "Sporting" or "Sporting Woman." And yet another possibility is if you discover that a town has an abundance of "dressmakers."

Often when you find the census records for a given workhouse or jail, you will discover the information provided indicates the job your ancestor had on the outside, which is seldom why he or she is now in jail. However, you now have more information to go on. **There are additional records that can be checked, including court records and state records, admission books for the place of confinement, and newspapers.**

Reminder

STATE AND COUNTY RECORDS

State and county records should always be searched regardless of whether you are searching for a skeleton or just searching for information on your family history. There are many instances where I have gone through a resource convinced that I would not find anything only to discover that it turned out to be a gold mine of information.

As you can see with the example of Benjamin Standerfer in "The Immortality of Infamy" on page 69, had I given up when I discovered that the majority of the entries in the index were to census records, which I had already gone through line by line, I would have missed the key entry on Benjamin that led to a great deal of information on him and his extracurricular activities. In addition, the court records supplied me with names of men who turned out to be brothers of Benjamin's, allowing me the avenue of researching Benjamin through these men since he refused to show up in the census records on his own.

This is just one example of the types of records you may discover. The trick

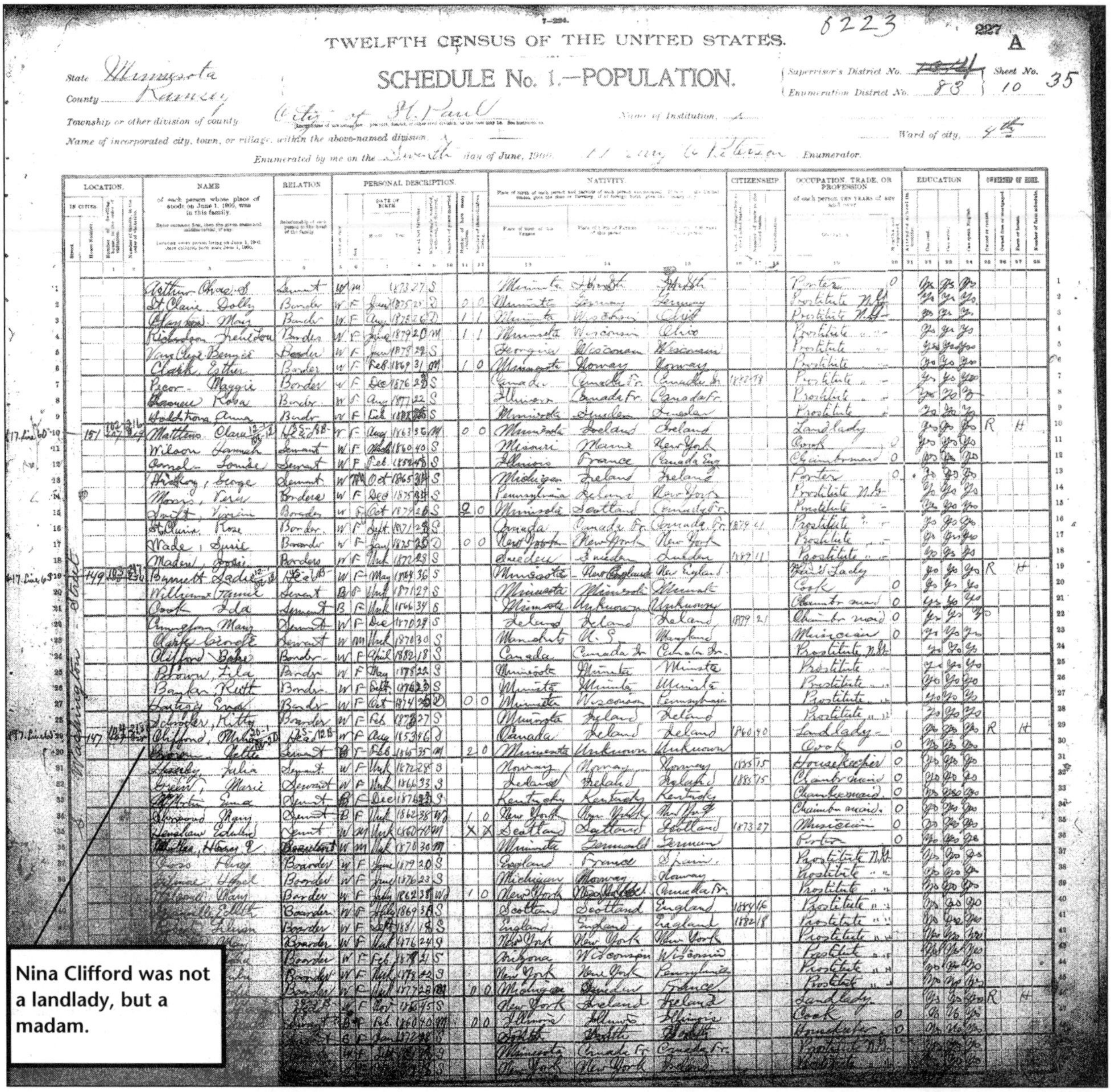

Figure 4-4
Nina Clifford wasn't the only "landlady" in St. Paul in 1900. The head of each household enumerated here was a landlady and the boarders were all prostitutes. (1900 Federal Census, St. Paul, Ramsey Co., Minnesota, T623, roll 783, sheet 10A.)

is not to exclude any possibilities. While I knew the county in which the family lived, I was open to looking in not only county records but also any record or resource from the state level as well. Of course, it helped that Benjamin was a particularly elusive ancestor. It is possible that had he shown up in the census records in 1860 and 1870, I would not have spent as much energy and creative analysis on the existing records. After all, I would have found the all-important age and place of birth in the census records. In my genealogical infancy, that would have been enough, and I would have moved on to another individual on the pedigree chart. Instead, he stubbornly refused to appear in the records,

THE IMMORTALITY OF INFAMY

Tracking down history on my ancestor Benjamin Standerfer has been my longest running headache. For many years he refused to be seen in the records. Of course, because of this I found I had to get creative fast. Out of desperation, I was introduced to some interesting records, including the Name Index to Early Illinois Records. When I first began looking in this index, it appeared to be an index to just the census records, and since I had already been through Moultrie County, Illinois, which is where the family had been for many years, I was not expecting to find much. Of course, Benjamin has always liked to stir things up, I now know, so I shouldn't have been surprised when I found a card with a source citation to a governor's order book. The governor's order book is where they have notices for arrest, among other things. In Benjamin's case, it was a request from the governor of Illinois to the governor of Iowa for the return of one Benjamin Standerfer. Needless to say, when I saw that, I knew he was mine. Thanks to a trip by a cousin to the county, we had the entire court file. What did Benjamin do? Well, he stole eleven dollars (two five dollar bills and a one dollar bill). A five hundred dollar bond was put up by his brothers, and he jumped bail. He was sentenced to a year in the state penitentiary with the first five days in solitary for jumping his bail. Of course, that wasn't the only thing Benjamin did. He would show up later on with more court records, this time in divorce court, but not with the wife I expected. He is my most colorful ancestor and has the thickest folder in my file cabinet.

even after having children, and researching him required a determination that I didn't know I had. In the end I was rewarded with an abundance of records on Benjamin and a realization that my paternal third great-grandfather was as colorful as they come. I have discovered at least three women he actually married, one who divorced him, another woman he lived with (while still married), and a potential fifth woman that he lived with, without benefit of clergy. He absconded with his wife's dower, and as we see, was not above taking money from others. Between the court case for the larceny, the court case for his divorce, and a 197-page pension application for his three months service in the Civil War, I have a lot of information on Benjamin and an interesting look into his life.

COURT RECORDS

If the census records indicate that your ancestor was incarcerated, then you will want to turn your attention to any county court records you can find. Generally trials are indexed by docket number. This means you must first get access to the docket, which is usually found in the courthouse in the clerk's office. Many of these dockets have also been microfilmed by the Family History Library. The docket details when a case was to come before the court and what

Definitions

DOWER

A *dower* is the legal provision for a married woman to be entitled to a portion of her husband's real estate (usually one-third) in the event he would die without a will. A wife had to release her right to dower in order for her husband to sell land with a free and clear title.

Research Tip

Internet Source

OUTLINED RECORDS

Detailed research outlines on each U.S. state, Canadian province, and many countries are available at the FamilySearch Web site <www.familysearch.org>. You will find the research outlines through the "Research Helps" link under the "Search" tab.

Important

Definitions

CIVIL VS. CRIMINAL

Criminal trials deal with violations of penal law, such as murder, larceny, or burglary. *Civil* trials pertain to private rights such as divorces, judgments, and liens.

happened to the case. You can determine if the case was tried or continued. The docket number assigned to the case is the key to getting access to the court file, or transcripts of the trial. While some dockets have been microfilmed by the Family History Library, do not be surprised if the docket you need has not. You may need to visit the county in question or hire a professional researcher to dig around in these records for you.

Remember that your ancestor may have been tried in another county than in the one in which he or she served the sentence. Depending on the severity of the crime, the individual may have been incarcerated in the state penitentiary. The records in question may no longer be found in the county in which the case was tried, either. Many states have begun to place older records in depositories that cover a region. So while the trial itself may have taken place in one county, the repository that now has the records may be in another county.

For those microfilmed by the Family History Library, you will want to pay close attention to the catalog entry. While the films are cataloged under the county in which the records cover, the repository of the original records may not be the county courthouse. If the microfilmed records do not go as far in years as you need, you should contact the regional repository in addition to the county courthouse to see which one currently has responsibility for the records.

Many people do not think to check divorce records, preferring to think that all of their ancestors lived happily ever after. While divorces were harder to get in earlier times, they did still take place. In some places the divorce records are filed with the vital records, especially on the state level. However, in many counties, the divorce records are found in the court records, and may be listed in the docket, especially the civil docket.

Remember that divorce records of the past were not a "no fault" scenario. In most cases one of the parties was accused of something—infidelity, physical abuse, or desertion, to name just a few. And while the docket may be easily available on microfilm, it may be necessary to contact the county courthouse for the actual court case. Of course, because the litigants could not just say "irreconcilable differences," you will often find that the transcript of the court case gives information about the individuals. Generally when there was a divorce, the party bringing the divorce would have had to supply witnesses to support the accusations against the other party, as in Figure 4-5 on page 71. For an historical look at divorce and its laws, read Glenda Riley's *Divorce: An American Tradition* (Lincoln: University of Nebraska Press, 1997).

NEWSPAPERS

Newspapers are certainly one of the resources that will offer the most when searching for an ancestor who may have broken the law. Of course, newspapers offer much more than just information on the colorful. They should be consulted for insight into the daily lives of our ancestors as well. Newspapers offer the news of the day, including births, marriages, deaths, sometimes divorces, and other court cases that may not result in incarceration of either party. They certainly offer a glimpse into the politics of the day.

In the case of tracking down a skeleton, newspapers may be your first indication of something running amiss in the life of an ancestor. Often when we find our ancestor in the more traditional records, such as vital records and censuses, we do not think to look anywhere else. However, by not looking in newspaper records and the other records already mentioned, you may miss out on all there is to know about your ancestor. Of course, there may be relatives who prefer that you not locate any juicy gossip on an ancestor. They belong to the "better left alone" camp. If they know there is something suspect in the family history, they may try to dissuade you from the pursuit of your ancestry.

Newspapers should be checked for upstanding, teetotaling ancestors as well. Names, dates, and places are fine, but most of us want to know more about our ancestors than just that. Rural newspapers often include stories about church gatherings or the fiftieth wedding anniversary of a couple in the town. Such an article may carry with it insight into the lives of the individuals, perhaps how they met and the trials they endured as they struggled to raise their family.

Reminder

When it comes to those individuals who might have spent time in jail, their jail time was often not more than a year or two, unless of course they were convicted of some heinous crime. Some may have spent as little as a couple of months while others spent a couple of years. **It is entirely possible for an ancestor to appear in the 1860 and 1870 census as the head of the family and have spent time in between those two census years incarcerated.** This is similar to what happened in the case of Benjamin Standerfer. Though he did not show up in the 1860 federal census, his incarceration in Illinois took place in 1864 and 1865. He was married again by 1867 and in the Kansas census by 1870. And while we can't all be as lucky as I was to discover the order of the Governor of Illinois to the Governor of Iowa, newspaper records may indicate similar information.

NATIONAL ARCHIVES AND THE ARCHIVAL RESEARCH CATALOG

The National Archives is like a repository for the nation—it is where federal records are found. When many think about the National Archives, they think about the main repository in Washington, DC. However, there are branches located throughout the country that also have a variety of records. The branches have microfilmed copies of the census records, some military records, and many other records both in microfilm and manuscript formats. You can get a list of the branches at the National Archives Records Center Web site <www.archives.gov/facilities/records_centers.html>.

A TREASURY OF RECORDS

The National Archives holds many different records from passenger lists to census records. They have military records, including service records and pension records. As you learned, they also have access to some records on our less-than-law-abiding ancestors. No one was as surprised as I was to see another Standerfer pop up in records dealing with larceny (see Figure 4-6 on page 73); after all, no other Standerfer has *ever* done anything wrong—*shhh*, I am forgetting about Benjamin for the moment.

In addition to the records of the National Archives, you may also want to investigate what records might be available from the Federal Bureau of Investigation. *Unlocking the Files of the FBI, A Guide to Its Records and Classification System* by Gerald K. Haines and David A. Langbart (Wilmington: Scholarly Resources, 1993) is a good book for learning what exists, what is available to the public, and what requires special clearance to view.

A large majority of the records housed with the National Archives detail the lives of everyday citizens, as we have seen already with the census records. Passenger lists and military records are some of the other records commonly requested from the National Archives. But there are many more record groups found in the National Archives—including those for the Federal Bureau of Investigations and the Justice Department. The National Archives also holds some records of U.S. District courts, as found in Record Group 21, Records of District Courts of the United States.

Some of these records have been cataloged in the National Archives online catalog—the Archival Research Catalog or ARC (see Figure 4-6 below), which was formerly known as the National Archives Information Locator, or NAIL. At the present time, about 13 percent of the National Archives holdings have been cataloged in the ARC. Some of the photographs and documents have been digitized and are viewable online through the Access to Archival Databases (AAD) system.

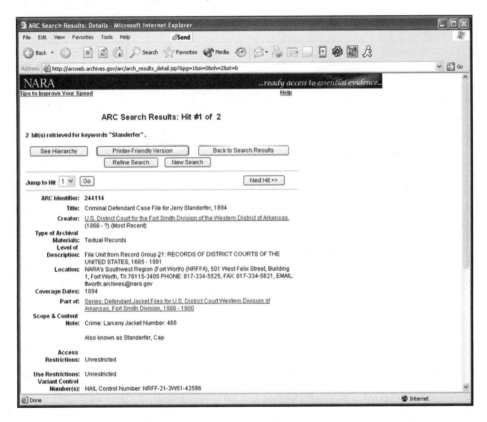

Figure 4-6
The ARC offers an online catalog of some of the holdings of the National Archives.

While the online catalog offers you some indication of the holdings of the National Archives and its many records centers, it is not complete. If you don't find what you were hoping to find, you may need to visit the National Archives or hire a professional researcher who is familiar with the Archives and it's many holdings and repositories.

PRISON RECORDS

Of course, if you have discovered that your ancestor was incarcerated you will definitely want to seek out prison records. Correctional institution records vary from institution to institution and from state to state. **However,**

Microfilm Source

when searching library catalogs, you may find one or more of the following, in some instances on microfilm:

- admission books
- biographical registers
- clemency files
- convict dockets
- death warrants
- descriptive registers
- discharge books
- lists of executions
- pardon books
- registers of prisoners

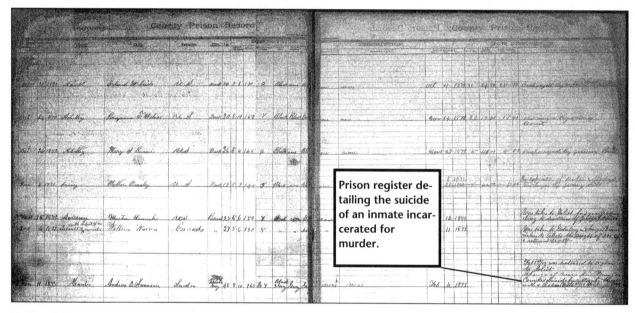

Prison register detailing the suicide of an inmate incarcerated for murder.

Figure 4-7
County prison record for Andrew Swanson, showing that he committed suicide. (Warren Co., Illinois, County Prison, Book A, page 9, FHL #1769733, item 3.)

Each record offers different information (see Figures 4-7 above and 4-8 on page 75). The admission books, registers of prisoners, and descriptive registers contain much the same information. They include information about the prisoner including name, date of entry to the institution, age, birthplace, occupation, physical description, crime, sentence, and number of convictions. They may also include county of residence, court of sentencing, date of sentence, and date of release or execution.

We often think that our male ancestors were the only ones being arrested and incarcerated. Of course, as was shown when I was discussing census records, there were crimes women committed as well. Criminal dockets or convict dockets, such as the one seen here, are not limited to men. However, the crimes for which women were arrested are usually different and less violent.

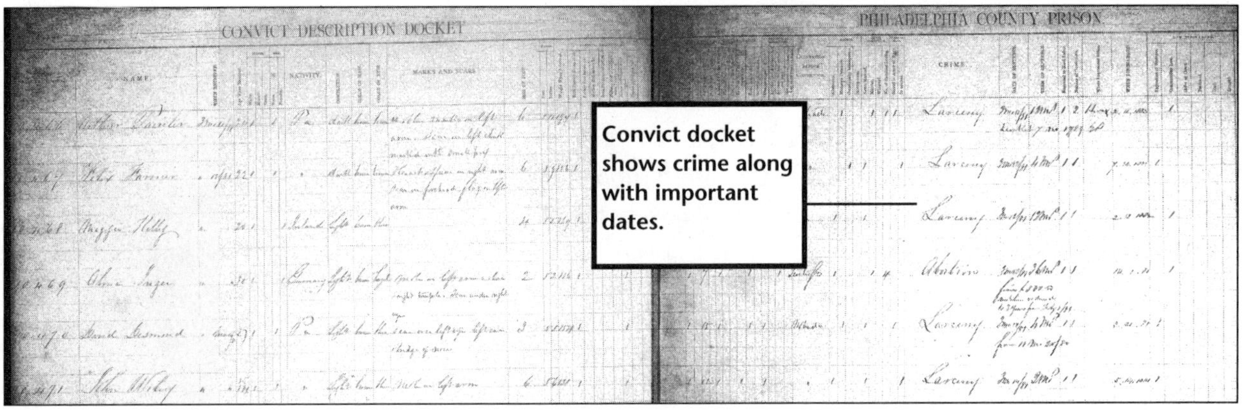

Convict docket shows crime along with important dates.

Figure 4-8
Dates shown in the convict docket entry offer important clues for finding court records. (Philadelphia, Pennsylvania, Convict Description Docket, 1880–1883, FHL #0974094.)

While many of the prison registers were forms, those filling them out often put additional information in the register or record. The List of Executions of the Philadelphia County Prison in Moyamensing is a perfect example. It is suspected that this executions list, which dates from 1839 to 1916, was compiled by prison agent George V. Meyer in 1916. The list of executions compiled by Meyer includes the number of the execution; the date of execution; the name of the inmate executed; his age, weight, and color; time of execution; murder victim; and the sheriff's name. Meyer also took some time to include details about the crime itself and how it happened or where it took place (Figure 4-9, below).

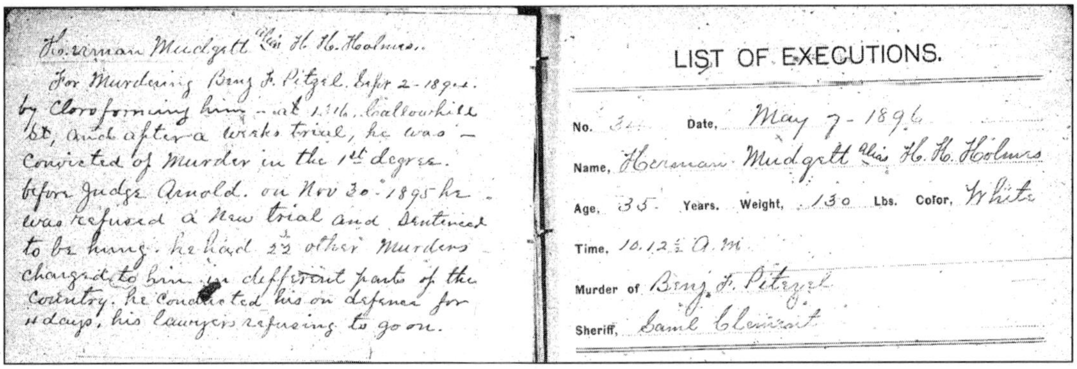

Figure 4-9
Execution entry for Herman Mudgett that sparked research into his history. (Philadelphia County, Pennsylvania, FHL #0975748, item 3.)

As with all the sources we use, we hope that the record will offer us additional information, pointing us in a new direction or toward another record. Working from the known to unknown, amassing documents on what is known supplies us with perhaps an age or place of birth that was previously unknown. And given the records that are often generated for those in prison, there may be more of an opportunity to find out about an individual.

THE DETAILS OF MURDER

In the case of Herman Mudgett's execution (see Figure 4-9 on page 75), not only does the record supply an alias, but the details shared as to the murder he was executed for give us the place of the murder as well as the detail about his having committed twenty-two other murders. Armed with this and his age, I was able to go out to the Internet and locate some information about him that helped me to identify him further and then locate him in census records, which lead me to published family histories.

TRUE CRIME BOOKS

Many people are fascinated by crime. This is certainly proven by the large collection of published books that deal with all different types of murders and other crimes. For someone to be included in such a book usually means that he was associated in some way with a horrific crime.

True crime literature is certainly not a resource that the average researcher will seek out unless, as was the case with Herman Mudgett, the researcher discovers that the crimes of the individual in question fall into the true crime category. And in the case of Herman Mudgett, not only were his crimes unspeakable, but he warranted his own book, *Depraved: The Shocking True Story of America's First Serial Killer* by Harold Schechter (New York: Pocket Books, 1996).

We can often find information on those accused of a type of crime, such as abortion or witchcraft, in books about the subjects. For example, there are many books about the witchcraft hysteria of 1692. Extensive research has also been undertaken on those accused of witchcraft in Europe. Such books often include transcriptions from court cases or other records.

Printed Source

True crime books are also a treasure trove of source citations. These books are often written by journalists, who document the facts as they are reported. If you do manage to find an ancestor included in a true crime volume, you will want to pay close attention to the sources used by the author of the book or chapter. You may find specific information on records about your ancestor. It is always best, especially if having to request documents via mail, when you can supply volume and page number. Source citations in true crime books, just as in genealogies, lead you to some of the very records of which you will want copies.

WEB SITES

For eager searchers, the Internet is truly a giant library. The key, of course, is in understanding how the Internet and various search engines and directories work, along with understanding how the sites have been cataloged and included in these different resources.

In genealogy, I turn first to the Internet to see what may have been made available online. There are many interesting sites of genealogical interest. When I discovered the Herman Mudgett entry in the list of executions of the Philadelphia County Prison and saw that he had supposedly committed twenty-two other murders, I suspected that there would be information available about him online. I was not disappointed. It took a few interesting searches to finally locate the information, but when I did, I had enough of a starting point to turn to more traditional genealogical resources for documenting his family history.

In addition to general Web sites that are posted by those who are either interested in the historical subject or in genealogy, there are many commercial sites that also offer information in the form of searchable databases.

Genealogy thrives on indexes. The more indexes we find, the more we want. Searchable databases are indexes in a fashion, though they often include a link to the page of an original document. In running the various searches on Herman Mudgett, I turned to the databases of Ancestry.com—

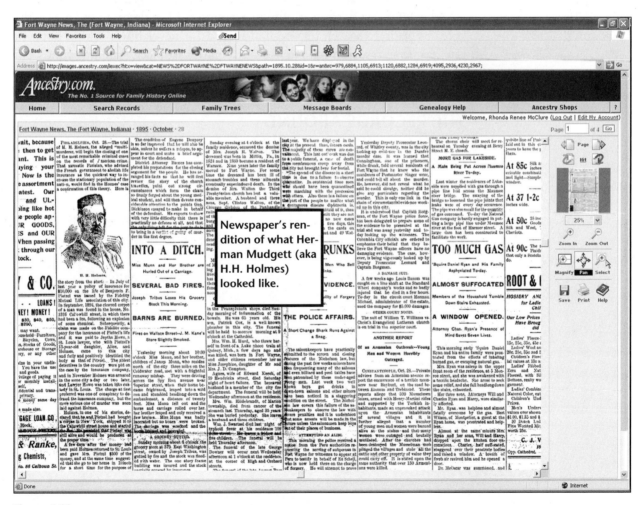

Figure 4-10

Newspaper article from *The Fort Wayne News* with a drawing of Herman Mudgett. © 2000–2002 MyFamily.com, Inc. Screen shot from Ancestry.com. Used with permission.

specifically their newspapers. I suspected that an individual such as Herman Mudgett would show up in some newspapers. I hoped that they were among those digitized and indexed by Ancestry.com. I found a number of articles. An entry in *The Fort Wayne News'* evening edition of 23 September 1895 mentioned his arraignment and that the date of the trial had been set. Given that the murder of Benjamin Pitzel had taken place in Fort Wayne, this was a reasonable expectation on my part, knowing that Ancestry.com had digitized some of the newspapers for Fort Wayne, Indiana. Additional entries were found for 28 October 1895, the start of the trial (Figure 4-10, page 77), and 4 March 1896, the sentencing.

Through general search engines, I can often find information on the individual or subject in question. In addition to locating information about Herman Mudgett, with general search engines, I found a wealth of information on "soiled doves" that aided me in locating census entries, along with additional information about the euphemisms used.

Important

Of course, the Internet is never the end of the search. For me it is the jumping-off point for the research. I generally run through the general search engines and the compiled databases, which are discussed in detail in chapter eight, before I begin to search for original records. It never hurts to find out who else has done research on a given individual or subject. And any time I can save some time, I jump at the chance.

THE RECORDS ABOUND

In researching family history in general, but certainly in the case of those notorious individuals who stepped outside the law, or who were accused of such, you are limited in your research only by your own creativity. Check all records that may exist. Don't assume that your ancestor isn't listed. Look what I found on Benjamin Standerfer by simply persevering with an index I was convinced might have entries on some of my other Standerfers but certainly none for Benjamin.

Of course, perhaps your infamous ancestor was actually of noble blood. But just because they were royal doesn't mean they weren't colorful.

FIVE

Royal and Noble Links

There is a fascination with royalty, even to this day. While the United States once fought a revolution to break free of the English monarchy, today's Americans are intrigued by the present English royals, and not just because of the scandals that result in them being written up in the tabloids every other week. To most of us who are on the outside looking in, it appears that royals have nothing but a life of luxury. We see present-day royals jetting off to Switzerland to ski or to the Mediterranean to swim, and it looks like they haven't a care in the world.

However, royals in history spent most of their time looking out for their lives. There was a lot of unrest in many of the countries ruled by monarchs, unrest that resulted in overthrows, incarcerations, and sometimes beheadings. And if the trusted officials of the household weren't plotting someone's demise, the state of the practice of medicine at the time may have contributed to an early grave, or in the loss of an only child.

MYTHS OF ROYAL CONNECTIONS

For genealogists, family stories are often full of potential relationships to royals. Determining if that story is true is what genealogists love to do, looking for clues and following the merry chase. Sometimes the stories turn out to be false, but in the end the research accomplished while on the trail of the elusive royal connection is something of which you can be as equally proud. While you may disprove one family tradition of a royal relation, it is more than possible that as your research progresses you will uncover another.

Sometimes the family lore isn't about a relationship to a given monarch, but instead to one of the household staff, ladies-in-waiting being a particular favorite among family traditions. Perhaps it is the romance of the "lady-in-waiting" persona that makes them one of the most popular characters in family history.

As a result of the various stories I've heard, I have broken down the stories of those with a family tradition of a royal relationship to the following three groups:

- those who are related to a monarch and his or her immediate family
- those who are related to a higher household staff, such as a lady-in-waiting
- those who are related to other household staff

"The Queen and I Are *This* Close"

The premise of the hilarious movie *King Ralph,* starring John Goodman, is that a terrible accident completely wipes out the British royal family. Genealogists are called in and the search is on to find someone with a blood tie to the throne. Enter a lounge singer, Ralph Jones, played by Goodman. You can't get much further from the throne than him. Of course the movie is filled with comedic situations where Ralph, who hasn't been raised with all the royal rules, gets himself into all sorts of problems. This movie speaks to our secret hope that we have a connection to royalty that might result in a similar situation for us. After all, many of us have dreamed of becoming royalty.

Of course in the real world, such things just don't happen. Dreaming doesn't make it so. Even if you have a direct relationship to today's monarchs, you need not hold your breath until they come calling. Having a royal connection, however, can make tracing that particular lineage a little easier to do. **Various books of royal relationships that have been published over the years offer both contemporary as well as historical lineages for those who think they may be related.** The better books also include bibliographies of the resources used in compiling the genealogies or Ahnentafels.

Printed Source

NUMBER CRUNCHING

An *Ahnentafel* is a type of ancestor table that gives each person a unique number. The first person in the table is given the number 1. The father of that person is given the number 2. The mother of that person is given the number 3. In searching later generations in the chart, to find any person's father, take the person's number and double it. Likewise, to find that person's mother in the table, take that person's number, double it and add one. So to find the parents of the mother mentioned above who was number 3, you take her number and double it to find her father (6); double it and add 1 to find her mother (7). You have seen a variety of Ahnentafels already in this book, and there is an extensive one at the end of this chapter detailing the ancestry of actors Joseph and Ralph Fiennes. Notice the numbers and how they grow with each new generation.

Of the royals of the twentieth century, I would venture to guess that none has been as popular as Diana, Princess of Wales. Perhaps it was the fairy-tale aspect of her marriage to Prince Charles that captured our imaginations, even though the story ended badly. Perhaps it was her shyness and her

GUIDES TO ROYALTY

Here are a few books that outline some of the royal lineages. It is a good idea to use these books as guides and try to verify the information as much as possible. Over the years some errors in the lineages have been discovered. They are, however, major resources in this area of genealogical research. Other books devoted to all aspects of royalty and heraldry are listed in the bibliography at the end of the book.

- Roberts, Gary Boyd. *The Royal Descents of 500 Immigrants to the American Colonies or the United States.* Baltimore: Genealogical Publishing Company, Inc., 2001.

- Stuart, Roderick W. *Royalty for Commoners.* 4th edition. Baltimore: Genealogical Publishing Company, 2002.

- Weis, Frederick Lewis. *Ancestral Roots of Certain American Colonists Who Came to America Before 1700.* 7th edition. Baltimore: Genealogical Publishing Company, 2002.

concern for common people that grabbed the attention of those around the world. Regardless, she brought the British monarchy into the twentieth century, making it personable and, in a way, hip. From her days as Shy Di until the night of her death, she captured the hearts of the world. She's been gone for more than five years and still people are fascinated by her.

In many ways she seemed to be just like the common people. She seemed accessible, and people wanted more. It is not surprising then, that along with an interest in her, an interest in her genealogy arose. Because her great-grandmother was American, she has many connections to colonial America. For today's researchers, her American ancestry means the potential for finding a common lineage and certainly a distant kinship with one of her many early New England, MidAtlantic, and Virginia roots.

The definitive work on Diana's American ancestors is Gary Boyd Roberts' and William Addams Reitwiesner's *American Ancestors and Cousins of The Princess of Wales* (Baltimore: Genealogical Publishing Company, Inc., 1984). Through this impressive compilation, genealogists have, at their fingertips, not only details of the ancestry of Diana, but also compressed Ahnentafels of many well known historical and notable individuals. Through these Ahnentafels, you may discover that you are not only related to the Princess of Wales but to many other notables as well, such as well-known Revolutionary War patriot Nathan Hale (see Figure 5-1 on page 83).

Of course, since the Princess is gone, the future King of England, Prince William, has captured the attention and hearts of the world. Reminding so many of his mother, with his blond hair and sensitive face, he adds another generation to his mother's relationships with those early forebears high-

AN ORGANIZATIONAL NOTE

Whether using *American Ancestors and Cousins of The Princess of Wales* (Baltimore: Genealogical Publishing Company, Inc., 1984) or his *Notable Kin* (New England Historic Genealogical Society, 1998–1999) volumes, it is important to understand the manner in which Gary Boyd Roberts displays the information. First, most of the time, he displays the information in what I call a "compressed Ahnentafel." He has included a lot of information in those three books. In order to do that and still keep the books to a reasonable size, he has omitted dates and includes just the names. Of course, once you have the names, you have something to work with so finding the dates and places becomes much easier. Second, you will need to pay close attention to the use of the semicolon as that is the character by which Roberts identifies the start of the next generation. Be aware that he usually doesn't have all of the parents for the previous generation. He usually has a specific lineage to either a Mayflower passenger or to show a connection to certain presidents or royalty in mind and concentrates on that lineage. Here is a sample taken from *American Ancestors and Cousins of The Princess of Wales*:

> 271. George Washington Gale Ferris Jr., 1859–1896, civil engineer, inventor of the Ferris wheel; George Washington Gale Ferris & Martha Edgerton Hyde; Jabez Perkins Hyde & Martha Edgerton; Jedediah Hyde Jr. & Elizabeth Brown . . .

Notice that in the above example he lists the parents of the primary individual, but then only the maternal grandparents. It takes the information in the direction of the common connection with the Princess of Wales and excludes any of the other names in each generation to keep the list of names to a minimum.

lighted in Roberts' and Reitwiesner's book. Girls all over have resurrected the dream of becoming a princess as William's face graces the cover of teen magazines right along with the faces of celebrities such as *NSYNC's Justin Timberlake and the Backstreet Boys' Nick Carter.

While I have talked about the British monarchy to this point, it is important to remember that most of the royal houses, because of the many arranged marriages from one country to another, are forever interrelated. If you find that you are related to one royal house, it is possible that you are related to other royal houses as well. Of the books previously mentioned, including Roderick W. Stuart's *Royalty for Commoners* and Gary Boyd Robert's *The Royal Descents of 500 Immigrants to the American Colonies or the United States*, there are many that include royal lineages from the different houses of Europe as well as the British royal line.

Great-Grandmother Was a Lady-in-Waiting

For every person I have found who is interested in claiming a monarch on the tree, I have found another individual with a family story claiming a

RELATIONSHIP OF PRINCE WILLIAM TO NATHAN HALE

Captain Joseph Strong

Elizabeth Strong	Siblings	Benajah Strong
Nathan Hale	1st cousins	Dr. Joseph Strong
	1st cousins once removed	Eleanor Strong
	1st cousins twice removed	Ellen Wood
	1st cousins 3 times removed	Frances Eleanor Work
	1st cousins 4 times removed	Edmund Maurice Burke Roche
	1st cousins 5 times removed	The Honorable Frances Ruth Burke Roche
	1st cousins 6 times removed	Diana, The Princess of Wales
	1st cousins 7 times removed	H.R.H. Prince William

Figure 5-1
Through his mother's American ancestry, Prince William, Britain's future monarch, is cousin to one of America's staunchest supporters of the colonies' independence.

connection to a lady-in-waiting for a queen or a princess. Of course, the ladies-in-waiting, as was the case with many of the other household staff, were usually of some noble connection, making them almost as important as royalty. In fact, most of those who are intrigued by the royals do not understand the difference between a royal and a noble, so that having a lady-in-waiting in their history is almost as good as having a king or a princess on the family tree. And of course there is the allure of being part of the inner circle. We all like to be on the inside, and when it comes to a queen or princess, there is no closer circle than that of the ladies-in-waiting.

Before we look at what is available on this subject, **let's first look at the term "lady-in-waiting."** It is actually a catchall phrase. A lady-in-waiting was a companion to the woman in question. She was supposed to accompany her majesty as needed and where appropriate. Her duties could vary based on whom she was serving. Some royals preferred to engage in a friendship while others required more work out of their ladies. While they are collectively known as ladies-in-waiting, there were many separate appointments for these women; each with their own titles and tasks:

- Mistresses of the Robes—a political appointment made by the current administration. She is the highest ranking lady-in-waiting and in charge of all of the ladies-in-waiting. She attends the Queen on important state functions.
- Ladies of the Bedchamber—the next ranking lady-in-waiting. There are usually eight appointed with two in waiting who usually attend the Queen at Court and on public occasions.
- Women of the Bedchamber—ranks below the Lady of the Bedchamber.

$\backslash$di$'$fin$\backslash$ vb

Definitions

There are usually eight appointed by the Queen with two in waiting who attend the Queen at Court and on public occasions.

- Maids of Honor—the lowest ranking lady-in-waiting. There are eight appointed by the Queen with two in waiting who attend the Queen at Court and on public occasions. This is the only lady-in-waiting required to be unmarried during her appointment.

Being appointed as a lady-in-waiting to the Queen required more than the Queen simply pointing her finger at the person. As can be seen in Queen Victoria's history, her many ministers often had some say into who could be selected. Sometimes when there was a change in the ruling party, at least in England, there was the chance that the Mistress of the Robes would be let go and a new one chosen. Perhaps this was because of the influence these women could have on the monarch and her duties; the elected ruling party wanted to make sure that the opposing party was not able to sway the monarch or have some unfair advantage when they were no longer the party in charge.

Usually those who were selected as ladies-in-waiting to the Queen had some noble upbringing. As a researcher you should expect to find a duchess as the Mistress of the Robes or a viscountess as the Lady of the Bedchamber. If your research has not uncovered any such noble connections, it is possible that your family story is not accurate, though this does not mean it's a complete fable.

While there are a few published lists of those who were ladies-in-waiting to queens and princesses, as well as other offices in the royal household, if you have accessed all of the usual resources, discussed later in this chapter, and have not found your ancestor mentioned, all is not lost. It is possible for your female ancestor to have been a lady-in-waiting and still not show up on any of these published lists. Ladies-in-waiting were not limited to the Queen, though that is who we think of first when discussing the subject. It is possible that your ancestor was a lady-in-waiting to one of the Queen's daughters or daughters-in-law. It is equally possible that your ancestor was a lady-in-waiting to a cousin of the Queen or King. Finally there are those ladies-in-waiting who were hired by a titled family.

Your family story may simply mention that great-great-great-grand aunt Lucretia was a lady-in-waiting. As the story is passed down from generation to generation, it gets changed, and eventually it is assumed or the story is changed to not only mention that she was a lady-in-waiting, but to whom she was "in waiting." And being human it is natural to assume the best, in this case a queen. Your family story may indeed show a connection to a queen, but as we have seen here there are many others to whom your ancestor could have been "in waiting."

In some instances such a position meant a better life, so do not be discouraged if your ancestress does not turn out to be a lady-in-waiting to the Queen. The travel alone for many of these women was perhaps more excitement than they could have hoped for. They may have met their husbands while in service. In fact, if your ancestor was a Maid of Honor then she had to be single and could not even be engaged. Upon her engagement she would have been released from her position as a Maid of Honor.

I mention the limitation of the Maid of Honor because we often try to force the existing facts to fit our family. Just as we try to force the facts when we are having trouble figuring out who our ancestor's parents were, we sometimes overlook something or grasp hold of a name because it is the same as that of our ancestor. Knowing that a Maid of Honor could not be engaged or married, should you find a Maid of Honor with the same name as your ancestress, you now have a ruler by which to gauge the probability of that person being your ancestor, especially if up to this point you have been unable to find the dates of birth or death of either your ancestor or the lady-in-waiting.

Warning

Is There a Doctor in the House?

Another popular position in the royal household, among family traditions, is that of an employee of some sort, such as a maid, musician, or physician. While not as glamorous as the lady-in-waiting, these people were often still in some contact with the royal family. Finding out whether your ancestor worked in the royal household can get a little confusing. There were those who worked in the royal household but for whom there may be no record. Generally these are individuals who were not paid by the Lord Chamberlain's department as the Queen's ladies-in-waiting were. Some of those who worked in the royal household would bring their own maid, paid for out of their own finances. As a result, while technically the maid was working in the royal household, she was not paid by the monarch and as such there may be no paper trail as to her employment within the royal household.

FINDING THE PROOF

While my ancestors were probably maids, if they ever even worked for the royal household, it is possible that you have family traditions about those who were of a higher station. It is possible you can find information about your ancestor. To ensure the best outcome of such research, it is necessary to know as much as possible about when your ancestor may have worked in the royal household. It is usually necessary to know which monarch your ancestor was working for in order to know where and when to search the records. When was your ancestor born? When did he marry? When did he die? If he held a position such as a physician, when did your ancestor become a physician? What do you know of where he studied and apprenticed? This could prove important in determining if your ancestor was indeed employed by the monarch.

With the Internet, we are finding more of this type of information available at our fingertips. **There are quite a few sites devoted to the various lists of employees of monarchs and royal households, as well as descriptions of the duties**

Internet Source

For More Info

SEARCH ENGINES

For detailed information about using search engines, see chapter four in *The Genealogist's Computer Companion* (Cincinnati: Betterway Books, 2001).

Important

DON'T KNOW MUCH ABOUT HISTORY

A project to record the history of each county in England from the early beginnings to present day is in progress. To find out more about this project, visit the Victoria County History Web site <www.englandpast.net/about.html>.

and lives of those who were in some way connected to the royal household through employment, such as a lady-in-waiting. Projects have resulted in the publishing of such lists in books and online. In some instances you will find that you can search by the name of your ancestor. But when working online, I have found that I often must have a working knowledge of when the individual was likely to have been employed in order to find him or her on a list. Sometimes by using a general search engine, such as Google.com <www.google.com>, to search the name of your ancestor, you may find the specific list upon which he or she is listed. This of course is determined by the capabilities and thoroughness of the search engine in question.

The Institute of Historical Research <www.history.ac.uk/welcome.html> was founded in 1921 and offers a place where scholars can meet to discuss and continue their research. The home to three different research centers, each with its own historic specialty, the Institute is certainly one of the first places that researchers will want to visit when researching anyone who may have worked in a royal household. As you will see, the Web site offers a number of impressive lists of office holders employed by some of the monarchs and their siblings. While the online list is far from complete, the Institute of Historical Research has published twelve volumes of office holders. This massive project was begun in 1972 with the *Treasury Officials 1660–1870* compiled by J.C. Sainty and has been rounded out with parts I and II of *Officials of the Royal Household 1660–1837*; part I is devoted to the Department of the Lord Chamberlain and part II includes the departments of the Lord Steward and the Master of the Horse.

Both of the last two volumes offer listings by appointment as well as an alphabetical listing of those given the appointments. In the list of appointments, you will find a little about the position and how a person was appointed, as well as some information about the salary received. In the alphabetical listing you will discover the outcome of the individuals who were appointed. Some individuals were removed from their positions. You may also learn when the individual died.

What is of particular interest is the list of references from which the various lists were compiled. Listed by repository and then by abbreviation in the book, a new world of resources is opened to anyone researching those who worked for the royal family up to 1837. As with any genealogical research it is a good idea to see what the availability is of those resources to see if you can gain further knowledge from the original records.

While the Institute has no plans to publish future books, this does not mean the organization is not continuing to amass information. Some of that information is now freely available on the Internet in the Institute's Research Tools section. Like the books, you will find that you are supplied with references to the original sources used. The lists of the appointments are a combination of the two sections found in the book. Under each appointment, you will find biographical information about the appointee, including any known termination in that position.

In 1837 Queen Victoria ascended to the throne and part of her house-

WAS SHE OR WASN'T SHE?

Recently there has been quite a bit of talk about the validity of Queen Victoria's ascension. There has been some question as to her legitimacy because of the introduction of the gene that carries the hemophilia disease. If the case could be made for her illegitimacy, that would put the current monarchy in jeopardy. Recently included in the History Channel *Time Machine* episode titled "Family History" it was explored in depth in *Queen Victoria's Gene: Haemophilia and the Royal Family* by D.M. Potts and W.T.W. Potts (Stroud: Allan Sutton, 1995). The premise is that because there appears to be no indication of hemophilia in the royal family until Queen Victoria, she must have been the result of an affair by her mother.

Genealogists have been interested in medical family trees for some time, and in the Holiday 2002 issue of *New England Ancestors*, the newsmagazine of the New England Historic Genealogical Society <www.newenglandancestors.org/>, Sally Ann Neale details her own research into hemophilia in her family history in "Hemophilia, A Genealogical Blood Trail." I found her article interesting and among other things it mentioned the fact that the gene can spontaneously mutate.

In reading the discussion about Queen Victoria, you are led to believe that such a mutation is highly improbable. Actually, according to the National Hemophilia Foundation <www.hemophilia.org/home.htm>, "One third of all cases of hemophilia A occur when there is no family history of the disorder. In these cases hemophilia develops as the result of a new or spontaneous gene mutation."

Without DNA testing, it is likely that Queen Victoria's legitimacy will continue to be discussed, but it does seem that there is strong evidence to show that she was not illegitimate.

hold has been identified and shared on Yvonne's Royalty Home Page <http://mypage.uniserve.ca/~canyon/royalty.html>. While she has not included all of the various positions for physicians and others, you will at least find lists of her ladies-in-waiting, as well as a lot of information about the duties and rules of being a lady-in-waiting. It is this type of information that we need in order to understand the possibility of our ancestor having worked in the household. For instance, if your ancestress was not a noble, it is possible that she worked in the household but not for the Queen. This would tell you that the information you seek may not have been published in the resources discussed. In fact, it is possible that you may never find a record that identifies your ancestress as a lady-in-waiting or for whom she was working.

OF NOBLE BIRTH

We have spent quite a bit of time on the royal household, primarily because it is the royal household to which most people are hoping to find a connec-

\di'fin *vb*

Definitions

tion. In the grand scheme of things though, the previously mentioned sources are just the tip of the mountain of resources. **There are those of royal birth and then there are those of noble birth.** In many instances the royal families turned to the noble families when marrying, which makes it possible for you to have some familial connection, especially if you have already identified a noble line. In most instances these marriages were the unions of the younger children of the monarch's household, those who did not expect to be in line for the throne.

ROYAL PAIN

Oh to be royal and in love. Maybe not. There seem to be hurdles to marrying your true love if you are a royal, especially if you are in line for the throne. To protect the throne from commoners though, some royals found they could marry their true love but the spouse and offspring were simply denied any claims to the titles or lands or throne. Such a marriage is referred to as a *morganatic marriage.*

For those researching British ancestry there are twelve royals from whom descents to present day have been compiled and are often easily identifiable.

1. Eleanor, daughter of John (1199–1216), who married Simon de Montfort
2. Edmund "Crouchback," Earl of Lancaster and Leicester, son of Henry III (1216–1272)
3. Eleanor, daughter of Edward I (1272–1307), who married Henry, Count of Bar, in France
4. Joan of Acre, daughter of Edward I (1272–1307), who married Gilbert de Clare, Earl of Gloucester
5. Elizabeth, daughter of Edward I (1272–1307), who married Humphrey de Bohun, Earl of Hereford and Essex
6. Thomas of Brotherton, Earl of Norfolk, and Marshal of England, son of Edward I (1272–1307)
7. Edmund of Woodstock, Earl of Kent, son of Edward I (1272–1307)
8. Lionel of Antwerp, Duke of Clarence, son of Edward III (1327–1377)
9. John of Gaunt, Duke of Lancaster, son of Edward III (1327–1377)
10. Edmund of Langley, Duke of York, son of Edward III (1327–1377)
11. Thomas of Woodstock, Duke of Gloucester, son of Edward III (1327–1377)
12. Mary, Queen-Dowager of France, daughter of Henry VII (1485–1509), who married Charles Brandon, Duke of Suffolk

Should you decide to trace the descents of any of these twelve individuals, you will soon discover that they intertwine through marriage. For instance, the great-great-granddaughter of Edmund "Crouchback" (number two above) married Lionel of Antwerp (number eight above).

GIRL POWER

In *Royal Descents: Scottish Records* (Walton-on-Thames, England: Chas. A. Bernau, 1908), the Reverend W.G.D. Fletcher says that the secret to success in finding a royal line is to work on the female lines. When you consider that it is the female lines that are always adding new surnames, and thus new lines, to the tree, this makes sense. Too often published genealogies concentrate only on the males, leaving the woman as forgotten side notes, when in fact your most interesting connections are often found through the women on your family tree.

As each successive generation is born and marries, we begin to see the marriages branching further out. We have royal family to royal family, royal to noble, then noble to noble, and finally noble to one of a lesser station. Eventually commoners are involved and a few drops of royal blood are seen intermixing with the blood of the common people. As a result it is possible for you and I to find that we have many noble and royal lineages if we take the time to pursue them.

Burke's Peerage is just one of the many useful sources when it comes to tracking a peer's lineage (see Figure 5-2 on page 91). In fact, you will often find *Burke's* cited as the source of information if a line does go back to a noble line. For additional books that have compiled the genealogies of the peerage, see the bibliography.

Books such as *Burke's Peerage* are easier to use when you already know the title of the peer. *Burke's* is arranged alphabetically by the title. For instance, the Earl of Hardwicke (Hardwicke being the part of the title that is alphabetized) will be found before the Baron of Saye and Sele. This is just one of the many books that have been published that include genealogies of those with some noble connection. Remember that not all of those included have a title; they may be included because they are descended from someone who is titled. This is the case with Joseph and Ralph Fiennes, brothers and actors. Because they are descended from the Baron of Saye and Sele, who is a Fiennes, they have been included in *Burke's Peerage*. While Joseph and Ralph are celebrities in their own right, they also have a number of nobles on the family tree as well as being descendants of royalty, including James II, King of Scotland. An Ahnentafel of the Fiennes has been included at the end of this chapter.

While you may find that there are coats of arms associated with these individuals, most often genealogists confuse coats of arms with family crests. In fact, you may have seen offers in the mail or when visiting your local mall enticing you to purchase a beautiful copy of your coat of arms, suitable for framing. Before you put down any money, you may want to learn a little more about heraldry, from which the coat of arms comes.

Warning

PEERAGE

Burke's Peerage has become a catchall phrase to indicate the many compiled publications from *Burke's* that outline in genealogical tables, the peerage and baronage of England, as well as the landed gentry of England, Scotland, and Ireland. These massive volumes have been published semiannually and often hold many wonderful clues to ancestry. The sheer magnitude of the volumes makes it possible to overlook an entry for an ancestor. Fortunately, *Burke's* has come onto the Internet <www.burkes-peerage.net/>. While it is a subscription site, the annual subscription fee is quite reasonable and offers you full text searching of:

- *Burke's Peerage & Baronetage* 106th edition

- *Burke's Landed Gentry Scotland* 19th edition

- The Irish records from *Burke's Landed Gentry* 15th edition (1937)

- *Burke's Landed Gentry England & Wales* 18th edition

- *Burke's Landed Gentry Ireland* 19th edition

- *American Families with British Ancestry* 19th edition

- *American Presidential Families*

A LOOK AT HERALDRY

Heraldry is an intricate subject. In fact, there are many books and Web sites available on it. You will find them listed in the bibliography at the end of the book.

Basically, heraldry was a method of identification. Historically it can be traced back to the twelfth and thirteenth centuries in Europe. While heraldry was used to a degree in military situations to identify friend or foe, there were more uses of heraldry for calling attention to the individual's stature.

Each shield includes certain personal devices that were registered and identified as belonging to and representing that individual. This is the most important point about a coat of arms: It was registered to an individual, not a family and not a surname. As the coat of arms was passed from father to son, it was usually altered in some way. A daughter was entitled to the coat of arms only if there were no male heirs. If you descend from a daughter then there is no coat of arms for you. However, you may discover that the wife of your ancestor had a small version of her husband's arms to which she had a courtesy right.

While you cannot claim the coat of arms because it was registered to an individual rather than a surname, heraldry is still a valuable resource to genealogists because of the need to prove a relationship. A person couldn't show up and simply lay claim to an arms. Proof of a right to that arms was

1877, Catherine Jane Jarvis, only dau. of late John Hildebrand Bond, of Belfast; she d. 3 Feb. 1880.

NOTE—**Heir presumptive**, Sir Henry Scudamore Stanhope, Bart.

ARMS—Quarterly erm. and gu.
CREST—A tower az. a demi-lion issuant from the battlements or, ducally crowned gu., holding between the paws a grenade fired ppr.
SUPPORTERS—Dexter, a wolf or, ducally crowned gu. Sinister, a talbot erm.
MOTTO—A deo et rege.
SEAT—Rockwood, Castle Derg, co. Tyrone.

Lineage.

THE family of Stanhope was originally from the North; the township so called is situate in Weardale, in the co. pal. of Durham.

JOHN DE STANHOPE of Rampton, Notts, j. u. 1373 (identified by Collins with John de Stanhope, burgess in Parliament for Newcastle, 1360); m. Elizabeth, dau. and heir of Stephen Maulovel, of Rampton, and eventual heir of the baronial family of Longvilers, of Tuxford, Notts. His descendant in the sixth generation,

SIR EDWARD STANHOPE, of Rampton, sheriff of Notts and Derby 23 HEN. VII., d. 1511, leaving Richard Stanhope, his eldest son and heir, who d. s. p. m. 1528. His second son,

SIR RICHARD STANHOPE of Shelford, Notts, knighted by HEN. VIII. at Hampton Court 1545, was imprisoned on a charge of conspiracy with the Duke of Somerset, 5 EDW. VI. and beheaded 26 Feb. 1552. His great-grandson,

SIR PHILIP STANHOPE (only son of Sir John Stanhope, by his 1st wife Cordell, dau. and heir of Richard, 3rd son of Sir Giles Alington, of Horseheath, co. Camb.) knighted at Whitehall 16 Dec. 1605, and by patent dated 7 Nov. 1616, created LORD STANHOPE, of Shelford, Notts, and 4 Aug. 1628, EARL OF CHESTERFIELD. His house at Shelford was garrisoned for the King during the Civil wars, under command of his son Philip, who lost his life 27 Oct. 1645, when the rebels took it by storm and burnt it to the ground; he d. 12 Sept. 1656, aged 72 (bur. in the church of St. Giles-in-the-Fields—M.I.), having m. 1st—in 1605, Lady Catherine, dau. to Francis, Lord Hastings, son and heir to George, 4th Earl of Huntingdon; she d. 28 Aug. 1636, having had with 2 daus. 11 sons, of whom,

[1] Henry, Lord Stanhope, K.B. whose line became extinct on the death of Philip Dormer, 4th Earl, "the celebrated Lord Chesterfield," 24 Mar. 1773.

[2] Hon. Arthur, of Mansfield Woodhouse, Notts. M.P. Nottingham, 1662; m. Mary dau. of Sir Henry Salusbury, Bart. (ext.), of Llewenny, co. Denbish. and had an only surviving son,

CHARLES, of Mansfield Woodhouse, d. 6 Mar. 1711/12, having m. 1674, Frances, only dau. of Sir Francis Topp, of Tormaton, co. Glouc. Bart. (ext.); she bur. 14 Jan. 1722, having had with other issue 2 sons,

(1) Michael, D.D. canon of Windsor, bp. 20 Dec. 1681; d. 8 bur. 20 July, 1737, having m. 29 June, 1714, Penelope, dau. of Sir Salathiel Lovell, Knt. one of the barons of the exchequer; she bur. 1 May, 1740, having had 2 sons,

/1/ Arthur Charles, of Mansfield Woodhouse, bp. 8 April, 1715; bur. 9 Mar. 1770, having m. 1st—Mary, dau. of Sir Andrew Thornhaugh, of Osberton, Notts.; she d. s. p. bur. 18 Mar. 1748. He m. 2ndly—25 Aug. 1750, Margaret, dau. and coheir of Charles Headlam, of Kexby, Yorks.; she bur. 3 Jan. 1764, having had an only son Philip. He m. 3rdly —2 Mar. 1767, Frances, dau. of Thomas Broad, of Fenton Vivian, co. Staff.; she d. s. p. 1811 (having re-m. 1782, to Rev. Thomas Bigsby, M.A. vicar of Beeston). His only son Philip, succeeded as 5th Earl, and his only grandson, George Philip Cecil Arthur, 7th Earl, d. unm. 1 Dec. 1871.

/2/ Ferdinand, d. 11 Feb. 1750, having m. 2 May, 1742, Mary dau. of   Phillips. His grandson, CYSTOM

CHARLES GEORGE, capt. in the army (3rd and youngest son of Adm. John Stanhope, R.N. by his wife Caroline, dau. of Digby Dent, Esq.), bp. 16 June, 1789; d. 22 Jan. 1833, having m. 6 Nov. 1820, Jane, eldest dau. of late Sir James Galbraith, Bart.; she d. 13 Jan. 1873, having had an only son,

George Philip, 8th and present Earl.

(2) Charles (4th son), bp. 29 Dec. 1700; d. 18 Mar. 1759 having m. Cecilia, dau. of Dutton Stede, of Stede Hill, Kent, and was grandfather of Adm. Sir Henry Edwyn Stanhope, created a BARONET 13 Nov. 1807, whose representative is heir presumptive to the Earldom of Chesterfield.

EARL CHESTERFIELD m. 2ndly, Anne, dau. of Right Hon. Sir John Pakington, K.B. (B. HAMPTON), of Westwood, co. Worc. widow of Sir Humphrey Ferrers, of Tamworth Castle; she d. 1677, having had an only son,

[3] Hon. Alexander, of Hartshorn, Derbyshire, gent. usher to the Queen, envoy extraordinary to Spain, 1689/1706; d. 20 Sept. 1707, having m. Catherine, dau. of Arnold Burghill, of Thingehill Parva, co. Hereford, and had 5 sons, of whom the eldest,

James, created EARL OF STANHOPE. (See that title.)

RICHARD WALTER CHETWYND, Viscount Chetwynd and Baron of Rathdowne (1717, I.), late 14th dragoons; s. his father as 7th Viscount 6 Dec. 1879; b. 26 July, 1823; m. 16 Mar. 1858, Harriet Johanna, eldest dau. of Walter Campbell, Esq. of Sunderland, N.B. and has a son and 2 daus.

[1] Hon. Richard Walter, K.O. 2nd Staff. mil. b. 27 Nov. 1859.
[2] Hon. Eleanora.
[3] Hon. Catherine Frances.

ARMS—Az. a chevron between three mullets or.
CREST—A goat's head erased arg. attired or.
SUPPORTERS—Two unicorns arg. each accolled with a chaplet of roses gu. having a chain of the same affixed thereto reflexed over the back.
MOTTO—Probitas verus honos.
SEAT—Marpoold, Exmouth.
TOWN HOUSE—25, Elvaston Place, S.W.

Lineage.

SIR JOHN CHETWYND, temp. EDW. III. (descended from Adam de Chetwynd, of Chetwynd, Salop, temp. HEN. III.), acquired the manor of Ingestre, Staff. by marriage with Isabel, dau. and heir of Philip de Mutton. His descendant,

SIR WALTER CHETWYND, of Ingestre, sheriff of Staff. 1607, by his wife Catherine Hastings, eldest dau. of George, 4th Earl of Huntingdon, and widow of Sir Edward Unton, of Wadley, Berks. Knt. had 2 sons, of whom the younger,

JOHN, of Rudge, near Bloreheath, Staff. M.A. Exeter Coll. Oxon. 1648, M.P. temp. CHARLES II. and JAMES II. By his wife, who d. 28 Feb. 1738, he had 3 sons, successive Peers.

(1) Walter, M.P. boroughs Stafford and Lichfield 1705-35, master of the buckhounds, temp. Queen ANNE, created BARON RATHDOWNE and VISCOUNT CHETWYND, of Berehaven, co. Cork, in the Peerage of Ireland, by patent dated 29 June, 1717, with limitation to the male descendants of his father, high steward for borough of Stafford 1717; d. 21 Feb. 1735, s. p. having m. Hon. Mary Berkeley, dau. and coheir of John, Viscount Fitzhardinge; she d. 3 June, 1741.

Figure 5-2
Page from 1881 edition of Joseph Foster's *The Peerage, Baronetage, and Knightage of the British Empire for 1881*, showing lineage of noble families.

required, and then, as has been mentioned, a change to the arms was required and would then be registered.

Genealogists owe a debt of gratitude to heraldry, at least when it comes to our English research. Because of the coats of arms and the need to prove entitlement to such, we have Heralds' Visitations.

In order to prove that an individual could use a coat of arms, it became necessary to record the right of that use, which was done by showing one's descent from the person who was originally entitled to that arms.

Sheriffs in each county compiled lists of the nobles, gentry, knights, and gentlemen in their area and these lists were then sent to the heralds. These individuals were then required to go before the heralds and show proof of their entitlement. While the proof could have been oral tradition, many of these individuals could back up their claims through records of the local church. These family trees were then recorded. The heralds undertook this project from 1530 to about 1686, over intervals of just a few years to thirty years.

Today these records are known as Heralds' Visitations and are perhaps more accessible than you may have thought. The original records are housed at the College of Arms. You can find a complete listing of the various visitations for each county in Sir Anthony Richards' *The Records & Collections of the College of Arms* (London: Burke's Peerage, 1952). You will also find that most of the visitations have been published, primarily by the Harleian Society.

Many people ignore this valuable resource because they do not understand the importance of the visitations. It is possible that researchers who

Warning

ARMS FOR SALE

You will find many places offering to sell you a family coat of arms. Be aware that while a person with the same surname as you is entitled to that coat of arms, it is not actually the "family" coat of arms.

HARLEIAN SOCIETY

The Harleian Society was founded in 1869. Its primary purpose was the publishing of the heraldic visitations. While a majority of the published volumes of the Harleian Society are available at the Family History Library, some of them on microfilm, you will not find them if you do an author search and use Harleian Society as your search term. Most of the published volumes had an editor, and it is this name for which you will need to search. Once you have found one such entry (if you would like, you can use the *Visitations of County Oxford 1566, 1574, 1634* by William Turner), you could then use the Series information, which is a hot link, to locate all the records associated with the society. Inquiries to the society should be addressed to

The Hon Secretary
Harleian Society
c/o College of Arms
Queen Victoria Street
London EC4V 4BT

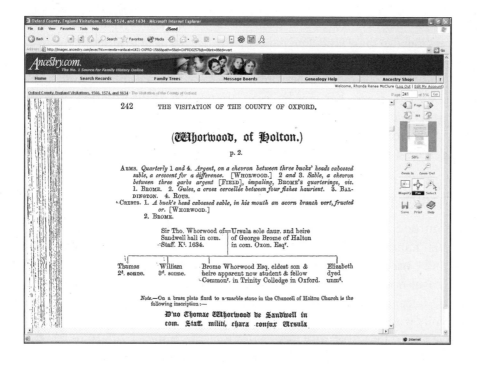

Figure 5-3
Digitized image of the Oxford County Visitions for England, 1566, 1574, and 1634, page 242. © 2000–2002 MyFamily.com, Inc. Screen shot from Ancestry.com. Used with permission.

have not spent much time working in the British records may be confusing the Heralds' Visitations with ecclesiastical visitations. Ecclesiastical visitations were visitations by either a Bishop or an Archdeacon to see how things spiritual and temporal were going with the given community. It is not unusual to find records relating to lists of clergy, school masters, or charities as a result of such visits. And while these may hold clues to aid you in your research, the Heralds' Visitations actually include pedigrees, something of great interest to any genealogist.

If the Family History Library has the volume in question only in book form, you cannot get it at your local Family History Center. This does not mean, however, that you cannot use the resources for the county from which your ancestors came. It just means you must look at some of the alternative formats in which the records now exist.

Ancestry.com has begun to make these records available as part of their online subscription site, which offers a UK and Ireland Records Collection. While they do not presently offer all of the published visitations that the Harleian Society has produced, they are certainly a good place to begin your online search for such records. Not only will you be able to view the digitized images of the pages as they were published by the Society, but you can also take advantage of the search functions at the site when searching for a specific individual or family (see Figure 5-3 above).

Another avenue to pursue in your search for visitation records is to see if they are available on CD-ROM for purchase. United Kingdom Genealogy <www.uk-genealogy.org.uk/> offers a number of them for sale. If you decide to purchase them, be sure to check out the available combined visitation CD-ROMs, as they may save you money if you find you want many of them.

Important

While you may never be able to claim the coat of arms, the visitations and the pedigrees found in those visitations may be just what you need to include extended, early lineage of a family on your own family tree. When combined with the information found in the many other published resources on notable and royal families, you can see that you have an abundance of information at your fingertips. The Internet resources offer you not only the convenience of researching from home, but also the option, especially in the case of *Burke's*, to search on a given individual, even when you do not yet know the title.

PUTTING THE RESEARCH TO WORK

I have introduced you to a number of different resources to aid you in your research of anyone royal or noble. We even discussed some of the resources that can be used when family stories talk about an ancestor having worked in the royal household. As I briefly mentioned, I've recently began to look into the lineage of actors Joseph and Ralph Fiennes. While I didn't have any family tradition to go on, I had found information on the Internet that discussed their ancestry to a degree. While the Internet offers much for genealogists, it is seldom the only thing I rely on when I am working on any family. As a result I took the information I found online and began to verify it.

Because the Web site mentioned that some of the information had come from *Burke's Peerage*, that was the first place I headed to see what I could learn about the ancestry of the two brothers. I was not disappointed. Unlike George Cokayne's *The Complete Peerage of England, Scotland, Ireland, Great Britain and the United Kingdom, Extant, Extinct, or Dormant*, which concentrates primarily on those with the titles, *Burke's* offers me the opportunity to see many descendants, including those that are now considered commoners. It also includes names of parents of spouses in many instances and offers me dates of birth, marriage, and death. By reading through the entry for the Baron Saye and Sele and paying attention to abbreviations that indicated I should turn to another section of the book, I was able to compile an impressive, though still in-progress, history for the brothers (see Figure 5-4 on pages 95-99).

KNOWING WHERE TO TURN

Of course, the trick is often knowing what records and resources will give you the information needed. The next chapter explores the different options when researching famous, notable, or infamous ancestors.

ANCESTORS OF JOSEPH AND RALPH FIENNES

This is an Ahnentafel of the direct lineage of brothers Joseph and Ralph Fiennes. To find the parent of an individual, take the number of that individual and multiply by two to find the father. Take the father's number and add one to find the mother. Not everyone listed has both parents.

Generation 1

1	**Joseph Fiennes** was born Joseph Alberic Fiennes on 27 May 1970 in Salisbury, Wiltshire, England and **Ralph Fiennes** was born Ralph Nathaniel Fiennes on 22 Dec. 1962 in Suffolk, England.

Generation 2

2	**Mark Fiennes** was born in 1933. He married Jennifer Anne Mary Alleyne Lash 14 Apr. 1962.
3	**Jennifer Anne Mary Alleyne Lash** was born in 1938. She died in 1993.

Generation 3

4	**Maurice Alberic Twisleton-Wykeham Fiennes** was born 1 Mar. 1907. He married Sylvia Joan Finlay 2 June 1932. Maurice was divorced from Sylvia in 1964. Maurice died in 1994.
5	**Sylvia Joan Finlay**
6	**Brig. Henry Alleyne Lash**

Generation 4

8	**Alberic Arthur Twisleton-Wykeham Fiennes** was born 4 Sept. 1865. He married Gertrude Theodosia Colley 9 Oct. 1895. Alberic died 28 Sept. 1919.
9	**Gertrude Theodosia Colley** died in 1934.
10	Major David Finlay

Generation 5

16	**Rev. Wingfield Stratford Twisleton-Wykeham-Fiennes** was born in Adelstrop, Gloucester, England, 1 May 1834. He married Alice Susan Yorke 6 Oct. 1863. He died 10 Oct. 1923.
17	**Alice Susan Yorke** was born in Asperden, Hertford, England, ca. 1837. Alice died 17 Feb. 1922.
18	**Henry FitzGeorge Colley** was born 1 July 1827. He married Elizabeth Isabella Wingfield 12 Aug. 1858. Henry died 24 Nov. 1886.
19	**Elizabeth Isabella Wingfield** died 18 Nov. 1903.

Generation 6

32	**Frederick Benjamin Twisleton-Wykeham-Fiennes, 16th Baron Saye and Sele** was born 4 July 1799. He married Emily Wingfield 4 June 1827. Frederick died in 1887.
33	**Emily Wingfield** died 20 June 1837.
34	**Very Rev. Hon. Grantham Munton Yorke** was born 17 Feb. 1809. He married Marian Emily Montgomery 10 Mar. 1830. Grantham died 2 Oct. 1879.
35	**Marian Emily Montgomery** was born in Calcutta, India, ca. 1801. Marian died 9 Sept. 1895.
36	**George Francis Colley** was born 11 Nov. 1797. He married Frances [--?--]. George died 9 May 1879.
37	**Frances [--?--]**
38	**Rev. William Wingfield** was born 21 May 1799. He married Elizabeth Kelly 14 Sept. 1830. William died 13 Mar. 1880.
39	**Elizabeth Kelly** died Mar. 1856.

Figure 5-4 continued on next page.

Generation 7	
64	**Archdeacon Venerable Thomas James Twisleton** was born 28 Sept. 1770. He married Charlotte Ann Wattell 26 Sept. 1788. He married Anne Ashe 7 June 1798. Thomas died 1824.
65	**Anne Ashe**
66	**Richard Wingfield 4th Viscount Powerscourt** was born 29 Oct. 1762. He married Catherine Meade 30 June 1789. He married Isabella Brownlow 9 Feb. 1796. Richard died 19 July 1809.
67	**Isabella Brownlow** died 5 Apr. 1848.
68	**Sir Joseph Sydney Yorke** was born 9 June 1768. He married Elizabeth Weake Rattray 29 Mar. 1798. He married Urania Annie [--?--] 22 May 1813. Joseph died 5 May 1831.
69	**Elizabeth Weake Rattray** died 29 Jan. 1812.
70	**Sir Henry C. Montgomery**
72	**John Pomeroy 4th Viscount Harberton**
76	**Richard Wingfield 4th Viscount Powerscourt** (redundant, see 66)
77	**Isabella Brownlow** (redundant, see 67)
78	**Rev. Thomas Kelly**
Generation 8	
128	**Thomas Twisleton 13th Baron Saye and Sele** was born 1735. He married Elizabeth Turner 14 June 1767. Thomas died in 1788.
129	**Elizabeth Turner** died 1 Apr. 1816.
132	**Richard Wingfield 3rd Viscount Powerscourt** was born before 24 Dec. 1730. He was baptized 24 Dec. 1730. He married Amelia [--?--] 7 Sept. 1760.
133	**Amelia [--?--]** died 11 Oct. 1831.
134	**Rt. Hon. William Brownlow**
136	**Charles Yorke** was born 30 Dec. 1722. He married Catherine Freeman 19 May 1755. He married Agneta Johnston 30 Dec. 1762. Charles died 20 Jan. 1770.
137	**Agneta Johnston**
138	**James Rattray**
144	**Arthur Pomeroy 1st Viscount Harberton** married Mary Colley 20 Oct. 1747.
145	**Mary Colley**
Generation 9	
256	**John Twisleton 12th Baron Saye and Sele** was born before 16 Jan. 1698. He was baptized 16 Jan. 1698. He married Anne Gardner 30 Dec. 1733. John died 1763.
257	**Anne Gardner** died 14 Jan. 1769.
258	**Sir Edward Turner 2nd Baronet of Ambrosden** married Cassandra Leigh.
259	**Cassandra Leigh**
264	**Richard Wingfield 1st Viscount Powerscourt** married Anne Usher 30 Aug. 1721. He married Dorothy Rowley 13 Apr. 1727. Richard died 21 Oct. 1751.
265	**Dorothy Rowley** died 21 July 1785.
272	**Philip Yorke 1st Earl of Hardwicke** was born 1690. He married Margaret Cocks.

Figure 5-4

273	Margaret Cocks
274	Henry Johnston
290	Henry Colley married Mary Hamilton.
291	Mary Hamilton
Generation 10	
512	Fiennes Twisleton 12th Baron Saye and Sele was born 1670. He married Mary Clarke 1692. Fiennes died 4 Sept. 1730.
513	Mary Clarke
514	William Gardner
518	William Leigh
528	Lewis Wingfield
530	Hercules Rowley
544	Philip Yorke married Elizabeth Gibbon.
545	Elizabeth Gibbon
546	C. Cocks married Mary Somers.
547	Mary Somers
582	James Hamilton 6th Earl of Abercorn married Elizabeth Reading 21 Jan. 1683/4. James died 28 Nov. 1734.
583	Elizabeth Reading died 19 Mar. 1754.
Generation 11	
1,024	George Twisleton married Cecil Twisleton.
1,025	Cecil Twisleton died in 1723.
1,164	Col. James Hamilton married Margaret [--?--]. James died 6 June 1673.
1,165	Margaret [--?--]
Generation 12	
2,050	Col. John Twisleton married Elizabeth Fiennes. John died 14 Dec. 1682.
2,051	Elizabeth Fiennes was born in 1613. She died in 1674.
2,328	Sir George Hamilton 1st Baronet of Donalong married Mary Butler 2 June 1629. George died 1679.
2,329	Mary Butler died Aug. 1680.
Generation 13	
4,102	James Fiennes 2nd Viscount Saye and Sele married Frances [--?--].
4,103	Frances [--?--]. She married secondly Rev. Joshua Spriggs in 1675. Frances died in 1684.
4,656	James Hamilton 1st Earl of Abercorn married Marian Boyd. James died 23 Mar. 1617/18.
4,657	Marian Boyd. She died 26 Aug. 1632.
4,658	Thomas Butler, Viscount Thuries
Generation 14	
8,204	William Fiennes 1st Viscount Saye and Sele married Elizabeth Temple.

Figure 5-4 continued on next page.

8,205	**Elizabeth Temple**
9,312	**Lord Claud Hamilton 1st Baron Paisley** was born in 1543. He married Margaret Seton 1 Aug. 1574. Lord died 1621.
9,313	**Margaret Seton** died before 18 Feb. 1616.
9,314	**Thomas Boyd 5th Lord Boyd**
Generation 15	
18,624	**James Hamilton 2nd Earl of Arran** was born in 1515. He married Margaret Douglas 23 Sept. 1532. James died 22 Jan. 1574/75.
18,625	**Margaret Douglas**
18,626	**George Seton 5th Lord Seton** was born ca. 1530. He married Isabel Hamilton 2 Aug. 1550. George died 8 Jan. 1585/6.
18,627	**Isabel Hamilton** was born ca. 1534. She died 13 Nov. 1604.
Generation 16	
37,248	**James Hamilton 1st Earl of Arran** was born in 1475. He married Janet Beaton before 1515. James died before 21 July 1529.
37,249	**Janet Beaton** died ca. 1522.
37,250	**James Douglas 3rd Earl of Morton**
37,252	**George Seton 4th Lord Seton** married Elizabeth Hay 10 Apr. 1527. George died 17 July 1549.
37,253	**Elizabeth Hay**
37,254	**Sir William Hamilton**
Generation 17	
74,496	**James Hamilton 1st Lord Hamilton** married Mary Stuart Apr. 1474. James died 16 Nov. 1479.
74,497	**Mary Stuart** was born ca. 1451. She married first Thomas Boyd, 1st Earl of Arran 26 Apr. 1467. She married James Hamilton, 1st Lord Hamilton Apr. 1474. Mary died ca. 1488.
74,498	**David Bethune**
74,504	**George Seton 3rd Lord Seton** married Lady Jane Bothwell 1506. George died 9 Sept. 1513.
74,505	**Lady Jane Bothwell**
Generation 18	
148,994	**James Stuart, James II, King of Scotland** was born in Edinburgh, Scotland, 16 Oct. 1430. He married Marie von Geldern in Edinburgh, Scotland, 3 July 1449. James died 3 Aug. 1460 in Roxburgh Castle, Scotland.
148,995	**Marie von Geldern**
149,008	**George Seton 2nd Lord Seton** married Margaret [--?--].
149,009	**Margaret [--?--]**
Generation 19	
297,988	**James Stuart, James I, King of Scotland** married Joan Beaufort.
297,989	**Joan Beaufort**
298,016	**John Seton Master of Seton** married Christian Lindsay 20 Jan. 1458/9. John died before 1476.

Figure 5-4

298,017	**Christian Lindsay** died in 1496.
Generation 20	
596,032	**George Seton 1st Lord Seton** married Margaret Stewart in 1436.
596,033	**Margaret Stewart**
Generation 21	
1,192,066	**John Stewart Earl of Buchan**

Figure 5-4

SIX

Finding Your Famous and Infamous Ancestry

Important

F ew of us set out to find a famous individual just for the fun of it. Usually we have heard a family story that hints that the individual is related. Finding information about the person is dependent upon what has made her famous. Historical notables are likely to have more information available about them, including a family tree, or at the very least some information about three or four generations of the family. If the person is a contemporary celebrity, books may yet be in progress or the information that has been found may not offer us as many family details as we would have liked. Likewise there are special publications devoted to publishing information about contemporary individuals. Such publications would not be of use when researching a historic notable.

The key to a successful search is in keeping your mind and options open. Too often we are convinced that such and such a publication won't have anything of use to our search, so we ignore it. Yet at a later date, we may consider the previously overlooked source in desperation only to discover that it had the clues we have been hunting for months. Don't ever ignore a source, no matter how obscure you think it might be. You never know when that source may result in a possible lead. I can't think of how many times I have found a tidbit here or there as I was reading an article about a celebrity. While I still seek out certain standard resources, I have learned—and yes, it was the hard way—that I must use all possible records and resources that I can access if I want to accomplish the goal of compiling the family history in question.

While our research is not always motivated by the possibility of finding a famous relative or ancestor, most people I know have some type of story about a possible connection to some famous individual. Such stories are usually about historic notables, as they have been passed down from one generation to the next. If you have the same surname as a celebrity, you may be wondering if there is a chance that you are related to that person in some way.

UP AGAINST A WALL

There are times when it seems like all your sources are coming up empty. It is at this time that you begin to turn to new sources, or revisit sources you haven't needed recently. This happened with my research of Dustin Hoffman's family history. While there are many Web sites, fan sites, and biographies about Dustin Hoffman, there is very little about his ancestry. In a last-ditch effort, as my deadline loomed large, I turned my attention to the *Reader's Guide to Periodical Literature*—an index to magazines. There are many articles that have been written about Dustin Hoffman, and some magazines that you would naturally turn to in hopes of finding additional information. Of all the magazine articles I read, and there were many, the most informative, and the one I almost passed up, was one in *Rolling Stone* in 1983. This article helped me to identify the year of death of his mother, which led me to more traditional records.

THE NAME'S THE SAME

By far the most common reason people think they are related to a notable figure is that they share the same surname as the individual in question. While this is certainly something that you will want to keep in mind, it is often not that simple. From experience, I have found that a connection usually isn't a result of the name held in common but rather through some other name or lineage a number of generations back. After all, if you were first cousins, you would definitely know it.

Another reason that "the name's the same" doesn't work, at least when it comes to those in the arts, is that many actors and other performers have changed their names. The name under which they now act or are known worldwide is not the name they were given at the time of their birth. In some instances the name has been changed to anglicize it. Others might have changed their name because the original wasn't "Hollywood" enough or it was too hard to remember or pronounce. Some actors change their name because there is already another actor going by that name. Regardless of the reason for

Reminder

THE NAME'S THE SAME—OR IS IT?

We are so used to expecting the name of a person to be the name they were born with, that assumptions are often made when it comes to the names of celebrities. Penny Marshall and Peter Marshall, at first glance, would appear to perhaps be related somewhere in the past. While nothing is impossible, when you realize that Penny Marshall's family name was actually *Masciarelli* with the family coming from Italy and Peter Marshall was born *Ralph Pierre LaCock* in West Virginia, you can see how the name is really no longer the same.

the name change, the fact remains that many of those that we watch on television or in movies or listen to on the radio may turn out to have a different original name than the one they're known by.

THE PLACE IS THE SAME

Other times you may find that you and a noted actor or actress share the same hometown, or that he or she shares that hometown with your parents or grandparents. Hometown heroes are shouted from the rooftops. There are streets named after them, and they often hold a place of prominence in the town. This phenomenon is becoming equally true of historically notable individuals as well, though you may need to look a little harder to find the information. Of course, with the prominence of travel channels and magazines, it has become a little easier.

HER KENTUCKY CONNECTIONS

Maysville, Kentucky, is the birthplace of Rosemary Clooney. When she returned to her hometown in Mason County, Kentucky, to marry Dante DiPaolo in 1997, you could say that the town welcomed her back with open arms. Genealogists researching the Clooney family can be thankful because the Mason County Genealogical Society published information about her marriage and about her family, with their many ties to Maysville. Best of all, there was a detailed genealogy of Rosemary's family included. Of course, since Rosemary was George Clooney's aunt, this means that anyone researching George Clooney's ancestry (see Figure 6-1 on page 103) had a head start on his paternal side. The information was found through a search of the newsletter and other genealogical publications listed in the Family History Library Catalog for Maysville. You can never exclude anything when researching your family history.

In addition to the pride of the town in question, the genealogical or historical society will often have extensive work on the family as well. While genealogists should always make it a point to concentrate on localities, with the Internet we often just plug a name into cyberspace and then move on if we don't find anything. Once you have learned a little about the celebrity in question using the tools discussed later in this chapter, you will then have a working knowledge of where to look for possible records and ancestry on an individual.

County histories are another locality-specific resource that may hold clues to the celebrity or historical figure in question. Sometimes in finding information about the celebrated individual, such as the lawyer or judge on a famous case, you may uncover information about your infamous ancestor as well. County histories have been published at many different times and for many different reasons. I have seen a number of those published in the latter part of the twentieth century that have been projects of local

ANCESTRY OF GEORGE CLOONEY
While his ancestry starts out in Kentucky, you can see that the generations take the lineage back to Ireland, Maryland, and Virginia.

Generation 1
1	**George Clooney** was born in Lexington, Fayette, Kentucky, 6 May 1961. He married Talia Balsam 1989. George was divorced from Talia in 1992.

Generation 2
2	**Nicholas J. Clooney** was born in Maysville, Mason, Kentucky, 13 Jan. 1934. He married Nina Bruce Warren Aug. 1959.
3	**Nina Bruce Warren** was born in Mason County, Kentucky, 24 Aug. 1939.

Generation 3
4	**Andrew Joseph Clooney** was born in Kentucky, 13 Oct. 1902. He married Frances Marie Guilfoyle. Andrew died 27 Aug. 1974 in Hamilton, Ohio.
5	**Frances Marie Guilfoyle** was born in Maysville, Mason, Kentucky, 25 Mar. 1909. She died 13 Dec. 1973.
6	**Marvin Jackson Warren** was born in Kentucky, ca. 1910. He married Dica Mae Edwards in Boyle County, Kentucky, 1938. Marvin died 15 May 1985 in Boyle County, Kentucky.
7	**Dica Mae Edwards** was born in Boyle County, Kentucky 1 May 1918.

Generation 4
8	**Andrew B. Clooney** was born in Kentucky, 25 June 1874. He married Crescentia Koch ca. 1900. Andrew died 31 Oct. 1947 in Maysville, Mason, Kentucky. His body was interred 3 Nov. 1947 in Washington, Kentucky, in St. Patricks Cemetery.
9	**Crescentia Koch** was born in Ohio, ca. 1876. She died 20 Jan. 1939 in Maysville, Mason, Kentucky.
10	**Michael J. Guilfoyle** was born in Mayslick, Mason, Kentucky, 14 Mar. 1876. He married Adelia Farrow in Covington, Kentucky, 1905. Michael died 15 June 1928 in Maysville, Mason, Kentucky.
11	**Adelia Farrow** was born in Mason Co., Kentucky, July 1884. She died 31 Dec. 1958 in Maysville, Mason, Kentucky.
12	**William M. Warren** was born in Green County, Kentucky, ca. 1879. He married Ida L. Chambers in Boyle County, Kentucky, 14 Nov. 1901.
13	**Ida L. Chambers** was born in Boyle County, Kentucky, Sept. 1884. She died 28 Sept. 1956 in Boyle County, Kentucky.
14	**Roy Edwards** was born in Boyle County, Kentucky, Dec. 1895. He married Nora Bell Perkins in Boyle County, Kentucky, 9 May 1917. Roy died 12 Aug. 1976 in Boyle County, Kentucky.
15	**Nora Bell Perkins** was born in Tennessee, ca. 1901. She died 6 Nov. 1987 in Boyle County, Kentucky.

Generation 5
16	**Nicholas Clooney** was born in Kilkenny Co., Ireland, ca. 1830. He married Bridget Byron in Mason Co., Kentucky, 24 May 1862.
17	**Bridget Byron** was born in Ireland, ca. 1835.
18	**Joseph A. Koch** was born in Ohio. He married Margaret Manns.
19	**Margaret Manns** was born in Ohio.
20	**Cornelius Guilfoyle** was born in Ireland, Jan. 1845. He married Rosanna Sweeney in Mayslick, Mason, Kentucky, 26 Aug. 1869.

Figure 6-1 continued on next page.

21	**Rosanna Sweeney** was born in Mason Co., Kentucky, 9 July 1854. She died 23 Nov. 1934 in Mason Co., Kentucky.
22	**Samuel Tully Farrow** was born in Mason Co., Kentucky, 23 July 1858. He married Louella Breckenridge Vanden ca. 1883. Samuel died 9 Sept. 1916 in Maysville, Mason, Kentucky. His body was interred 11 Sept. 1916 in Maysville, Mason, Kentucky, Maysville Cemetery.
23	**Louella Breckenridge Vanden** was born in Maysville, Mason, Kentucky, 1 Dec. 1860. She died 26 Jan. 1935 in Maysville, Mason, Kentucky. Her body was interred 28 Jan. 1935 in Maysville, Mason, Kentucky.
26	**John M. Chambers** was born in Tennessee, Aug. 1862. He married Lucy A. [--?--] ca. 1882. John died 2 Oct. 1913 in Boyle County, Kentucky.
27	**Lucy A. [--?--]** was born in Kentucky, July 1866. She died 10 Mar. 1937 in Boyle County, Kentucky.
28	**James Jack Edwards** was born in Boyle County, Kentucky, 11 Dec. 1858. He married Dicy Florence Bandy in Boyle County, Kentucky, 13 Feb. 1894. He married Hattie E. Rodes in Boyle County, Kentucky, 19 Sept. 1898. James died 23 Apr. 1931 in Boyle County, Kentucky.
29	**Dicy Florence Bandy** was born ca. 1868. She died Jan. 1896 in Kentucky.
30	**Unknown Perkins** married Jane Gray.
31	**Jane Gray**
Generation 6	
42	**Michael Sweeney** was born in Ireland, ca. 1828. He married Mary D. [--?--].
43	**Mary D. [--?--]** was born in Ireland, ca. 1824. She died before 1880.
44	**John B. Farrow** was born in Kentucky, Dec. 1833. He married Martha Jane Bramel 6 Aug. 1857.
45	**Martha Jane Bramel** was born in Kentucky, June 1840.
46	**Preston B. Vanden** was born in Ohio, 17 Feb. 1815. He married Adelia Cooper.
47	**Adelia Cooper** was born in Ohio, ca. 1820.
52	**Abraham Chambers** was born in Tennessee, Nov. 1827. He married Susanna [--?--] ca. 1846.
53	**Susanna [--?--]** was born in South Carolina, Feb. 1824.
56	**Mason Edwards** was born in Kentucky, ca. 1810. He married Lucy Whitehouse ca. 1856.
57	**Lucy Whitehouse** was born in Kentucky, ca. 1823.
58	**Ansel L. Bandy** was born in North Carolina, 23 Sept. 1838. He married Mary Ann Burgess in Davidson County, Tennessee, 7 Apr. 1864. Ansel died 1 Oct. 1906.
59	**Mary Ann Burgess** was born in Tennessee, 2 Sept. 1844. She died 12 Dec. 1904.
Generation 7	
88	**Orson Dogan Farrow** was born 15 Feb. 1805. He married Elizabeth O. Bruer 6 Apr. 1829.
89	**Elizabeth O. Bruer**
90	**Samuel Bramel** was born in Maryland, 21 July 1801. He married Mary Jane Taylor 19 Apr. 1836.
91	**Mary Jane Taylor** died before 1880.
104	**Unknown Chambers** married Nancy [--?--]
105	**Nancy [--?--]** was born in South Carolina, ca. 1790.
116	**William Bandy** married Dicie Green.
117	**Dicie Green**

Figure 6-1

Generation 8	
176	**William Farrow** was born in Virginia, 18 Apr. 1771. He married Elizabeth Shore in Fayette Co., Kentucky, 1793. He married Nancy [--?--] after 1826. William died 26 Dec. 1846 in Fleming Co., Kentucky.
177	**Elizabeth Shore** was born in Virginia, 20 Aug. 1775. She died 5 Sept. 1826 in Fleming Co., Kentucky.
180	**Samuel Bramel** married Mary Soletha Southern.
181	**Mary Soletha Southern**
Generation 9 (6th-great-grandparents)	
352	**Joseph Farrow** was born in Prince William Co., Virginia, ca. 1742. He married Elizabeth Masterson. Joseph died ca. 1784 in Loudon Co., Virginia.
353	**Elizabeth Masterson** was born ca. 1744.

Figure 6-1

genealogical societies. These histories often include sections devoted to the biographical and genealogical information of those who have ties to that county or community. While it usually costs money to submit your narrative, many individuals take advantage of this to share the information they have gathered, especially if their ancestors were early pioneers to the area. You can usually count on the compilers of such a county history to include information, sometimes detailed genealogical facts as well, on anyone who is famous and from that area.

Celebrities and historical figures didn't burst forth "fully grown." Most were born into the same obscurity as you and me (see Figure 6-1 on pages 103-105). These humble beginnings are often the place where your research of a celebrity will concentrate, at least at the start. Of course, to know where to turn you must first understand what resources are available that can give you the initial information you need to begin to trace the ancestry of a famous individual.

Infamous individuals are often approached from a different research angle. In many cases the infamous individual was not a celebrity. If he or she was, then the family has probably made peace with the deed in question and embraced the famous villain. More often than not though, you stumble across some hint of a scandal or a shady past as you are progressing in your family tree. As we saw in chapter three, you never know when a colorful ancestor will pop up. No one expects to find intrigue in a deed record, and yet that is exactly one of the places where it may be found.

In addition, many digitization projects are making it possible for us to run searches of newspapers from long ago. There are bound to be some completely unexpected headlines that appear when searching, perhaps long forgotten stories of sadness or shame.

If you are interested in learning more about a given individual, because you recognize that they have done something newsworthy, regardless of whether it was good or bad, or you suspect you are related to someone famous, there are a number of good resources that you should make it a point to turn to each time you begin such a search.

Reminder

KNOWING WHERE TO BEGIN

In genealogy, the rule of thumb is to work from the known to the unknown. This works when we are doing our own research—after all, we can easily obtain our birth certificate. We can talk to our parents. We can get records either about them or from them and so on. When it comes to researching a famous actor or a long deceased icon of history, you do not have the same opportunities. Instead you must turn to published resources to see what is already known about the person. In some cases you will find a lot of information and in other times you will discover that very little has been previously published. Don't get discouraged though, even if the information is small. Sometimes you need only a crumb to go forward.

YOU CAN FIND ALMOST ANYONE

There are certain resources that you can turn to regardless of whether you are interested in a contemporary or historical person. While I would like to tell you these resources will answer all of your questions, this is not always the case. I mentioned crumbs before because sometimes they're all we have to work with—just tiny bits of information compiled only through our ingenuity and perseverance. Yet, all that hard work makes you truly appreciate the family tree that you compile. The other record types included here may prove more useful when looking for a more obscure "fifteen minutes of fame" type of ancestor.

BIOGRAPHIES

Biographies are an excellent resource for both contemporary as well as historically significant individuals. I have found biographies to be a better resource than autobiographies when it comes to looking for clues about the parents and grandparents of the subject.

Autobiographies, perhaps because they are written by the subject, seem to focus exclusively on the individual. Once in awhile you may find that

---

GO WITH WHAT YOU FIND

In his autobiography, Charlton Heston didn't give as many exact dates and places as I have sometimes found in biographies, yet he did offer more identifying information than I have found in many other autobiographies (see Figure 6-2 on page 107). You often must read and reread the early chapters of biographies or autobiographies to make sure you haven't overlooked any important dates or indications of ages of the main individuals. When combined with research in traditional records, you may find that you know more than you thought.

ANCESTRY OF CHARLTON HESTON

Armed with the information in his autobiography, it was possible to turn to census and vital records and put together the beginnings of a family history including identifying Charlton's real maternal grandfather. More research will certainly allow this tree to grow.

Generation 1

1   **Charlton Heston** was born in Chicago, Cook, Illinois, 4 Oct. 1923. He married Lydia Marie Clark in North Carolina, 17 Mar. 1944.

Generation 2

2   **Russell Whitford Carter** was born in Illinois, 19 Sept. 1897. He married Lilla Charlton ca. 1921. Russell was divorced from Lilla ca. 1933. Russell died Sept. 1966 in Michigan.

3   **Lilla Charlton** was born in Illinois, July 1899. She married Chet Heston after 1933. Lilla died Mar. 1994 in Chicago, Cook, Illinois.

Generation 3

4   **John B. Carter** was born in England, ca. 1866. He married Katie Beatrice Clark ca. 1895.

5   **Katie Beatrice Clark** was born in Springfield, Illinois, 5 Aug. 1868. She died 21 Dec. 1936 in Richfield, Roscommon, Michigan.

6   **Charles George Christopher Baynes** was born in Montreal, Montreal, Quebec, 20 Nov. 1872. He married Marian E. Charlton in Chicago, Cook, Illinois, 4 Feb. 1896.

7   **Marian E. Charlton** was born in Ontario, Canada, Apr. 1871.

Generation 4

10   **Wallace William Clark** married Margarett A. Canady. Wallace died before 1910.

11   **Margarett A. Canady** was born in Indiana, 26 Mar. 1845. She died 13 Jan. 1926 in Richfield, Roscommon, Michigan.

12   **George Aylmer Baynes** was born in Quebec, 28 Feb. 1848. He married Elizabeth Griffin in Montreal, Montreal, Quebec, 14 June 1870.

13   **Elizabeth Griffin** was born ca. 1853 in Quebec.

14   **James Charlton** was born in England, 15 May 1832. He married Mary Drysdale ca. 1859. James died 19 Nov. 1913 in Chicago, Cook, Illinois. His body was interred 21 Nov. 1913 in Hamilton, Northumberland, Canada.

15   **Mary Drysdale** was born in Canada, 6 Sept. 1836. She died 28 Oct. 1913 in Chicago, Cook, Illinois. Her body was interred 31 Oct. 1913 in Hamilton, Northumberland, Canada.

Generation 5

22   **Phila A. Canady** married Nancy J. Wolfe. Phila died before 1880.

23   **Nancy J. Wolfe** was born in Indiana, ca. 1824.

24   **William Craig Baynes** was born in Quebec, ca. 1810. He married Elizabeth Chase Harvey.

25   **Elizabeth Chase Harvey**

28   **Unknown Charlton** married Mary Athey.

29   **Mary Athey**

30   **Alexander Drysdale** was born in Scotland, ca. 1804. He married Catherine Frazier.

31   **Catherine Frazier**

Figure 6-2

the autobiographer mentions, almost in passing, his or her parents and perhaps gives you a tiny glimpse into the home of his or her childhood. More often than not, though, this glimpse is all you get. Often the autobiography is written with a specific purpose in mind. The book may have been written to share something major that the person has recently gone through, or the focus may have been on the most important time in the person's life up to this point. Regardless, autobiographies do not usually supply as much family history information.

Biographies, on the other hand, are designed to give you a real understanding of the subject. As a result, while the book may open at the time the celebrity is discovered or at some other middle point in his life, at some point most biographers go back and tell you the story of when the person was born. Often it is at this point that the author of the biography will devote some time to when and where the parents were born, how they grew up or met each other,

DON'T BELIEVE EVERYTHING YOU READ

In researching Lizzie Borden, I came across a book called *Lizzie Borden: The Legend, the Truth, the Final Chapter* by Arnold R. Brown (Nashville: Rutledge Hill Press, 1991) in which he poses the idea of a different person who was responsible for the death of Lizzie's parents, a William Borden who he says is the illegitimate child of Andrew Borden. In reading the book, it appeared that the author had done quite a bit of research. Unfortunately, my faith in the research hit a sudden issue when the author began to make assumptions based on what he found in the vital records. While it is natural to make certain assumptions, he listed the following birth records for a Charles Borden and his two wives, Phebe Hathaway and Peace:

- Hannah H. Borden, born 21 Sept. 1844, mother listed as Phebe

- Eliza A. Borden, born 21 May 1848, mother listed as Phebe

- Eliza Borden, born 23 May 1850, mother listed as Phebe

- (Male) Borden, born 27 Dec 1860, mother listed as Peace

- Joseph H. Borden, born 27 Dec 1861, mother listed as Peace

He goes on to say "There are no birth records for William S. or Charles, and there is no explanation for why there are two Elizas.

"The available information from the Fall River City Clerk's office is not as complete, nor does it fit together as neatly as we might hope. 'Male' Borden is more likely to be Charles than William because William's death certificate gave his age in 1901 as forty-five, which would put his birth in 1856" (296).

He uses this supposed missing record to infer that under a law still on the books today in Massachusetts, William is illegitimate and that explains why he is not listed. Actually it is more than William who is not listed. The vital records alone leave many questions. When combined with the census records though, it appears that his assumption about (Male) Borden is incorrect and I suspect that (Male) Borden and Joseph H. Borden are one in the same, given that they had the same birth date, just one year apart. It is also possible that the first Eliza Borden as found in the birth records died and the family elected to name the next daughter Eliza as well, a common practice. The 1850 census also shows an Amanda M. Borden that he has not mentioned at all in his book.

The 1850 Fall River, Bristol Co., Massachusetts, census of the family of Charles and Phebe indicates that children were as follows: Charles was born ca. 1838 (age twelve), Amanda M. was born ca. 1843 (age seven), Hannah H. was born ca. 1845 (age five), and Eliza was born ca. May 1850 (age one month). The 1860 census shows the family of Charles and Peace with Borden children Chas A. (age twenty-two), Hannah (age fifteen), Eliza (age eleven), and William (age seven), as well as Bassett children (perhaps Peace's prior marriage?) Chas. (age thirteen), Edwin (age eleven), and William (age seven). The 1870 census shows Charles and Peace with Eliza (age twenty), William L. Bassett born ca. 1854 (age sixteen), and Joseph H. (age nine). A search of the 1870 census index for Massachusetts revealed a seventeen-year-old William Borden enumerated in the third Ward of Taunton, also in Bristol County, and this could be the son of Charles.

While it is still possible that William was illegitimate, the fact that the author drew assumptions from limited records has forced me to question the validity of his arguments as to William's parentage and his accusation of William as the actual murderer of Andrew and Abby Borden. The research completed in vital records seems limited, it appears his conclusions are based on incomplete information, and I am left to wonder if further research would have painted a different picture about William.

and so forth. I have seen some outstanding genealogical information included in biographies, sometimes going back three or four generations.

Good biographies cite sources used in compiling the information reported in the book. When it comes to the dates of births, marriages, and deaths, I pay close attention to the footnotes or endnotes to see where the information came from. I'm happy when I see that the author has spent time digging in the records that I would need to look at. I will still examine the records, but through the source citations the job of finding them has been made considerably easier.

Biographies, like all of the other resources mentioned in this chapter, are what genealogists consider a source of secondary information. **Secondary information is the information supplied by individuals who were not present at the**

\di'fin *vb*

Definitions

events being reported. In a biography, this usually means the compiler of the information has viewed some records or other information and has drawn conclusions that are now being shared with you, the reader.

The inaccuracies I have seen in biographies generally come either from inexperience with the records that genealogists use all the time or a heavy reliance on other secondary information. I have seen biographies where the author has compiled a biography solely on information found in interviews with the celebrity. While you would think that the interviews would be accurate, people often misquote dates of events by a day, month, or year. Such misinformation was one of the problems I encountered when working with the information found about Dustin Hoffman's mother.

Once in a while I see a biographer use the same records that genealogists use, such as birth records, but she either uses them incorrectly or misinterprets the information to draw a conclusion that may be misleading or flat-out wrong. These types of mistakes are often not apparent to me until I begin to use those same records in conjunction with the other records that genealogists rely on. Seldom does a genealogist rely on a single record when it comes to deciphering the ancestry of a person.

Today, in addition to the more traditional published biographies, we have individuals publishing online biographies. When it comes to celebrities I have discovered that enamored fans are most apt to put up such a Web page. I've seen similar pages for historical individuals as well, though with those from history you have a good chance of finding some scholarly articles online, too. I have seen many graduate students publish their papers after they have submitted them to their professors. Such articles are often cited, making them a valuable source of information with regards to potential records and resources.

FAMILY HISTORIES

Like so many of the other resources genealogists have used, family histories have changed dramatically over the years. In the past we had to search out published family histories, visiting many libraries or getting others to visit them in our stead. Today's technology is bringing many of these histories to us online, allowing us to easily peruse them at our leisure (see Figure 6-3 on page 111).

Warning

Family histories can be a double-edged sword. **They are compiled by family historians with all manner of experience.** Some researchers, eager to share what they found, publish perhaps before they are ready, not having verified their information in the most reliable resources available. In some instances, the compiler, in a zeal to find a connection to a famous individual, may have forced a round ancestor into a square pedigree. Unless we take the time to evaluate the information in a family history by comparing it to the records that are available, we run the risk of perpetuating the error.

There are times that family histories don't include the famous individual, even though the person is related and was famous at the time the family

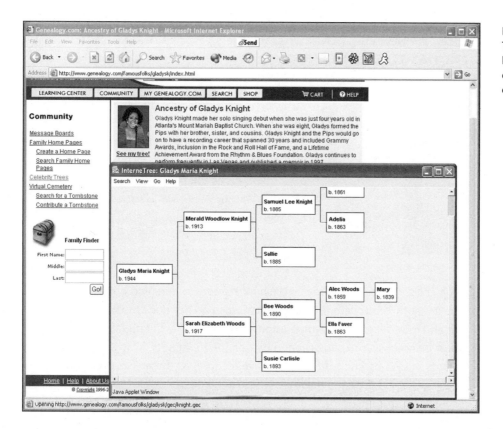

Figure 6-3
Technology is making genealogical information more accessible. © 2002 Genealogy.com. Used with permission.

history was compiled. Other family histories do not call attention to the famous individual in any way. When you are conducting research in a family history, then, it becomes important to look not only for the famous individual but also for her parents and grandparents as well. You never know where in the line the compiler stopped.

BIOGRAPHICAL DICTIONARIES AND WHO'S WHO

When it comes to those who have distinguished themselves in one way or another, it is always possible you will find them in a biographical dictionary or a Who's Who compilation. There are Who's Who directories on high school students, women, people across the United States, people in a specific region of the United States, and people of a particular ethnic background, to name just a few. Some are easier to find than others.

There are times that one of the more specialized publications should be the focus of your research. Because the volume focuses just on women or just on those who have excelled in medicine, it is possible that you will find the individual you are seeking. The information found in a Who's Who usually includes the date and place of birth, names of the parents, name of spouse and children, educational institutions attended, employment, and perhaps more.

The entry for actor John Carradine provided me with a lot of information. I learned when and where he was born, which allowed me to turn my

HE HAS TO BE THERE

Mario Anzuoni/SplashNews

In sharing my professional interest in celebrity family history with a colleague, he mentioned that he knew that the ancestry of Matt Damon could be found in one of the published Damon family histories. I was thrilled, to say the least, but it would be a year before I would find out just which family history it was in. Why? Matt Damon himself was not mentioned. Richard A. Damon Jr., compiler of *The Damon Family of Wayland, Massachusetts* (Camden: Penobscot Press, 1997), stopped the direct line of Matt Damon with the listing of his father as a child. I broke one of my cardinal rules in my researching of this, in that I looked at the book without being prepared. I had not done my homework, and when I didn't find Matt Damon listed, I could not identify his father, though after being given the page citation by Gary Boyd Roberts, it was obvious to me that it was his parents and I should have recognized them. The problem was that once I had done my preliminary research I did not return to this volume. It is essential that we progress in our research in an orderly manner so as not to waste time as happened in this instance.

For More Info

MARQUIS WHO'S WHO PUBLICATIONS

Marquis Who's Who directories include a number of specialty publications devoted to ethnic and industry-specific directories. You can find a list of all of their publications at <www.marquiswhoswho.com/>.

attention to birth records. Knowing his parents' names, including his mother's maiden name, made it easier to verify I had the correct birth record when I got it. The other information included offered me some insight into his life and offered possible localities in which I could pursue additional research.

Biographical dictionaries are similar to the Who's Who though they are often written in a more narrative style, with less abbreviation. They are usually devoted to a given occupation or ethnic background, and are also frequently focused on a specific town, county, or state, as opposed to encompassing all of the country. They are often published more frequently. Biographical dictionaries are more apt to include those who are not famous. Good news for those who are trying to find information on their cobbler or cigar maker ancestor. To find biographical dictionaries, you may need to plan a visit to the locality where your ancestor was living. Get familiar with the repositories in the area.

Finding individuals mentioned in the Who's Who and some biographical dictionaries has been made much easier with the availability of the *Biographical and Genealogical Master Index* (BGMI). Begun in the 1970s and compiled by Mirana C. Herbert and Barbra McNeil, the first edition was published in 1980, and the most recent was published in 1995. Unlike the Who's Who publications that come out yearly, this index of those and other

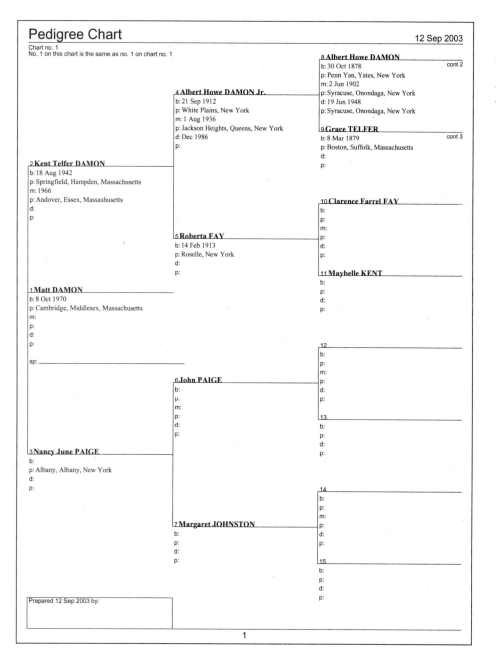

Pedigree Chart   12 Sep 2003

Chart no. 1
No. 1 on this chart is the same as no. 1 on chart no. 1

8 **Albert Howe DAMON**
b: 30 Oct 1878   cont 2
p: Penn Yan, Yates, New York
m: 2 Jun 1902
p: Syracuse, Onondaga, New York
d: 19 Jun 1948
p: Syracuse, Onondaga, New York

4 **Albert Howe DAMON Jr.**
b: 21 Sep 1912
p: White Plains, New York
m: 1 Aug 1936
p: Jackson Heights, Queens, New York
d: Dec 1986
p:

9 **Grace TELFER**
b: 8 Mar 1879   cont 3
p: Boston, Suffolk, Massachusetts
d:
p:

2 **Kent Telfer DAMON**
b: 18 Aug 1942
p: Springfield, Hampden, Massachusetts
m: 1966
p: Andover, Essex, Massashusetts
d:
p:

10 **Clarence Farrel FAY**
b:
p:
m:
p:
d:
p:

5 **Roberta FAY**
b: 14 Feb 1913
p: Roselle, New York
d:
p:

11 **Maybelle KENT**
b:
p:
d:
p:

1 **Matt DAMON**
b: 8 Oct 1970
p: Cambridge, Middlesex, Massachusetts
m:
p:
d:
p:

sp:

12
b:
p:
m:
p:
d:
p:

6 **John PAIGE**
b:
p:
m:
p:
d:
p:

13
b:
p:
d:
p:

3 **Nancy June PAIGE**
b:
p: Albany, Albany, New York
d:
p:

14
b:
p:
m:
p:
d:
p:

7 **Margaret JOHNSTON**
b:
p:
d:
p:

15
b:
p:
d:
p:

Prepared 12 Sep 2003 by:

1

Figure 6-4
Knowing the names of a celebrity's parents or grand-parents may be essential when working with compiled family histories.

biographical sources is only updated periodically. BGMI concentrates on those individuals who were alive and important in the nineteenth and twentieth centuries (see Figure 6-5 on page 115).

This index is a relatively recent resource compared to many of the other resources that genealogists frequently use. **When it comes to finding someone who has been published in a biographical dictionary or record, using it saves major time,** provided the researcher understands the purpose of the volumes. It is not designed to supply you with the biography but instead to lead you to the biographies as found in other publications, some of which you might not know even exist.

While the index has been available in some public libraries, and is avail-

Timesaver

WHO'S WHO ENTRY

Who's Who in America, 38th Edition, 1974–1975, p. 504:

CARRADINE, JOHN RICHMOND, actor; b. N.Y.C., Feb. 5, 1906; s. William Reed and Genevieve Winifred (Richmond) C.; student Episcopal Acad., Phila., Graphic Arts Sch., Phila.; children—Bruce John, John Arthur, Christopher John, Keith Ian, Robert Reed. Debut, St. Charles Theater, New Orleans, 1925; appeared in numerous motion pictures, 1928–, numerous stage plays, 1945–; organizer own repertory co. playing Hamlet, Shylock and Othello. Mem. A.F.T.R.A., Actors Equity Assn., Screen Actors Guild. Clubs: Players, Channel Island Yacht. Home: 4220 Harbor Blvd., Oxnard, CA 93030. Office: % Paul Kohner Inc., 9169 Sunset Blvd., Los Angeles, CA 90069.

WHERE TO LOOK

In a word—everywhere. You will find that there are records on the town level in some instances, perhaps at a town hall. Many of the records will be on the county level at the county courthouse. Still others will be found on the state level at the state vital statistics office, for example. Of course, there are many different public and specialty libraries where genealogy can be found. This is especially true when looking for biographical information. Collections and published biographical resources are usually found in public libraries, as well as genealogical and historical societies. Sometimes, you will find what you want at the state archives or state historical society. When you need to know what records may be found where, you will want to check out what these books tell you about the locality you are researching.

- Bentley, Elizabeth Petty. *The Genealogist's Address Book*. 4th edition. Baltimore: Genealogical Publishing Company, Inc., 1998.

- Eichholz, Alice, editor. *Ancestry's Red Book: American State, County & Town Sources*. Revised edition. Salt Lake City: Ancestry, Inc., 1992.

- *The Handy Book for Genealogists*. 10th edition. Everton Publishers, 2002.

You may find that in reading these books that you learn that the state in question has set up regional archives or repositories. If so, then you may find that in addition to town, county, and state repositories, you must also turn your attention to the regional repository.

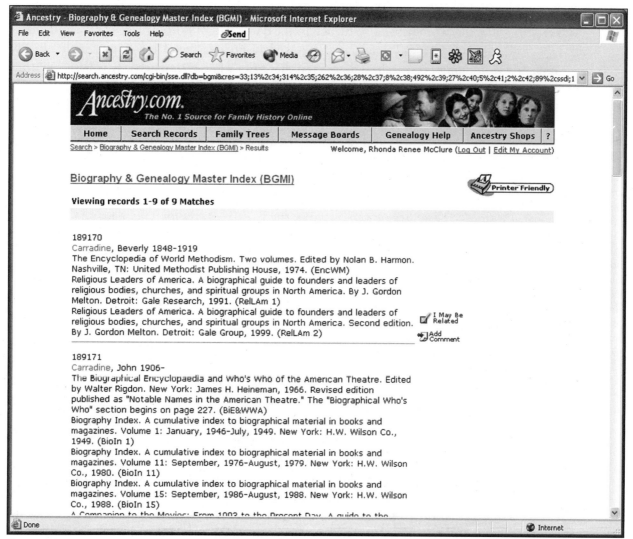

Figure 6-5
Biography & Genealogy Master Index entries lead you to other biographical resources. © 2000–2002 MyFamily.com, Inc. Screen shot from Ancestry.com. Used with permission.

able at the Family History Library, it has also made its way online as part of the subscription offerings at Ancestry.com. There is a disclaimer on the site stating that they have not included any living individual who was born after 1920 in an effort to protect privacy of living individuals. Yet, I have still saved myself time in that I learned of specific titles of biographical publications I could then search for in online library catalogs.

Of course, like published biographies and family histories, it is always possible that the information included in the Who's Who may be incorrect. Usually errors creep in during the data entry or typesetting phase of the publication.

About a year ago, while I was putting together a tree on actress Sissy Spacek, I was going through my preliminary resources, many of which are discussed in detail in this chapter. I had amassed information from celebrity

For More Info

ONLINE LIBRARY CATALOGS

For finding library catalogs that are available online, you will want to start with LibDex.com <www.libdex.com/>. You can find more about online library catalogs in chapter six "Library Research from Home" in *The Genealogist's Computer Companion* (Cincinnati: Betterway Books, 2001).

type databases, and searched the Internet for "fan sites" and other published biographies. I also turned to the databases of both Ancestry.com and Genealogy.com, which are discussed in greater detail in chapter eight. In my initial research, I discovered that Sissy's father and actor Rip Torn's mother were siblings. In the hope of finding anything that would help me jump-start the research on this family, I put in Thelma Torn's name into Ancestry's database, originally expecting only to find entries in the Social Security Death Index and the Texas Death Index. While I did find both of these, I discovered that Ancestry was showing an additional hit under its Biography & History heading. Because the name was such an unusual one, I went to look and see what it was.

The entry turned out to be the BGMI listings for Thelma, and told me she was mentioned in *Who's Who of American Women* for the years 1964–65, 1966–67, 1968–69, 1970–71, and 1973–74. I was able to get the information from the sixth edition, 1970–71. It confirmed that she was born when and where I thought, and listed her parents, including her mother's maiden name. This information helped me immensely in identifying Sissy's paternal lineage back four generations to the early 1800s, where I was stopped simply because the families came from Moravia and deadlines did not permit me to devote any more time to the research (see Figure 6-6 on page 117). While this publication was immensely helpful, it also included a typo. Her parents are listed as "Arnold A. and Mary (Cervenka) Space." Her birth record clearly listed her surname as Spacek, and given the rest of the information that I had amassed at that point I realized that the Who's Who had a typo on her maiden name.

While these biographical resources are some of the first places I turn for information, I have also found that I can sometimes get useful information from other publications as well, including periodicals. Finding the periodicals with the information I want requires the use of two special resources.

WILSON *READERS' GUIDE TO PERIODICAL LITERATURE*

I know that some of you are scratching your heads, trying to figure out why this title sounds vaguely familiar. Probably the last time you used this bunch of green books you were in high school or college working on a research paper, one that required you to use multiple sources, including magazines.

I once took a young friend to the library with me. She was a senior in high school at the time but was interested in genealogy and was intrigued by what I did at the library. On that particular trip, in addition to using more traditional genealogical resources, I needed to find magazine articles about the Salem Witchcraft Trials of 1692. When we got to the library, I made a beeline for the volumes in the *Readers' Guide*, explaining that after I got what I needed there we would move on to the genealogy and audiovisual departments. As she saw the books I was beginning to grab, her eyes got

ANCESTRY OF SISSY SPACEK
Generation 1
1   **Sissy Spacek** was born in Smith County, Texas, 25 Dec. 1949.
Generation 2
2   **Edwin Arnold Spacek** was born in Granger, Williamson, Texas, 3 July 1910. He married Virginia Spilman. Edwin died 7 Jan. 2001 in Virginia, at 90 years of age.
3   **Virginia Spilman** was born 18 Dec. 1917.
Generation 3
4   **Arnold A. Spacek** was born in Fayetteville, Fayette, Texas, 16 Sept. 1886. He married Mary Cervenka in Williamson County, Texas, 17 Sept. 1907.
5   **Mary Cervenka** was born in Granger, Williamson, Texas, 24 Feb. 1889. She died 26 Sept. 1970 in Williamson County, Texas.
Generation 4
8   **Frank J. Spacek** was born in Moravia, Dec. 1853. He married Julie Gloekner in Fayette County, Texas, 16 Nov. 1875. Frank died before June 1929.
9   **Julie Gloekner** was born in Germany, 2 Jan. 1854. She died 14 June 1929 in Granger, Williamson, Texas.
10   **Josef Cervenka** was born in Hukvaldy, Austria, 28 Feb. 1865. He married Anna Machu in Granger, Williamson, Texas, 2 Sept. 1884. Josef died 11 Aug. 1943.
11   **Anna Machu** was born in Senince Usti, Vsetin Valley, Moravia, 13 Apr. 1865. She died 26 Feb. 1937 in Ballinger, Rummels, Texas.
Generation 5
16   **Frank Spacek** was born in Moravia, ca. 1816. He married Antonia. Frank died before 1900.
17   **Antonia** was born in Moravia, June 1832.
18   **William Gloekner** married Johanna Kirsch. William died before 1900.
19   **Johanna Kirsch** was born in Austria, Feb. 1830.
22   **Pavel Machu** was born in Moravia, Jan. 1834. He married Rozina Talica ca. 1856. Pavel died before Jan. 1920.
23   **Rozina Talica** was born in Moravia, 16 Nov. 1840. She died 28 May 1920 in Granger, Williamson, Texas.

Figure 6-6
Biographical sources can help get a pedigree started.

wide, and she turned and looked at me. Her comment? "You mean people actually use these after high school?" I chuckled and assured her that people did indeed use them.

Here I am twelve years later still turning to them not only for historical subjects, such as Salem, but also when I am in need of interviews and articles about individuals, both historical and contemporary. On some occasions when I'm stumped, I have even left the Family History Library in Salt Lake City to use the *Readers' Guide* and magazine collection at the public library a few blocks away.

While the *Readers' Guide* is often a more effective resource when it comes to researching a historic event or a specific event, I have found that articles about individuals sometimes hold the clues I need. My motto when I am researching a celebrity

Research Tip

or historical figure is to leave no stone unturned. If time permits, I try to exhaust all resources available to me from different repositories and avenues, both on and offline.

Like the Who's Who publications, at the present time the *Readers' Guide* is not priced so that individuals can access it. Most public libraries have the actual published volumes, which come out each month and then are combined into a single yearly volume at the end of the year. They index periodicals on different subjects from gardening to racecars and everything in between. Using the *Readers' Guide* I have found useful interviews in magazines such as *People, Time, Life, American Heritage,* and many more (see Figure 6-7 below). I still maintain the most amazing find was the information I found about Dustin Hoffman's mother in an article about him in *Rolling Stone,* a magazine I was almost convinced wouldn't have the information I needed. While he still remains my genealogy enigma, it answered a couple of important questions for me.

Figure 6-7
Taking notes is important, especially when dealing with mainstream resources such as the *Reader's Guide.*

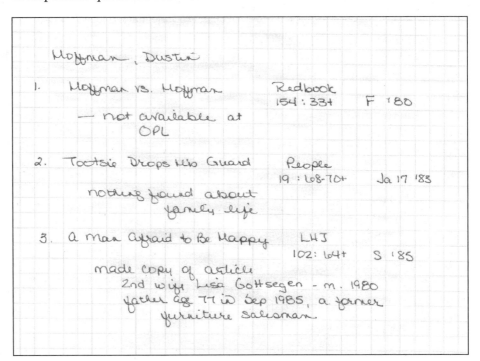

PERSI

While the *Readers' Guide* is my resource for mainstream magazines, when it comes to genealogical periodicals, I turn to PERSI, the *Periodical Source Index* compiled by the Allen County Public Library in Fort Wayne, Indiana. Designed to help genealogists know which periodicals have records and genealogical information about a specific surname, person, locality, or record type, this massive and ongoing project published its first volumes in 1985. At that time it was necessary to look in multiple volumes, those that were first published and then each subsequent yearly update.

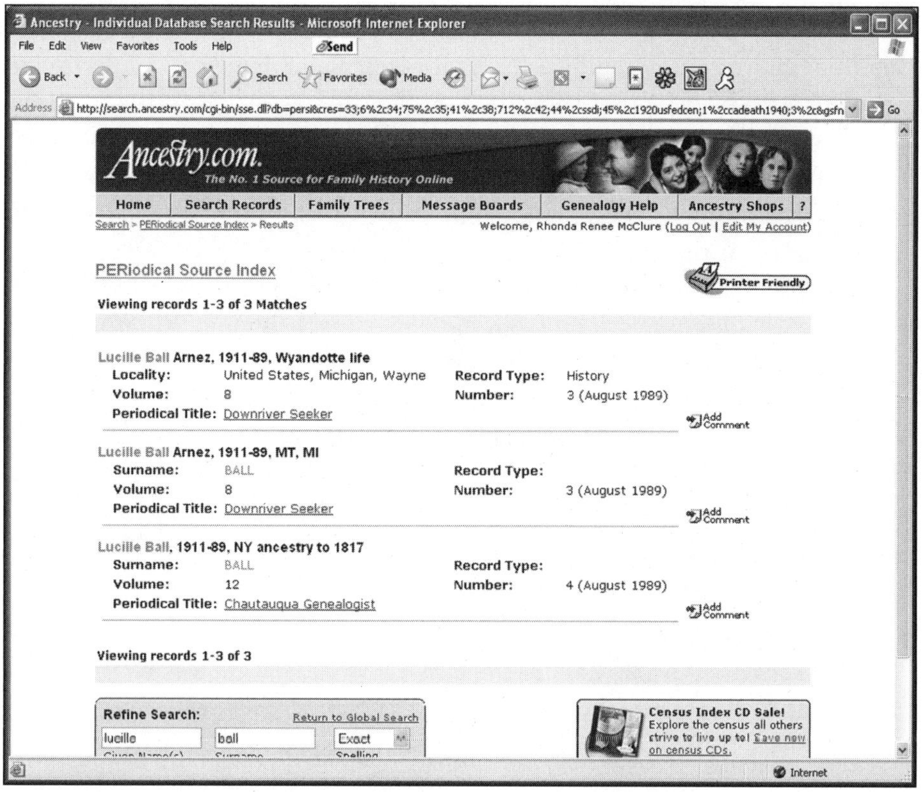

Figure 6-8
PERSI is a big time saver when it comes to searching for family history in genealogical periodicals. ©2000–2002 MyFamily.com, Inc. Screen shot from Ancestry.com. Used with permission.

At one point there were about twelve volumes I had to look through before I could say with certainty that I had truly found all the entries indexed in PERSI.

A few years ago, Ancestry.com formed a partnership with the Allen County Public Library and published PERSI on CD-ROM. There was much rejoicing in the genealogical community. Searching the CD-ROM was much faster and, through the nature of the computer searching mechanisms, it offered us ways to locate entries we had not found when we only had the books available.

Now Ancestry.com makes the PERSI index available as part of their U.S. Records Collection, one of the subscriptions they offer through their Web site <www.ancestry.com/>. There have been times when I found myself with just a few days to compile a celebrity tree, usually as a result of a change in the *Biography* episode lineup on A&E cable television. As a result I needed all the advantages I could get. Online searching of databases is one of those advantages, and knowing which genealogical periodicals may already have some of the information, even if my search has to take place at midnight, helps (see Figure 6-8 above).

Resources like the *Readers' Guide* and PERSI help me to focus my research in specific publications based on the information I need at the time. When combined with BGMI, I find I have an index to most of the published resources that are likely to offer me biographical information about almost anyone who has done anything noteworthy.

NEWSPAPERS

One final major type of publication that researchers in general underutilize is newspapers. Newspapers should be on the shortlist of resources to check when researching noteworthy people. Even those who have a limited fame, their "fifteen minutes," may end up in the newspaper, and it may be through the information in the newspaper that you find the tidbit needed to take the genealogy of that person back another generation.

Of course, the first thing that we think of when it comes to newspapers are the obituaries. Obituaries differ from the single line death notice that we often see in today's newspapers. The obituary was a declaration of the life of the recently departed. It often mentions the struggles the individual overcame. It usually mentions when the deceased settled in the area where he was living when death came. You may also find that the names of the immediate survivors, parents, siblings, and children—including married names of daughters—are listed. Seldom do grandchildren or great-grandchildren get listed though they are usually identified by the number still living.

ONLINE OBITUARIES

Finding obituaries usually means finding newspapers. However, you can find some online obituaries. The easiest way to see if an obituary exists online is to do a search for the deceased person's name in a general search engine—such as Google.com <www.google.com/>—and adding the word *obit* or *obituary*.

When looking for a celebrity or someone associated with a celebrity, you may want to check Obits.com <www.obits.com/>.

Another place to look is the various subscription sites, including Ancestry.com <www.ancestry.com/> and Genealogy.com <www.genealogy.com/>.

Finally, be sure to search for the newspaper by name in the general search engines. You may discover that they have put their obituaries online, as does *The New York Times* <www.nytimes.com/>, though the newspaper may require a membership to view its archives.

Reminder

Newspapers, though, are much more than just a source of obituaries. When it comes to the famous and infamous, they are sometimes your sole glimpse into the life of that person. In the case of the infamous, in reporting the crime, you may also learn about the background of the individual. Reporters will refer to childhood if they think it explains why the person has committed the crime or if they are questioning how such a good child could turn out so bad in the end. In articles on the famous, you can learn about their background, including when they were born. You may likewise learn about every wedding and divorce as well as the announcement of each birth of a child of the celebrity.

Finding these entries sometimes requires patience. While I have found an impressive index to *The New York Times*, published in yearly volumes and available at many public and university libraries, most local newspapers are seldom indexed for the general news stories. Genealogical and historical societies will often create abstracts or indexes to items like the obituaries, but seldom do I see indexes to the whole paper. As a result you must either have an idea of the event in question or simply spend some time getting close and personal with the newspapers for the town in question.

ONLINE DATABASE

The New York Times is one of the few newspapers that is complete and is available online with a full-text search as well as digitized images of each issue. Your public library may already have access to this database, one of those available from ProQuest <www.proquest.com/> as a subscription to libraries and institutions. Members of The New York Genealogical and Biographical Society also have access through their Web site <www.nygbs.org/>.

Before you begin to look at the pages of the newspaper, you must first find the newspaper you need. There are some good finding aids mentioned in "Newspaper Finding Aids" on the next page that will help you in this endeavor. The Internet is also beginning to play a major role in the availability of information in newspapers, both from the past and the present. When it comes to the current issues, you will find that the obituaries are one of the sections that are usually included on the site. They may also be searchable. Some newspaper sites will show you this information for free, while others will show you only the most current issues for free. Issues put in the archive require you pay a subscription fee to access.

Of the finding aids mentioned, the *Gale Directory of Publications and Broadcast Media* is one of the best resources for identifying the newspaper of a given town or community and when it is published, along with providing contact information. There may be times when it becomes necessary to visit the newspaper and see if you can get permission to go through its morgue.

When you wish to find which newspapers are available in microfilm or microfiche and where they are located, then *Newspapers in Microform* publications for both the United States and foreign countries should be your first stop. **You will find that many of these newspapers are now part of the holdings of the states' historical societies, archives, or libraries.** You will also find that many of these newspapers are available through interlibrary loan.

Like many of the other records that hold genealogical information, newspapers are entering the digital age. While many newspapers now offer an online version of the paper, many of them for free, those newspapers of the past are also becoming available online, mostly through subscription services such as Ancestry.com <www.ancestry.com/> and NewspaperArchive.com <www.newspaperarchive.com/>.

\di'fin\ *vb*

Definitions

PAPER MORGUE

A *paper morgue* is where the publisher of a newspaper has stored the old issues of the newspaper.

Library/Archive Source

NEWSPAPER FINDING AIDS

- *Chronological Index of Newspapers for the Period 1801–1852 in the Collections of the Library of Congress* compiled by Paul E. Swigert in 3 volumes, plus supplement—mostly of the newspapers in the Library of Congress' Newspaper Reference Room, listed by year, then by state, then by city, and then by title.

- *Editor & Publisher International Year Book* is published each July and contains names, addresses, and other details about newspapers currently published in the United States, Canada, United Kingdom, Ireland, and Europe, plus other foreign countries. It is found in larger libraries.

- *Gale Directory of Publications and Broadcast Media* is the professional's reference. It is found at most libraries. Now available online <www.galegroup.com/> for libraries. Your library may have a subscription.

- *Newspapers in Microform, United States, 1948–1983.* The dates are not the dates of the newspapers covered, which in fact includes newspapers in the United States from 1704 to 1972.

- *Newspapers in Microform, Foreign Countries, 1948–1983.* The dates of coverage for this foreign equivalent is 1655 to 1972.

- *United States Newspaper Program National Union List* is available on microfiche through the Family History Library.

Library/Archive Source

INTERLIBRARY LOAN

Books and microfilm you can use through *interlibrary loan* come from another library willing to loan the book to your library for a brief period of time. Usually you are required to use the reference work within the library; it cannot be taken home and used.

The benefit of these types of online resources is that they are being indexed in addition to being digitized. For a genealogist this offers the chance to do a blanket newspaper search and discover stories about individuals in many different newspapers for a wide variety of reasons. While it often seems that today's news is all bad, and there are stories of crime, devastation, and suffering in these older newspapers, I have found that they also include society news and gossip—some of the best information we can sometimes find about our ancestors, even the less than famous.

In researching the Carradine family, my preliminary information indicated that the Carradine brothers' great-grandfather was the Reverend Beverly Carradine. He is known for his involvement in early Methodism. He was a traveling preacher, holding large outdoor revivals in tents. In running a search of Beverly Carradine at Ancestry.com, I found the expected census index entries, but I also found three entries in digitized newspapers, two in the *Washington Post,* and one in *The Atlanta Constitution.*

I went first to *The Atlanta Constitution* which was published for 24 April 1909 and found a small mention of "one of the biggest revivals ever held in this [Emanuel] county" being conducted by Dr. Beverly Carradine. While this newspaper entry didn't give me anything new in the way of ancestry, it did tell me that Beverly Carradine, who was born in 1848, was still alive and preaching.

I next turned my attention to the two entries in the *Washington Post* dated 9 and 13 June 1915. On page four of the issue published on June 9 I found a detailed article about a gathering of Southern men and women who were celebrating the anniversary of the birth of Jefferson Davis. Among other names, I found that a "cross of honor was conferred upon the Rev. Beverly Carradine, Company K, Wood's Mississippi Cavalry." The issue of the newspaper published on June 13 had a similar story but established that this gathering was the 107th anniversary of the birth of Jefferson Davis (see Figure 6-9 below).

Figure 6-9
You never know what information you might glean from a mention in a newspaper. © 2000–2002 MyFamily.com, Inc. Screen shot from Ancestry.com. Used with permission.

Again, while the newspaper didn't tell me where Beverly Carradine was born, it did tell me that he fought in the Civil War and that he was part of the Confederacy. I knew this because of the cross of honor, but also because the article included his company and unit so it was easy enough to find out more (see Figure 6-10 on page 124).

While many of the previously mentioned resources are useful regardless of the claim to fame of the individual you are researching, there are many unique resources when it comes to searching for information on those from Hollywood—the movie and television personalities. Many of these sources are available online and offer perhaps more than you wanted to know about your favorite celebs. But when it comes to whether or not you are truly related to one of these individuals, you will soon agree that you want as much information as possible—the more the better.

\di'fin\ *vb*

Definitions

WHAT IS A "CROSS OF HONOR?"

The *Southern Cross of Honor* was conceived by Mrs. Alexander S. Erwin in July, 1898, after attending a reunion of Confederate Veterans held in Atlanta, Georgia. It honors the military or civil service and material aid given by soldiers and regular citizens.

ANCESTRY OF THE CARRADINE BROTHERS	
The Carradine family, in an attempt to learn more about the Carradine line, has led me on a merry chase. To date, I have been able to take the family back to George R. Carradine, but he has been a particularly difficult person to isolate in the records.	
Generation 1	
1	**Robert Carradine** was born in San Mateo, San Mateo, California, 24 Mar. 1954. **Keith Carradine** was born in San Mateo, San Mateo, California, 8 Aug. 1949. **David Carradine** was born in Hollywood, Los Angeles, California, 8 Dec. 1936.
Generation 2	
2	**John Carradine** was born Richmond Reed Carradine in New York City, New York, New York, 5 Feb. 1906. John died 27 Nov. 1988 in Milan, Italy. He married Ardanelle McCool Cosner in 1935 (David's mother). He married Sonia Henius Sorel in 1945 (Keith and Robert's mother). He married Doris Rich in 1957. He married Emily Cisneros in 1974.
Generation 3	
4	**William Reed Carradine** was born in Dalton, Georgia, ca. 1871. He married Genevieve Winifred Richmond in New York City, New York, New York, 3 Feb. 1905.
5	**Genevieve Winifred Richmond** was born in Milford, Otsego, New York, ca. 1885.
Generation 4	
8	**Beverly Carradine** was born in Yazoo City, Yazoo, Mississippi, 4 Apr. 1848. He married Laura Reed in Yazoo County, Mississippi, 4 July 1869. Beverly died 23 Apr. 1931 in Western Springs, Cook, Illinois.
9	**Laura Reed**
10	**Horace Richmond** married Winifred Ryan.
11	**Winifred Ryan**
Generation 5	
16	**Henry Francis Carradine** was born in Yazoo City, Yazoo, Mississippi, 7 June 1808. He married Mary Caroline Hewitt 10 Sept. 1835. Henry died 8 Mar. 1854.
17	**Mary Caroline Hewitt** was born in Washington, District of Columbia, 5 June 1819. She died in 1881.
Generation 6	
32	**George R. Carradine**
34	**James Hewitt** married Caroline Grayson.
35	**Caroline Grayson**

Figure 6-10
Newspapers can help you identify details of an individual's life that help in compiling a family tree.

CELEBRITY RESOURCES

Warning

Paparazzi are forever snapping photos of celebrities, which are then sold to magazines, newspapers, and other places. The Internet has also brought all sorts of information about celebrities into our homes, much from fan sites. The key in using these resources, though, is in understanding that misinformation published in one place is often copied to many other sites. **I have discovered that many fan sites have "borrowed" the biographical write-up they**

found at some other site. If the first source is wrong about something, then it can be wrong in many places.

As a result there are some specific reliable sites I start with whenever I begin the research on a new celebrity. **Most of these sites are available for free.** Some offer information about the lives of celebrities, while others share information about the final resting place of those who are no longer with us.

Money Saver

- Biography.com <www.biography.com/>—Offers short biographies on a variety of celebrities. Not limited to just actors and actresses.
- E! Online <www.eonline.com/>—Offers biographical information about mostly actors and actresses, among other information. Often includes the names of parents, siblings, and children of the celebrity.
- Find A Grave <www.findagrave.com/>—A massive database of famous, infamous, and common individuals with burial information and many photographs of tombstones.
- Hollywood Underground <www.hollywood-underground.com/>— Offers information about the final resting place of the famous buried in and around Los Angeles. This is a good site if you are thinking of visiting the cemetery in person.
- The Internet Movie Database (IMDB) <www.imdb.com/>—A database with a lot of information about those in the movie and television industry. Not just limited to actors and actresses, the database includes behind-the-scenes people as well. The site offers a more in-depth database for a yearly subscription fee.
- The Margaret Herrick Library of the Academy of Motion Picture Arts and Sciences <www.oscars.org/mhl/>—While not a database, the library is a repository of much that has been printed about the industry and those who have worked in it.
- Variety.com <www.variety.com/>—Offers a searchable database of articles and other entries about the motion picture and television industry. In order to read the full articles you must become a subscriber.

Sometimes I find a lot of information with these sites, and sometimes I find none. It depends largely on the information that is readily available about the person and how popular the person is. Let me also say that these sites are not genealogical sites. I use many compiled genealogy sites, which are discussed in chapter eight. These sites are devoted strictly to the entertainment business and offer me the first clues that allow me to jump-start a new research project. I also rely heavily on the resources I discussed earlier in this chapter, especially biographies, for that initial research.

My goal is to find enough identifying information to turn my attention to the more traditional genealogical sources, including vital records, census, published family histories, and more. To do this, I must have a working knowledge of the individual. If that individual was born within the last thirty years or so I must also hope I find enough generations to get me back so that the traditional records will be of value. Privacy laws, which are

Figure 6-11
The Margaret Herrick Library of the Academy of Motion Picture Arts and Sciences in Hollywood, California.

THE MARGARET HERRICK LIBRARY

Named after a former Academy Librarian and long-time Executive Director, the Library of the Academy of Motion Picture Arts and Sciences is a library of all things having to do with motion pictures. The library's holdings offer researchers books, periodicals, pamphlets, clipping files, still photographs, and screenplays in addition to the special collections. Open to the public, you will need to have a valid photo ID to gain access and to request resources. You are limited to paper, pencil, and a laptop computer—and, yes, you can take your power cord—with all other items you may need to be placed in one of the lockers. There is a great deal of information about the library on their Web site <www.oscars.org/mhl>.

While the library is open to the public, the special collections area is limited to those with a specific project, such as the publishing of a book, as the information in the files is often one of a kind. While I was in Los Angeles, I had called ahead of time to see if I could get permission to use certain folders of specific individuals. In talking with the special collections librarian, it was necessary for me to explain the nature of my project. She was quite helpful and had not only the folders I requested, which were various files in the Vincent Minnelli collection containing personal correspondence and various miscellaneous pages about individuals in the family, but also a couple of folders from the George Cukor collection that had a detailed family history compiled by George's father, along with George's attempts to verify the information.

Even without the holdings of the special collections department, researchers will find that the clipping files and biographies that are on the shelves are full of information about not only actors and actresses, but also many important behind-the-scenes people, including directors. Unfortunately, with the exception of the detailed listing of the special collections, which is available online, you will have to wait until you get to the library to search their library catalog, and the catalog does not include the clipping files. If you want to access the clipping files, you simply fill out a request form and they will let you know what they have. Many of the clipping files are extensive and are divided by years. Some of the clippings have been put on microfiche.

Copies vary in cost according to how they are made. The library makes all copies with the exception of those items on microfiche. When they made copies of items for me from clipping files on Elizabeth Montgomery, Tyrone Power, and Liza Minnelli, they tried to fit as many clippings on a page as they could.

When you get ready to leave, you will have to present everything in your arms for review. This is to protect the collection to ensure that nothing is inadvertently removed. The search will include opening your computer.

The Library is located at 333 South La Cienega Boulevard in Beverly Hills. Depending on how you get there, you may have quite an adventure. I discovered that many of the taxi drivers knew about the street, but not where the library was located. It is just north of Olympic Boulevard in the Beverly Hills section of the La Cienega, which does continue beyond Beverly Hills. The library is open on Monday, Tuesday, Thursday, and Friday from 10 A.M. to 6 P.M.

discussed in chapter seven, sometimes put a few speed bumps in my way—the records I need are not readily available in all states.

Half the fun for me in researching the famous is that initial rush as I begin the search. What will I find in my favorite databases? Will the research start out easy or will it be filled with frustrations? Will the lack of information available on the Internet send me off to the library to look for obscure interviews in magazines indexed in the *Readers' Guide*?

Most of the time, you and I cannot just pick up the phone and call the celebrity to ask about the information we have found. We must turn to sources like those discussed in this chapter to help us in identifying the necessary information about the person, such as birth, marriage, death, and names of parents, siblings, and spouses. With this information we can begin to turn to more traditional resources and eliminate those with the same name who are, in fact, the parent, sibling, or spouse of the celebrity.

While I have researched more than a hundred celebrity trees for one reason or another (the compiling of a tree, determining a celebrity relationship, authoring an article), I have only been able to directly communicate with one of the celebrities in question. Sure, it makes the job a little more challenging in some instances, but at least you know that it can be done. Once you have found the identifying information in the sources discussed in this chapter, you are ready to tackle the more traditional record types which are discussed in the next two chapters, record types that will help you further begin to build the celebrity tree as well as your own.

SEVEN

Finding Famous Folks and Their Ancestors in Original Records

O nce you have found some information about the celebrated individual, the next step is to begin to compile a family history on that person. After all, you will most often discover the connection a few generations back on both your lineage and that of the famous person. While this chapter discusses finding well-known individuals and their families in the various records, remember that the same methods apply when you are researching your own family. Each of the records and resources used are the same ones used for any genealogical research. Even the section on name changes is pertinent to genealogical research. I know many people who have uncovered a name change in their own family tree.

"YOUR NAME—NO, I MEAN YOUR *REAL* NAME"

I am astounded at some of the birth names of celebrities and the subsequent names they have changed to, mostly because I am usually wrong about which is which. Some names, I am convinced, were given to them by an agent or a studio, only to discover that the celebrities were born with the name. Tyrone Power comes to mind, as does Errol Flynn. Both of these princes of the silver screen embodied Hollywood and the romance of their era. I was easily convinced that their names were created to grab the public, the result of hours of hard thinking by motion picture bigwigs, but I was wrong.

Finding the birth name of a celebrity is usually easier than searching for your own ancestors who have changed their names. Most of the biographical sources discussed in the previous chapter will reveal the birth name of a celebrity if it is different from the name they use now, and once you find the birth name, you are off and running, right?

While the various GEDCOM databases discussed in chapter eight are likely to list both the birth and celebrity names, making a search there easier, you will find that in some records you need to check for just the birth name. Other records will require you to check for the birth and celebrity or new names. For instance, when you find yourself looking for the death record of an individual, if it is a man you need to look for the birth name as well

REALLY, WHAT'S YOUR NAME?

Often, the first step with celebrity research is finding the birth name of the celebrity. Here are a few sites to help you with that.

- Stage Names
  www.fiftiesweb.com/dead/real-names-1.htm

- Celebrity's Real Names
  www.usfamily.net/web/wpattinson/otr/celeb/celebn.shtml

- Famous Name Changes
  www.famousnamechanges.com/html/welcome.htm

- Real Names of Celebrities
  www.angelfire.com/la/stagenames/

Research Tip

as the name he went by on the stage or screen. In a few instances you may discover a hybrid of the two names. **If you are looking for a death record on a woman, you need to look under her stage name, her legal given name with either her stage last name or her married last name, and her given stage name and her married last name.** That's a lot of names to keep track of.

If I find myself in such a situation I make a list of all the possible permutations of the name and then I go through that list systematically. And of course, if name changes weren't bad enough, I need to also keep in mind possible spelling variations. While they are not as common with more recent records, it still happens from time to time, more frequently now that I am dealing with digitized records. Typos have crept into the various online indexes. Keeping a list that I can check off as I work through a database or an index means I can say at the end of the search that I have exhausted it for all the variations I have on the name—at least those I have identified or suspected up to that point.

I mentioned that some stars have changed their name to make it sound more Hollywood. We saw a few of those name changes in chapter six when I was discussing the fact that "the name's the same" isn't always an indication of relationship, a fact that you should remember whether you're doing celebrity research or general genealogical research. Too often we find ourselves out on a limb because we jumped to include a person whose name was the same, only to find that the records we uncover as the research progresses don't support that conclusion.

People in general have changed their names for other reasons. One of the most common is to anglicize the name—to be more American—after immigrating. A perfect example of this is Irving Berlin. All of us know him as Irving Berlin. When he was born though, he was Israel Beilin.

I found him listed on the S.S. *Rhynland* from Antwerp, Belgium, to New York City, arriving in 1893 with his family (see Figure 7-1 on page 131). Of

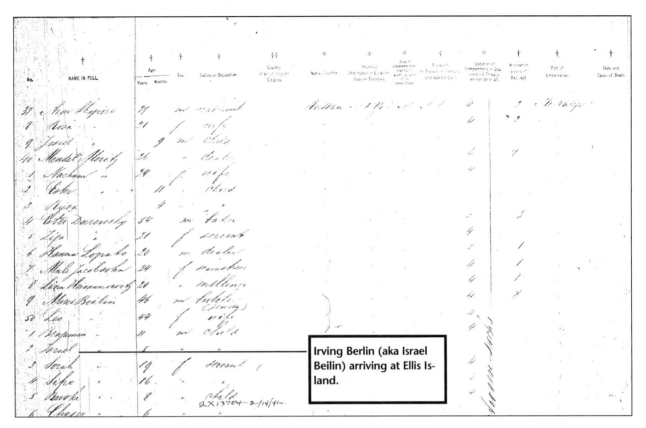

Irving Berlin (aka Israel Beilin) arriving at Ellis Island.

Figure 7-1
Passenger manifest showing the family of Irving Berlin (who at the age of five was named Israel Beilin) as they arrived at Ellis Island.

course, if I had searched for him as Irving Berlin on the Ellis Island Web site <www.ellisislandrecords.org/>, I would have gone away disappointed.

Tracing Irving Berlin's genealogy has frustrated me on more than just the name. There was the name change, which I was aware of, but the spelling variations of the *Beilin* name had me wondering if I had overlooked the family in one or more records. Irving has lead me a merry chase through the years, as has his father Moses and his mother Lena. In the 1900 census, I found the family under the surname spelling of *Baline*, though Irving is still going by the given name of Israel. By 1912, as listed in the New York City directory, I find a twenty-four-year-old Irving living on his own and listed as Irving Berlin. Fortunately I took a moment to scan the rest of the Berlin list as I discovered his mother had adopted the same surname and was listed as the widow of Moses.

My problem has been that Moses has stubbornly refused to appear in any of the records he should. Given that Lena is listed as his widow in 1912, I've searched the New York City death index from 1912 back to about 1900 and have been unable to locate Moses. I suspect that it is because he is listed under some variant spelling I have not as yet come up with or deciphered. Until then, I have little more to go on for Moses than what I found in the 1900 census (see Figure 7-2 on page 132).

When the name is anglicized as was the case with Irving Berlin's, it is

Internet Source

THE NAME WAS CHANGED AT ELLIS ISLAND

Names being changed at Ellis Island is only a myth. To read more about it, visit the INS Web site's History, Genealogy, and Education section <www.immigratio n.gov/graphics/aboutus/ history/articles/ NAMES.htm>.

ANCESTRY OF IRVING BERLIN	
There are times when the records or the lack of them mean we don't have a lot to begin with. Sometimes, if our immigrant ancestor was a recent ancestor such as a parent or grandparent, you will find yourself going back to the "old country" pretty quickly. More and more is coming out of some of the old Eastern Block countries that used to be sealed off because they were under Soviet rule.	
Generation 1	
1	**Irving Berlin** was born Israel Beilin in Mogilov, Belurus, 11 May 1888. Irving immigrated, 14 Sept. 1893. Destination: New York City. He married Dorothy Goetz ca. 1912. He petitioned the court to become a citizen in New York City, New York, New York, 15 Oct. 1917. He married Ellin Mackay in Manhattan, New York, New York, 4 Jan. 1926. Irving died 22 Sept. 1989 in New York.
Generation 2	
2	**Moses Beilin** was born in Russia, Jan. 1846. He married Lena Jarchin prob. in Russia, ca. 1875. Moses immigrated, 14 Sept. 1893. Destination: New York City. Moses died by 1912.
3	**Lena Jarchin** was born in Russia, Aug. 1849. She resided in Bronx, New York, New York, 1 June 1915. Lena died 21 July 1922 in Bronx, New York, New York.
Generation 3	
6	Jacob Jarchin

Figure 7-2
Sometimes there just isn't much information to find on an ancestor.

Warning

either the English translation of the surname or letters are dropped from the spelling of the name. The dropping of letters is more common with the eastern European immigrants. Many of their names have a number of silent consonants which were dropped to make the spelling and pronunciation of the name easier when they came to America.

Celebrities often change their names altogether. In fact, the new name seldom resembles the birth name. In some cases it is because the birth name didn't impart the persona or impression that the studios or the entertainment business was trying to sell. Like selling a product, it is all in the packaging, and that includes the name. Billions of dollars are poured into the marketing of different products that we buy on a regular basis. In many ways, we are buying the "product" of the celebrity. We have a preconceived notion of what that person is like and the name is often part of our preconception.

Other times the name hasn't really been changed, but rather a portion of it was dropped or omitted. A great example of this is Tom Cruise. His birth name is Thomas Cruise Mapother IV. From a genealogical standpoint, knowing he was Thomas the fourth made researching his paternal line a lot easier. I knew that I was looking for a long line of Thomas Cruise Mapothers, four generations worth (see Figure 7-3 on pages 134-135).

The mystery of Thomas Cruise Mapother, born in 1876, stays with me, and every so often I pull it out and try to figure out why I can't find him in the records.

HEADING FOR THE RECORDS

Once you know the names you are searching for and have done some homework either with the resources discussed in chapter six or in your own

WHO'S THOMAS CRUISE MAPOTHER'S FATHER?

Russ Einhorn/SplashNews

While Tom Cruise is the fourth generation to carry the name of Thomas Cruise Mapother, there are questions surrounding the first Thomas Cruise Mapother. Other researchers have linked this Thomas as the son of Dillon H. Mapother and Marie Cruise. The problem? Dillon H. Mapother dies in 1874, which is two years before Thomas is born. Searches in the 1880 census index on CD-ROM do not reveal a Thomas Mapother. What they do show is a family of a Thos. O'Mara, age forty-five, with wife Mary, age thirty-seven, born in New Jersey, a son Thos., age three, and three individuals whose relationships are not identified, Dellia Mapother, female, age eighteen, Weble Mapother, male, age seven, and Henry Mapother, male, age sixteen.

By all accounts, it appears that after the death of her husband, Dillon H. Mapother in 1874, Mary remarried to Thomas O'Mara. The will of Dillon H. Mapother specifically mentions his *three* children, though their names are not included in the will. I suspect that Dellia Mapother, listed in the 1880 census, is actually Dillon E. Mapother, the eight-year-old boy listed in the D.H. Mapother home in the 1870 census. It is apparent when looking at the 1880 census page that the F for female has been inked over the M for male that was already there.

So, if Thomas O'Mara is the first Thomas Cruise Mapother, why did he change his name? And will I ever be able to find records proving that Thomas Cruise Mapother born in 1876 is the same as Thos. O'Mara who shows up in the 1880 census? The search continues, and it's always in the back of my head as I try to find another angle to work to solve this mystery.

family, gathering records and talking to other family members as discussed in chapter two, then it is time to turn your attention to the records for the time and place of each event you have presently identified.

What you will quickly discover is that records vary from place to place. They vary sometimes from town to town or county to county within a given state. They certainly vary from state to state, and when it comes to working in different countries, you will find that the same record type may be called something entirely different—vital record (births, marriages, and deaths in the United States) vs. civil registration (births, marriages, and deaths in the United Kingdom). The information recorded for a birth, for instance, may be as little as the name of the child, birth date, and names of the parents, minus a maiden name for the mother. Another jurisdiction or state may be more thorough, listing the maiden name of the mother, and the birthplaces and ages of both parents. You may find that while one county began record-

Reminder

ANCESTRY OF TOM CRUISE
For a detailed look at the ancestry of Tom Cruise, complete with full source citations, check out his family history as it has been published at AncestorChronicles.com <www.ancestorchronicles.com/cruise.htm>.

Generation 1

1	**Tom Cruise** was born Thomas Cruise Mapother IV, in Syracuse, New York, 3 July 1962. He married Mimi Rogers 9 May 1987 in San Miguel, California. Tom was divorced from Mimi Rogers Jan. 1990. He married Nicole Kidman in Telluride, Colorado, 24 Dec. 1990. Tom was divorced from Nicole Kidman in Los Angeles, California, 8 Aug. 2001. He adopted two children while married to Nicole.

Generation 2

2	**Thomas Cruise Mapother III** was born 13 Oct. 1934 in Jefferson Co., Kentucky. He married Mary Lee Pfeiffer in Jefferson Co., Kentucky, in 1957. He was divorced from Mary Lee Pfeiffer in Jefferson Co., Kentucky, 1 Aug. 1975. Thomas died 9 Jan. 1984 in Jefferson Co., Kentucky.
3	**Mary Lee Pfeiffer** was born in Jefferson Co., Kentucky, 22 Sept. 1936.

Generation 3

4	**Thomas Cruise Mapother II** was born in Louisville, Jefferson, Kentucky, 15 Dec. 1907. He married Catherine Reibert. Thomas died 17 Jan. 1986 in Jefferson Co., Kentucky.
5	**Catherine Reibert** was born in Louisville, Jefferson, Kentucky, 21 May 1912. She died 26 Apr. 1993 in Louisville, Jefferson, Kentucky.
6	**Charles Conrad Pfeiffer** was born in Kentucky, Jan. 1894. He married Comala R. Ramser ca. 1915. He died in Jefferson Co., Kentucky, 5 March 1953.
7	**Comala R. Ramser** was born in Kentucky ca. 1897.

Generation 4

8	**Thomas Cruise Mapother** was born in Louisville, Jefferson, Kentucky, 29 Dec. 1876. He married Anna Batman in Louisville, Jefferson Co., Kentucky, 9 January 1907. Thomas died 12 Apr. 1939 in Louisville, Jefferson, Kentucky. His body was interred 14 Apr. 1939 in Kentucky, St. Louis Cemetery.
9	**Anna Batman** was born in Louisville, Jefferson, Kentucky, 20 July 1877. She died 29 Nov. 1968 in Jefferson Co., Kentucky.
10	**William Reibert** was born in Kentucky, May 1877. He married Charlotta Louise Voelker in Kentucky, Aug. 1907. William died 20 Nov. 1957 in Jefferson Co., Kentucky.
11	**Charlotta Louise Voelker** was born in Louisville, Jefferson, Kentucky, 15 Nov. 1884. She died 30 Dec. 1975 in Jefferson Co., Kentucky.
12	**Lee Norbert Pfeiffer** was born in Louisville, Jefferson, Kentucky, 6 June 1868. He married Anna J. Shea in Louisville, Jefferson, Kentucky, 24 Nov. 1892. Lee died 10 Mar. 1948 in Louisville, Jefferson, Kentucky.
13	**Anna J. Shea** was born in Springfield, Kentucky, 24 Nov. 1872. She died 30 Nov. 1917 in Louisville, Jefferson, Kentucky.
14	**Joseph C. Ramser** was born in Kentucky, Oct. 1870. He married Suzie A. Mackey in Louisville, Jefferson, Kentucky, 17 Apr. 1894.
15	**Suzie A. Mackey** was born in Louisville, Jefferson, Kentucky, 9 Nov. 1872. She died 21 Dec. 1947 in Louisville, Jefferson, Kentucky.

Generation 5

18	**Thomas J. Batman** was born in Kentucky, Feb. 1853. He married Elvira Tompkins. Thomas died 29 March 1933 in Jefferson Co., Kentucky.

Figure 7-3

19	**Elvira Tompkins** was born in Louisville, Jefferson, Kentucky, 28 Aug. 1854. She died 18 June 1910 in Louisville, Jefferson, Kentucky.
20	**Adam Reibert** was born in Baltimore, Baltimore, Maryland, 27 July 1851. He married Francisca Boesser in Louisville, Jefferson, Kentucky, 21 Aug. 1873. Adam died 19 Nov. 1911 in Louisville, Jefferson, Kentucky.
21	**Francisca Boesser** was born in Louisville, Jefferson, Kentucky, Mar. 1853.
22	**John Voelker** was born in Indiana, Jan. 1863. He married Louisa Steadle ca. 1883. John died 3 Jan. 1922 in Jefferson Co., Kentucky.
23	**Louisa Steadle** was born in Kentucky, July 1860. She died 16 Sept. 1946 in Jefferson Co., Kentucky.
24	**Charles Conrad Pfeiffer** was born in Schenechtady, New York, 20 Nov. 1837. He married Julia Gould before 1 June 1860. He married Mary Rosella Hawkins before 1865. Charles died 6 Aug. 1926 in Louisville, Jefferson, Kentucky.
25	**Mary Rosella Hawkins** was born in Kentucky, ca. 1842.
27	**Mary Brown**
28	**George Ramser** was born in France, Feb. 1835. He married Kate [--?--] ca. 1860.
29	**Kate [--?--]** was born in Indiana Nov. 1846.
30	**Gerald Mackey** married Bridget Quinn.
31	**Bridget Quinn**
Generation 6	
38	**Robert William Tompkins** married Susanna E. Dean.
39	**Susanna E. Dean**
40	**George Raibert** was born in Germany, ca. 1810. He married Katherine.
41	**Katherine** was born in Germany, ca. 1814.
42	**Frank Boesser** married Mary [--?--].
43	**Mary [--?--]**
48	**Christopher Pfeiffer**
51	**Margaret [--?--]** was born in Ireland, ca. 1822.

Figure 7-3

ing births and deaths in 1877, another county didn't begin recording the same records until much later, and these records were often not recorded at the state level until the early 1900s. For help in identifying what records may exist and when recording began, check out the listings in the bibliography at the end of this book.

It won't be long before you are asking yourself why some records are open for any year while others are closed. There appears to be no standard across the states or countries as to what records should be available. In many ways this is actually a plus to genealogical researchers. While you will find frustration in some states and counties, you will jump for joy at how fast your research progresses in others.

So what prevents you from accessing some of the records? Most states and countries have privacy laws on the books. These laws are designed to keep

Internet Source

RESEARCH HELPS

Don't forget there is a lot of great information in the Research Helps section—found under the Search Tab—at the FamilySearch Web site <www.familysearch.org/>.

the records of those who are still living private and not freely accessible. In genealogical terms this usually amounts to frustration. Different records are closed for different spans of years. Many states have a fifty-year or longer waiting period on birth and marriage records, while others are closed for one hundred years. Death records are often not closed for as long. Some have a one hundred-year limit on them before you can access them. Many federal records have a seventy-two year protection, and others are protected until the person in question has died and you can prove that he or she is dead.

As we look at the different record types, I will discuss the potential availability of each.

VITAL RECORDS AND CIVIL REGISTRATION

Vital records, known as civil registration in some countries, are the first records that everyone thinks of when they begin to search a family tree. In some instances, though, it is one of the harder records to get. Birth and marriage records are often sealed for extended periods of time due to privacy laws. They are, though, usually the most informative records available—at least the more recent ones. Perhaps you are sensing a catch-22 situation: The more recent ones are also the ones that are more apt to be unavailable.

Important

You should always get copies of any records you can, even if you think you already know all of the information on the record (see Figures 7-4 on page 137 and 7-5 on page 138). You will be relying on this information to show you where to turn next in your research. Getting in the habit early is one of the best practices to cultivate.

While the records themselves may be closed for years, I have discovered that I often have access to indexes, usually on microfilm, that cover more

---

SEPARATE BUT EQUAL

Most of us have heard this saying at least once in our lives, maybe while sitting in history class. We thought it just applied to schools. I have found that it often applied to the records as well. Too many times I have found myself frustrated as I discovered that only white marriages were microfilmed, or that the only index available was to the white marriages. Many times, usually when working in Southern states, you will find this to be a problem. And then there is what I call the demarcation year of 1865. Many of the records that other researchers rely heavily on are not available before this date for those researching African-American ancestry. Instead you must first try to identify the slave owner and then hope that the plantation records have survived and are accessible before you can begin to put together the family before 1865. Fortunately, there are a number of good books on this subject, including Franklin Carter Smith's and Emily Anne Croom's *A Genealogist's Guide to Discovering Your African-American Ancestors* (Cincinnati: Betterway Books, 2003).

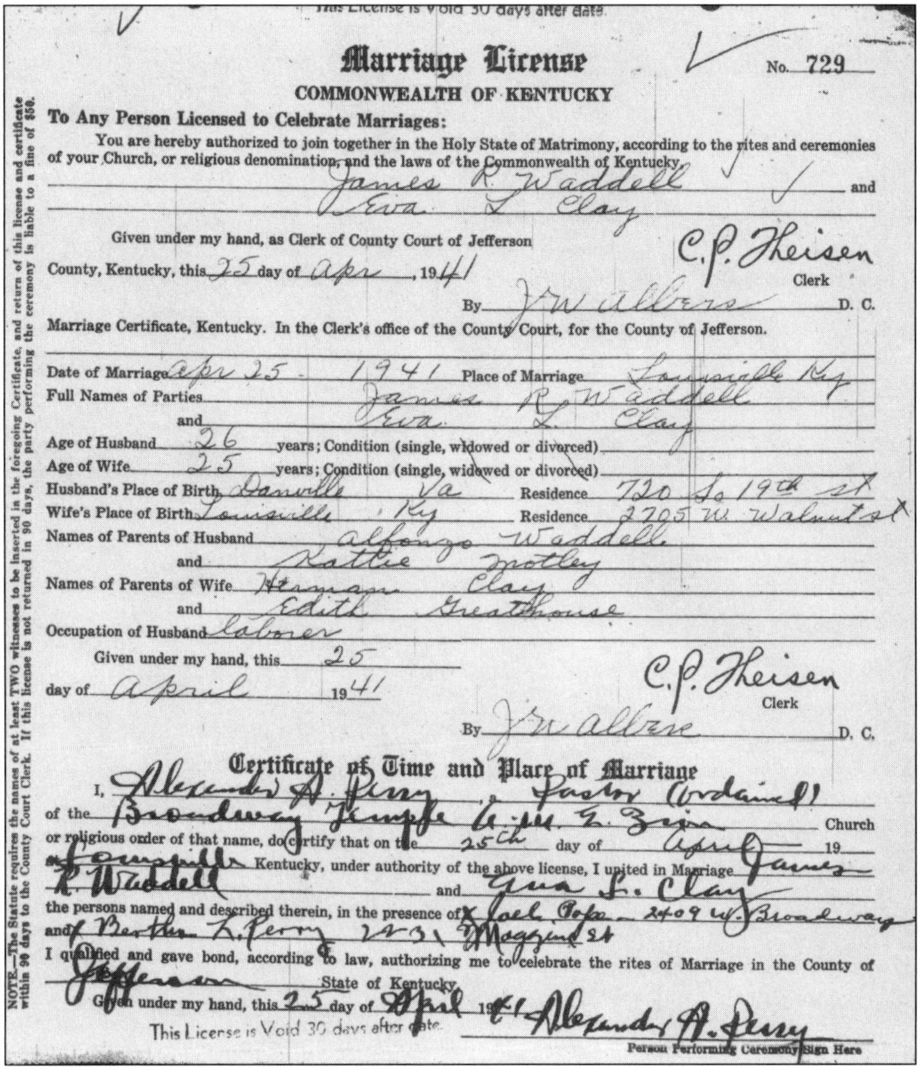
This License is Void 30 days after date.

Marriage License

COMMONWEALTH OF KENTUCKY

No. 729

To Any Person Licensed to Celebrate Marriages:

You are hereby authorized to join together in the Holy State of Matrimony, according to the rites and ceremonies of your Church, or religious denomination, and the laws of the Commonwealth of Kentucky, James R. Waddell and Eva L. Clay

Given under my hand, as Clerk of County Court of Jefferson County, Kentucky, this 25 day of Apr 1941

C. P. Theisen Clerk

By J. W. Albers D. C.

Marriage Certificate, Kentucky. In the Clerk's office of the County Court, for the County of Jefferson.

Date of Marriage Apr 25 1941 Place of Marriage Louisville Ky

Full Names of Parties James R. Waddell

and Eva L. Clay

Age of Husband 26 years; Condition (single, widowed or divorced)

Age of Wife 25 years; Condition (single, widowed or divorced)

Husband's Place of Birth Danville Va Residence 720 So 19th st

Wife's Place of Birth Louisville, Ky Residence 2705 W. Walnut st

Names of Parents of Husband Alfonzo Waddell

and Hattie Motley

Names of Parents of Wife Herman Clay

and Edith Greathouse

Occupation of Husband laborer

Given under my hand, this 25 day of April 1941

C. P. Theisen Clerk

By J. W. Albers D. C.

Certificate of Time and Place of Marriage

I, Alexander A. Perry, Pastor (Ordained) of the Broadway Temple A. M. E. Zion Church or religious order of that name, do certify that on the 25th day of April 19 at Louisville Kentucky, under authority of the above license, I united in Marriage James R. Waddell and Eva L. Clay the persons named and described therein, in the presence of Joel Pope 2409 W Broadway and of Bertha L. Perry 2231 Magazine St

I qualified and gave bond, according to law, authorizing me to celebrate the rites of Marriage in the County of Jefferson State of Kentucky.

Given under my hand, this 25 day of April 1941 Alexander A. Perry

Person Performing Ceremony Sign Here

This License is Void 30 days after date.

NOTE—The Statute requires the names of at least TWO witnesses to be inserted in the foregoing Certificate, and return of this license and certificate within 90 days to the County Court Clerk. If this license is not returned in 90 days, the party performing the ceremony is liable to a fine of $50.

Figure 7-4
Marriage records for African Americans, such as this one for Muhammad Ali's aunt, are often segregated, but may hold a great deal of information. (Certificate No. 729, Louisville, Kentucky.)

years. For instance, the birth index in Moultrie County, Illinois, that is available on microfilm at the Family History Library goes into the 1980s, the time when the Family History Library microfilmed it. The same is true of the Index to Civil Registration of England and Wales.

Some of the state vital record offices are now offering online indexes so that individuals who have need of a vital record can do the search and get the necessary identifying information, such as the exact date of the event, the date of filing, and the all-important certificate number. Sending this information in when you request a record makes it easier for a clerk to locate the record.

Two other online options that prove quite useful are VitalRec.com <www.vitalrec.com/>, where you can learn about record availability by country, state or province, and county, and VitalChek.com <www.vitalchek.com/>, a site devoted to offering methods of ordering vital records. Some states and county courthouses have begun to offer an online ordering option, and

Figure 7-5
Armed with the information on the pedigree chart, begin to request all available vital records.

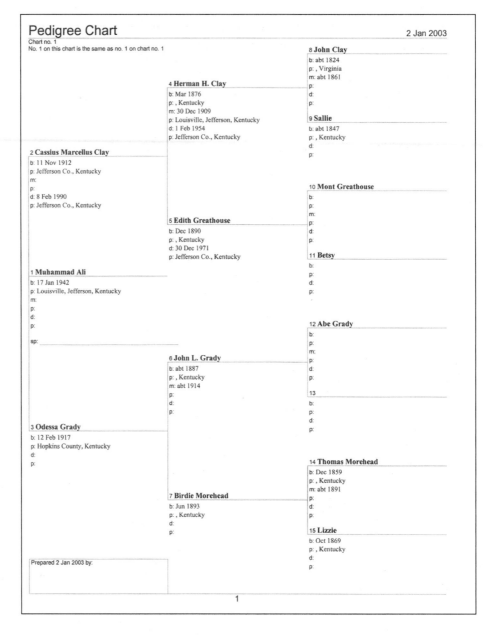

with a nominal processing fee, you can order the record through the site. It can cut weeks off the delivery time of the requested vital record.

CENSUS RECORDS

The next most used record would probably be the census record. Census records have always been popular resources among genealogists, but with the recent digitization of these records, some with accompanying new indexes, they have become even more popular.

You may already be somewhat familiar with the census record. In April 2002, the 1930 U.S. Federal Census was released. It caused quite a stir, and many newspapers and other media outlets picked up on the story, no doubt

ADOPTION AND BIRTH CERTIFICATES

When a child is adopted, formally and legally, a new birth certificate is created. It is known as an amended certificate, and it takes the place of the original birth certificate that was recorded at the time of the birth of the child—which is then sealed in with the court file of the adoption, sometimes never to see the light of day again. The amended certificate usually does not have any special identification to let you know that it is not the original. Usually the only clue is when the certificate was filed. If it was filed some years after the date of birth, this may suggest an amended certificate, which is not to be confused with a delayed birth certificate. A delayed certificate will be labeled as such and was usually the result of no certificate having been filed at the time of the birth. Delayed birth certificates were common once things like Social Security began because people needed to be able to prove that they had reached a certain milestone age.

Because adoption is such a unique situation, it is not fully addressed in this book. There are some great Web sites to guide you with your research should you discover an adoption:

- ABCgenealogy: Adoption www.abcgenealogy.com/Adoption

- Adoption.com www.adoption.com

- Adoption.org Neighborhood www.adoption.org

- Adoption Triad Outreach www.adoptiontriad.org

wondering why folks were getting excited about a record that was seventy-two years old. For genealogists this was a much anticipated record release. Every ten years, the next decennial census is released. For many, the 1930 census meant possibly finding a parent or a grandparent listed. I was at a library recently, and a woman actually found herself on the page. She was thrilled.

Census records are an enumeration of the households of a country. They are usually compiled in an effort to determine the population of the country for a number of different reasons, including amassing an army and redistricting political divisions to make things fair in the government (see Figures 7-6 on page 140 and 7-7 on page 141).

The United States is not the only country to have taken a census. In fact most countries have taken one or two enumerations over the years. Discovering whether or not they have survived and the availability of the records can usually be found in how-to books about the country in question, or in the previously mentioned research outlines published by the Family History Library.

For instance, England has taken decennial censuses for many years. Like the United States, England has a privacy law that protects those enumerated for a set number of years. At the present time you can view up through the

\di'fin\ *vb*

Definitions

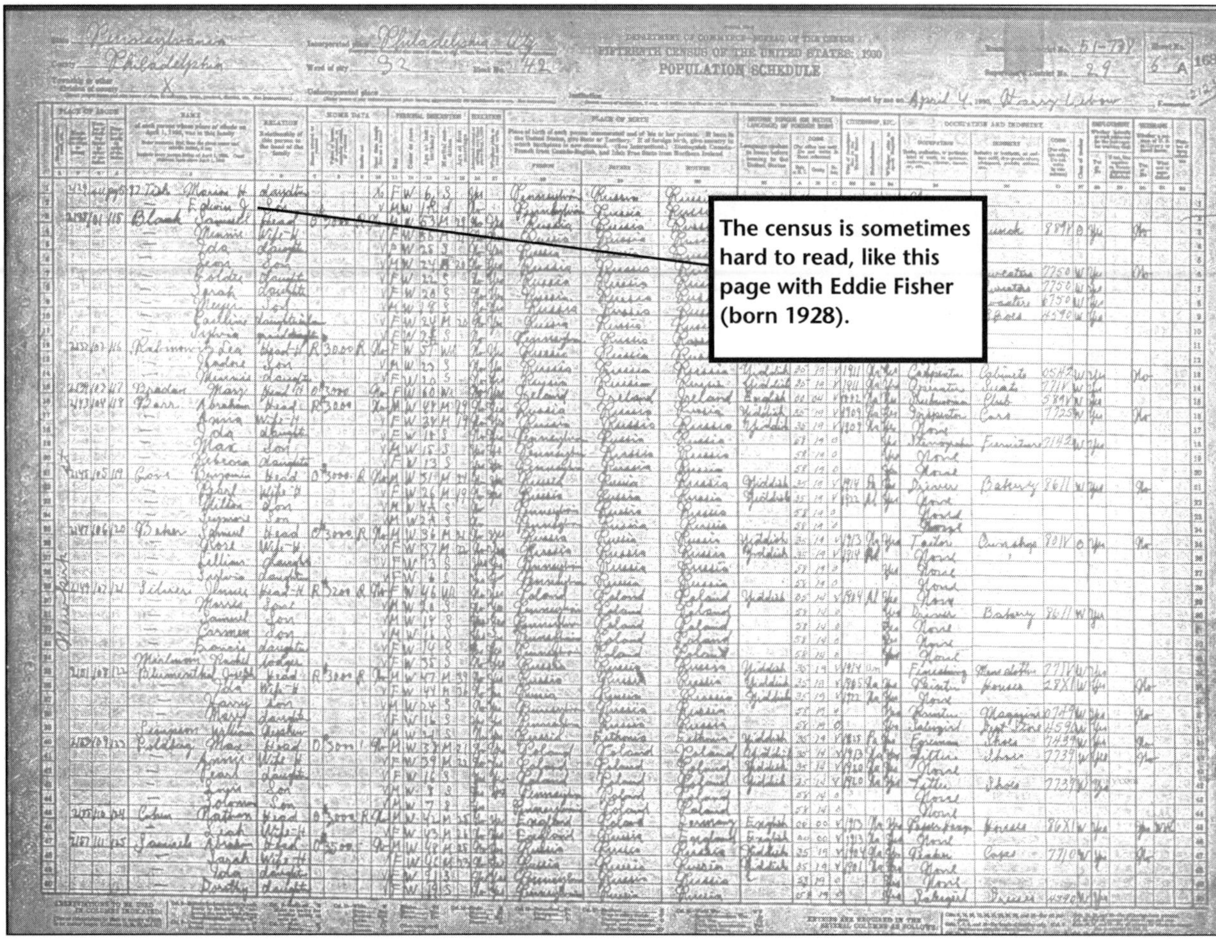

> The census is sometimes hard to read, like this page with Eddie Fisher (born 1928).

Figure 7-6
The 1930 census is opening up research for a new generation. (Philadelphia, Philadelphia, Pennsylvania, T626, roll 2114, Enumeration District 51-718, sheet 6A.)

BE SURE TO GET THE MOST FROM THE CENSUS

The census is one of the most used resources, especially now that the images have been digitized and are available online through the subscription sites of both Ancestry.com <www.ancestry.com/> and Genealogy.com <www.genealogy.com/>. The problem is that many people don't understand all that the census page holds or how best to use it. They also aren't aware of the many other census records, both federal and state, that may be of help. For a good overview of the census records, see Kathleen W. Hinckley's *Your Guide to the Federal Census* (Cincinnati: Betterway Books, 2002).

1901 census for England. Canada has also released their 1901 census. The Family History Library, who indexed the 1880 U.S. Census and published the resulting index on some fifty CD-ROMs, has completed similar projects

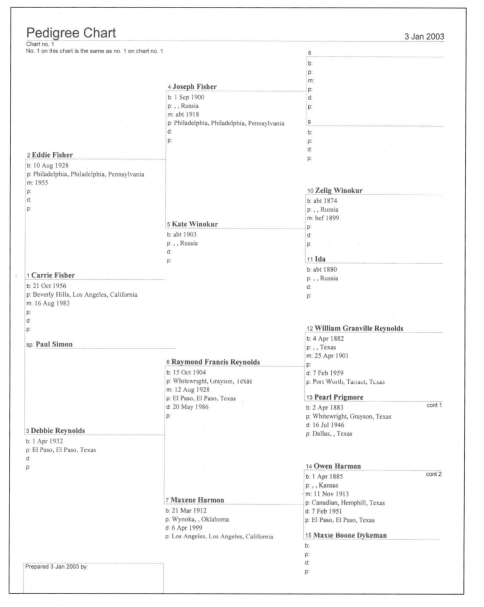

Pedigree Chart

3 Jan 2003

Chart no. 1
No. 1 on this chart is the same as no. 1 on chart no. 1

4 Joseph Fisher
b: 1 Sep 1900
p: , , Russia
m: abt 1918
p: Philadelphia, Philadelphia, Pennsylvania
d:
p:

8
b:
p:
m:
p:
d:
p:

9
b:
p:
d:
p:

2 Eddie Fisher
b: 10 Aug 1928
p: Philadelphia, Philadelphia, Pennsylvania
m: 1955
p:
d:
p:

10 Zelig Winokur
b: abt 1874
p: , , Russia
m: bef 1899
p:
d:
p:

5 Kate Winokur
b: abt 1903
p: , , Russia
d:
p:

11 Ida
b: abt 1880
p: , , Russia
d:
p:

1 Carrie Fisher
b: 21 Oct 1956
p: Beverly Hills, Los Angeles, California
m: 16 Aug 1983
p:
d:
p:

sp: **Paul Simon**

12 William Granville Reynolds
b: 4 Apr 1882
p: , , Texas
m: 25 Apr 1901
p:
d: 7 Feb 1959
p: Fort Worth, Tarrant, Texas

6 Raymond Francis Reynolds
b: 15 Oct 1904
p: Whitewright, Grayson, Texas
m: 12 Aug 1928
p: El Paso, El Paso, Texas
d: 20 May 1986
p:

13 Pearl Prigmore   cont 1
b: 2 Apr 1883
p: Whitewright, Grayson, Texas
d: 16 Jul 1946
p: Dallas, , Texas

3 Debbie Reynolds
b: 1 Apr 1932
p: El Paso, El Paso, Texas
d:
p:

14 Owen Harmon   cont 2
b: 1 Apr 1885
p: , , Kansas
m: 11 Nov 1913
p: Canadian, Hemphill, Texas
d: 7 Feb 1951
p: El Paso, El Paso, Texas

7 Maxene Harmon
b: 21 Mar 1912
p: Wynoka, , Oklahoma
d: 6 Apr 1999
p: Los Angeles, Los Angeles, California

15 Maxie Boone Dykeman
b:
p:
d:
p:

Prepared 3 Jan 2003 by:

Figure 7-7
Carrie Fisher's pedigree chart.

on the 1881 census for England, Scotland and Wales, and Canada. All of these census indexes are available for sale on CD-ROM, but they are also available online, and freely searchable, as part of the databases of the FamilySearch Web site <www.familysearch.org/>.

Books such as Kathleen W. Hinckley's *Your Guide to the Federal Census* (Cincinnati: Betterway Books, 2002) and Mark D. Herber's *Ancestral Trails* (Baltimore: Genealogical Pub., 2000) offer useful information to understanding the census for the United States and England respectively. By reading such books, you'll save yourself time when it comes to working with the census records for these two countries. You will understand the strengths and weaknesses of this resource, what information you should expect to get from the census, and what might mislead you in your research. For those working in other countries that also have a census, you should be able to find a how-to guide that talks about the census and any of its peculiarities for a particular country.

CEMETERY RECORDS

Cemetery records and the records associated with the burial of an individual are other valuable resources for your research. I have seen tombstones that not only include the dates of birth and death but also include the place of birth, as did Darryl Zanuck's (see Figure 7-8 on page 143). There are many other hints to the life of an ancestor that may also appear on the tombstone itself, such as religious affiliation. You may learn of specific fraternal organizations to which the person belonged. I have also seen military insignia or the inclusion of a soldier's rank, company, and regiment. Any extra insight into the life of an ancestor or person can help you in locating additional records on that person. Few tombstones are as thorough in sharing the life of the person as Darryl Zanuck's, but I never pass up the opportunity to view the tombstones of my ancestors.

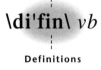

Reminder

When we think of a cemetery we naturally think of tombstones, but there are many other records and resources associated with the death of an individual that might also prove useful in our research. For more information, see Sharon De-Bartolo Carmack's *Your Guide to Cemetery Research* (Cincinnati: Betterway Books, 2002). (See Figures 7-9 and 7-10 on page 144 for another example of a famous tombstone and ancestry.)

SOCIAL SECURITY DEATH INDEX

When you find yourself working on the early generations of your ancestry or that of a famous individual from the twentieth century, it is extremely possible that you will need death dates of individuals who have passed away after 1960. Because of the privacy laws that exist in many states, you may not be able to get the death certificate of a person without already possessing a great deal of information or until a certain number of years has passed. This frustration can sometimes be alleviated to a degree by working with the Social Security Death Index (SSDI).

\di'fin\ *vb*

Definitions

The SSDI is a database of deaths reported to the Social Security Administration. While Social Security got its beginnings in the 1930s, with the first benefits paid out in the late 1930s, the SSDI was not computerized until 1961. This means that the bulk of the entries found in this resource are for those who died after 1961. Many people have confused the SSDI as a master index to deaths in the United States since the founding of the country, but like many other useful records and resources, it has limitations. People with certain occupations, such as railroad workers, are excluded, as are most individuals who died before 1962. It was not created with genealogists in mind and as such our wants and wishes, such as adding pre-1962 deaths, will not bring about changes as they may in databases created for or by genealogists.

The good news about the Social Security Death Index is that it is one of

A LIFE STORY

A tombstone can hold a wealth of information. I have seen instances where a tombstone tells the entire life story of the individual. One such tombstone is that of producer Darryl F. Zanuck, best known for such films as *The King and I* and *The Snows of Kilimanjaro*, whose daughter Darrylin shared with the world in an immortal way the many accomplishments of her father:

DARRYL FRANCIS ZANUCK

Born Wahoo, Nebraska, September 5, 1902

Passed on Palm Springs, California, December 22, 1979

Co-Founder, President and Producer of 20th Century Fox Studio. Doctor of Humanities, University of Nebraska, Lincoln, Nebraska, Mason 50 years receiving the highest degree. In his lifetime, received such a host of degrees, diplomas and awards from all over the world, that it is impossible to state them all. Private, World War I overseas, 14 years old. World War II Colonel, active duty overseas. U.S. Signal Corp, Algiers. Listed below are a few of the service ribbons and decorations he was proudly authorized to wear: Victory Medal (WWI); Medal of French Legion of Honor with Rouge Rosette (WWI); Asiatic Pacific Campaign Ribbons and European-Africa-Middle Eastern Campaign Ribbons.

A man who used his imaginative, creative genius to deliver inspiration through his celebrated motion pictures. He imparted a lifetime message of decency, love, patriotism, justice, equality and hope throughout the nation and the world. Beloved husband, father, grandfather and great-grandfather. I love you, Daddy—you will never be forgotten.

—Darrylin

Figure 7-8

ANCESTRY OF JIMMY STEWART	
Generation 1	
1	**Jimmy Stewart** was born in Indiana Co., Pennsylvania, 20 May 1908. He married Gloria Hatrick in Brentwood, Los Angeles, California, 9 Aug. 1949. Jimmy died 2 July 1997 in Los Angeles, Los Angeles, California.

Figure 7-9

Generation 2	
2	**Alexander M. Stewart** was born in Indiana Co., Pennsylvania, 19 May 1872. He married Elizabeth Ruth Jackson in Indiana Co., Pennsylvania, 19 Dec. 1906. Alexander died 28 Dec. 1961 in Indiana Co., Pennsylvania.
3	**Elizabeth Ruth Jackson** was born 16 Mar. 1875. She died 2 Aug. 1953.
Generation 3	
4	**James Maitland Stewart** was born in Pennsylvania, 24 May 1839. He married Virginia Kelly. He married Martha A. [--?--] ca. 1888. James died 16 Mar. 1932.
5	**Virginia Kelly** was born in Pennsylvania, ca. 1847. She died before 1888.
6	**Samuel McCartney Jackson** was born in Pennsylvania, Sept. 1833. He married Mary E. Wilson ca. 1868.
7	**Mary E. Wilson** was born in Pennsylvania, Nov. 1844.
Generation 4	
8	**John Kerr Stewart** was born in Indiana Co., Pennsylvania, 19 Nov. 1785. He married Elizabeth Hindman Armstrong in Indiana Co., Pennsylvania, 16 Mar. 1815. John died 22 Feb. 1870 in Indiana Co., Pennsylvania.
9	**Elizabeth Hindman Armstrong** was born in Franklin Co., Pennsylvania, 17 Nov. 1789. She died 9 Apr. 1867 in Indiana Co., Pennsylvania.
10	**Unknown Kelly** married Eliza [--?--].
11	**Eliza [--?--]** was born in Pennsylvania, ca. 1816.
12	**Unknown Jackson** married Elizabeth [--?--].
13	**Elizabeth [--?--]** was born in Pennsylvania, ca. 1807.
14	**John McConnell Wilson** was born in Clarion, Clarion, Pennsylvania, 20 Oct. 1812. He married Ruth Goheen ca. 1833. John died 22 Mar. 1877 in Clarion, Clarion, Pennsylvania.
15	**Ruth Goheen** was born in Pennsylvania, ca. 1813.
Generation 5	
16	**William Stewart** married Margaret Getty.
17	**Margaret Getty**
18	**Alexander Armstrong** married Lena Ann Hindman.
19	**Lena Ann Hindman**
28	**Robert Wilson** married Sarah McConnell.
29	**Sarah McConnell**

Figure 7-10
Even celebrities sometimes carry a family name. Jimmy Stewart was named after his paternal grandfather.

THE SOCIAL SECURITY DEATH INDEX

Each entry in the SSDI offers you valuable genealogical information. The entry for Anthony Sinatra, father of Frank Sinatra, offers the following information:

Name: Anthony Sinatra

Birth Date: 4 May 1894

Death Date: Jan. 1969

Last Residence: 07024 (Fort Lee, Bergen, NJ)

Last Benefit: none specified

SSN: 140-32-5246

State Issued: New Jersey

Many people mistake the Last Residence field as the place of death for the individual. While in many instances it is, this is not always the case. The Last Residence field is the legal address of the individual, as far as the Social Security Administration is aware. If the person recently moved or died while they were on vacation or otherwise traveling, they could easily die hundreds of miles away, in another state or country. What the Last Residence does offer you, though, is perhaps a new locality of which you were previously unaware to search for records, including death, cemetery, and obituary.

the few searchable databases that is available for free. You will find the SSDI available at the following major genealogical sites:

- Genealogy.com: www.genealogy.com—only through its FamilyFinder search, cannot search the SSDI by itself
- FamilySearch: www.familysearch.org
- Family Tree Legends: www.familytreelegends.com
- New England Ancestors: www.newenglandancestors.org
- RootsWeb: www.rootsweb.com

In addition to supplying you with the death dates of certain twentieth century individuals, the SSDI also offers you a way to get valuable information about a person's birth and parents. While you often can't request copies of a person's death records because of the privacy laws, you can contact the Social Security Administration with the information found in the SSDI and request a copy of the SS-5 form of the individual you located.

The SS-5 form is the application for a social security number. The form has fields for an individual's full name, place and date of birth, work history, and the full names of the parents, including the maiden name of the mother. This is much of the same information you would find on the death certificate (see Figures 7-11 on page 146 and 7-12 on page 147).

Figure 7-11
SS-5 forms, such as this one for Ron Howard's mother, offer names of parents and the birthplace of applicants.

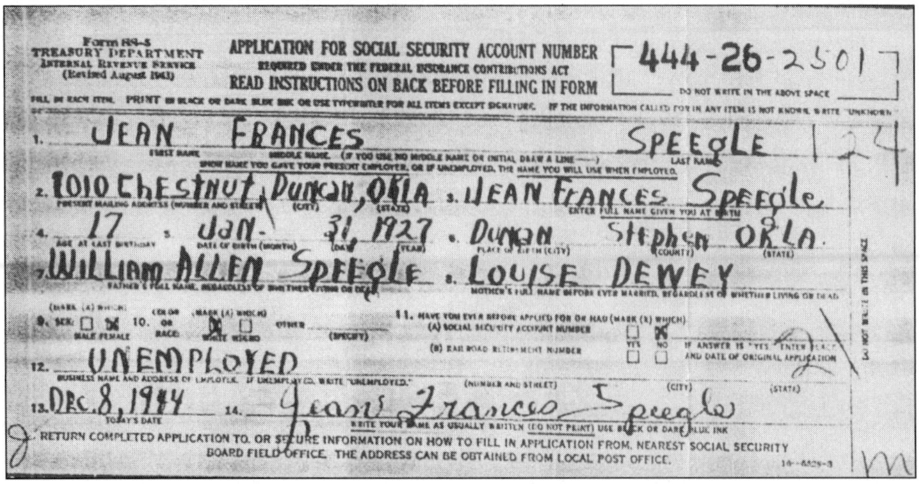

Form SS-5
TREASURY DEPARTMENT
INTERNAL REVENUE SERVICE
(Revised August 1943)

APPLICATION FOR SOCIAL SECURITY ACCOUNT NUMBER
REQUIRED UNDER THE FEDERAL INSURANCE CONTRIBUTIONS ACT
READ INSTRUCTIONS ON BACK BEFORE FILLING IN FORM

444-26-2501
DO NOT WRITE IN THE ABOVE SPACE

FILL IN EACH ITEM. PRINT IN BLACK OR DARK BLUE INK OR USE TYPEWRITER FOR ALL ITEMS EXCEPT SIGNATURE. IF THE INFORMATION CALLED FOR IN ANY ITEM IS NOT KNOWN, WRITE "UNKNOWN"

1. JEAN (FIRST NAME) FRANCES (MIDDLE NAME. IF YOU USE NO MIDDLE NAME OR INITIAL DRAW A LINE ——) SPEEGLE (LAST NAME)
SHOW NAME YOU GAVE YOUR PRESENT EMPLOYER, OR IF UNEMPLOYED, THE NAME YOU WILL USE WHEN EMPLOYED.

2. 1010 Chestnut (PRESENT MAILING ADDRESS (NUMBER AND STREET)), Duncan (CITY), OKLA (STATE)
3. JEAN Frances Speegle (ENTER FULL NAME GIVEN YOU AT BIRTH)
4. 17 (AGE AT LAST BIRTHDAY)
5. Jan. (DATE OF BIRTH (MONTH)) 31, (DAY) 1927 (YEAR)
6. Duncan (PLACE OF BIRTH (CITY)) Stephen (COUNTY) OKLA. (STATE)
7. William ALLEN SPEEGLE (FATHER'S FULL NAME, REGARDLESS OF WHETHER LIVING OR DEAD)
8. LOUISE DEWEY (MOTHER'S FULL NAME BEFORE EVER MARRIED, REGARDLESS OF WHETHER LIVING OR DEAD)
9. SEX: (MARK (X) WHICH) MALE ☐ FEMALE ☒
10. COLOR OR RACE: (MARK (X) WHICH) WHITE ☒ NEGRO ☐ OTHER (SPECIFY)
11. HAVE YOU EVER BEFORE APPLIED FOR OR HAD (MARK (X) WHICH)
(A) SOCIAL SECURITY ACCOUNT NUMBER YES ☐ NO ☒
(B) RAILROAD RETIREMENT NUMBER YES ☐ NO ☐
IF ANSWER IS "YES" ENTER PLACE AND DATE OF ORIGINAL APPLICATION
12. UNEMPLOYED (BUSINESS NAME AND ADDRESS OF EMPLOYER. IF UNEMPLOYED, WRITE "UNEMPLOYED.") (NUMBER AND STREET) (CITY) (STATE)
13. DEC. 8, 1944 (TODAY'S DATE)
14. Jean Frances Speegle (WRITE YOUR NAME AS USUALLY WRITTEN (DO NOT PRINT) USE BLACK OR DARK BLUE INK)
RETURN COMPLETED APPLICATION TO, OR SECURE INFORMATION ON HOW TO FILL IN APPLICATION FROM, NEAREST SOCIAL SECURITY BOARD FIELD OFFICE. THE ADDRESS CAN BE OBTAINED FROM LOCAL POST OFFICE.
DO NOT WRITE IN THIS SPACE

All of the above mentioned Web sites that offer the SSDI also provide a letter you can print out and mail to the Social Security Administration to request a copy of the SS-5 form for someone found in the SSDI.

OTHER RECORDS

In addition to these basic records, there are many other records and resources that genealogists use to re-create a family history. These include original records, such as land records and probate records like wills. With a full spectrum of resources at your fingertips, you can gain a good overall view of the life of an individual, as well as some indication as to the migration of the person or his or her family.

Important

While genealogists flock to certain record types and resources, there is really no resource that should be overlooked. Using all available resources is even more important when working with celebrities or historical figures. You never know what you will find. In chapter six we talked about newspapers and magazines. While you are more apt to find information about a celebrity or famous person in some of the mainstream publications that are indexed in the *Readers' Guide to Periodical Literature*, the PERSI index of genealogical periodicals is also valuable. When it comes to original records, I check all that are available to me—I never know what record will hold the clue I need. A tombstone may lead me to military records, which may lead me to vital records. Or an obituary may lead me to land records which help me determine when a family arrived in a given state or county, which may then lead me to county land records.

The bibliography in the back of the book includes a number of useful books that will supply you with detailed information about all the records discussed in this book as well as some others. Different research situations call for different records or research approaches.

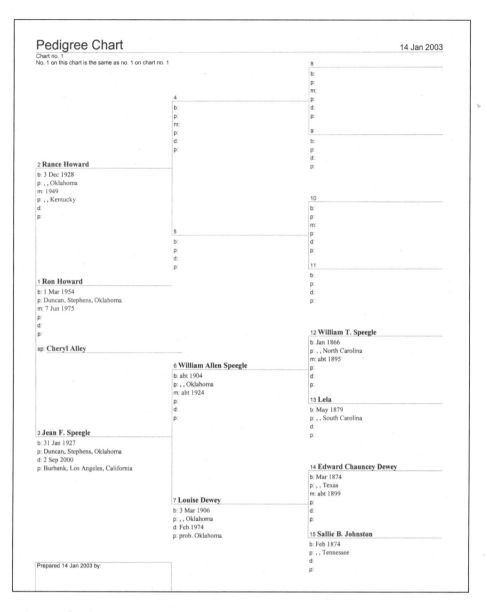

Pedigree Chart   14 Jan 2003

Chart no. 1
No. 1 on this chart is the same as no. 1 on chart no. 1

2 Rance Howard
b: 3 Dec 1928
p: , , Oklahoma
m: 1949
p: , , Kentucky
d:
p:

1 Ron Howard
b: 1 Mar 1954
p: Duncan, Stephens, Oklahoma
m: 7 Jun 1975
p:
d:
p:

sp: **Cheryl Alley**

3 Jean F. Speegle
b: 31 Jan 1927
p: Duncan, Stephens, Oklahoma
d: 2 Sep 2000
p: Burbank, Los Angeles, California

4
b:
p:
m:
p:
d:
p:

5
b:
p:
d:
p:

6 William Allen Speegle
b: abt 1904
p: , , Oklahoma
m: abt 1924
p:
d:
p:

7 Louise Dewey
b: 3 Mar 1906
p: , , Oklahoma
d: Feb 1974
p: prob. Oklahoma

8
b:
p:
m:
p:
d:
p:

9
b:
p:
d:
p:

10
b:
p:
m:
p:
d:
p:

11
b:
p:
d:
p:

12 William T. Speegle
b: Jan 1866
p: , , North Carolina
m: abt 1895
p:
d:
p:

13 Lela
b: May 1879
p: , , South Carolina
d:
p:

14 Edward Chauncey Dewey
b: Mar 1874
p: , , Texas
m: abt 1899
p:
d:
p:

15 Sallie B. Johnston
b: Feb 1874
p: , , Tennessee
d:
p:

Prepared 14 Jan 2003 by:

Figure 7-12
Working from information found on the SS-5 forms of Ron Howard's mother and maternal grandmother allowed me to identify some of his ancestry quickly.

SO MANY RECORDS, SO LITTLE TIME

Few of our family members, unless they, too, have been bitten by the genealogy bug, appreciate the thrill and excitement we experience when we are hot on the trail of an ancestor. As a result we often have little time to devote to this hobby—real life and all that it requires often gets in the way. While I encourage you to always turn to the records discussed in this chapter and any other original records that may prove useful, there are some resources that can help focus your search or offer you a lot of information in a short amount of time. Compiled genealogies are designed to show you the compiled results of the research of others in these records we have just explored. Let's take a look at compiled genealogies, what you can learn from them, and what you should watch out for when working with them.

For More Info

ANSWERS ON THE DOUBLE

There are times when all we want is a quick answer about a particular record or research technique. We don't want to have to read an entire book or even a chapter of a book. It's these times when Marcia Melnyk's *The Genealogist's Question & Answer Book* (Cincinnati: Betterway Books, 2002) comes in handy.

Shortcuts: Compiled Genealogies

A compiled genealogy, as I am using the term here, is any family history that details more then one generation. Many of the records discussed in earlier chapters are associated with a given person at a given time. The record concentrates on an event in the life of that individual. When many of these events are gathered together by a researcher and put into a database or on a family group sheet and pedigree chart, a compiled genealogy has begun.

Compiled genealogies are the conclusions arrived at by individuals doing research. These genealogists have looked at many different resources and evaluated what the resource tells them. They enter the names, dates, and places for the events of each person and begin to link the people together into familial units based on the information found in these records. For instance, because the marriage record (see Figure 8-1 on page 149) says that Irving Berlin's parents are Moses Berlin and Leah Lipkin, the researcher enters these names into the database or on the family group sheet and pedigree chart, which may then be shared with others in a variety of ways, many of which we will discuss here in this chapter. Of course, as we saw earlier Irving's original surname was *Beilin*.

The Internet plays a major role in the world of compiled genealogies. Many databases we will examine in this chapter are compiled genealogies, though they may not be published as the standard family history book. I have separated the compiled genealogies into three different types:

- Published family histories—books devoted to family lineages
- Web published family histories
- GEDCOM databases—databases to which researchers can upload data files created from their own genealogy programs

Each of these types of genealogies has both good and bad points, which you should keep in the back of your mind as you begin to evaluate the information found in them. There is no actual perfect compiled family history as they are all secondary evidence, the result of the analysis and experience of another researcher. Because the experience of researchers

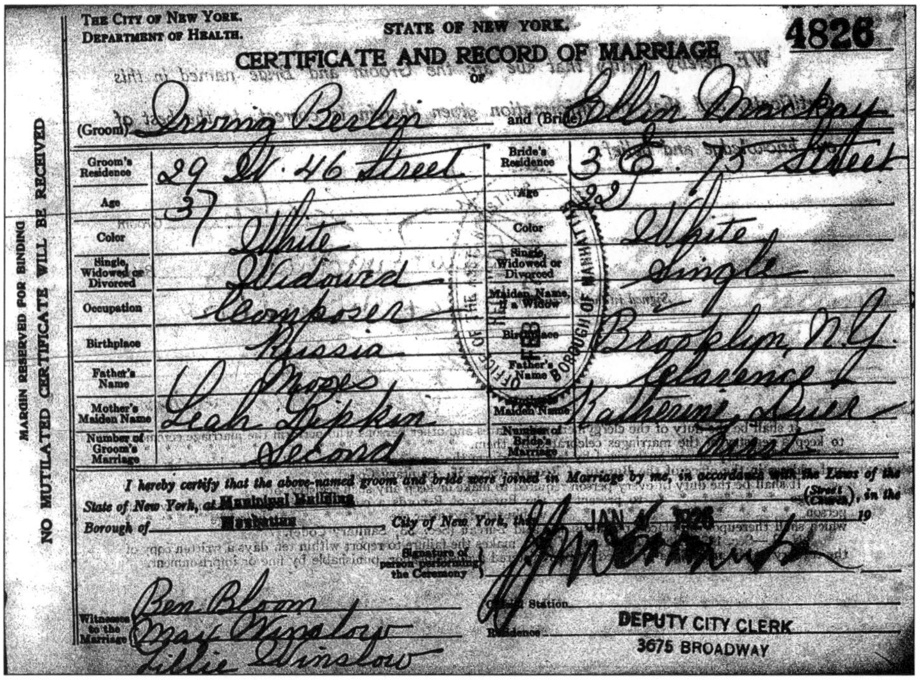

The City of New York.
Department of Health.
STATE OF NEW YORK.
4826
CERTIFICATE AND RECORD OF MARRIAGE
of
(Groom) Irving Berlin and (Bride) Ellin Mackay

Groom's Residence	29 W. 46 Street	Bride's Residence	3 E. 75 Street
Age	37	Age	22
Color	White	Color	White
Single, Widowed or Divorced	Widowed	Single, Widowed or Divorced	Single
Occupation	Composer	Maiden Name, if a Widow	
Birthplace	Russia	Birthplace	Brooklyn, N.Y.
Father's Name	Moses	Father's Name	Clarence
Mother's Maiden Name	Leah Lipkin	Mother's Maiden Name	Katherine Duer
Number of Groom's Marriage	Second	Number of Bride's Marriage	First

I hereby certify that the above-named groom and bride were joined in Marriage by me, in accordance with the Laws of the State of New York, at Municipal Building (Street), in the Borough of Manhattan City of New York, this JAN 4 1926 19

Signature of person performing the Ceremony

Witnesses to the Marriage: Ben Bloom, May Winslow, Lillie Winslow

DEPUTY CITY CLERK
3675 BROADWAY

MARGIN RESERVED FOR BINDING
NO MUTILATED CERTIFICATE WILL BE RECEIVED

Figure 8-1
It is important to verify anything found in compiled genealogies with many different original records.

can vary widely, so too does the analysis and accuracy of the information found in all of these resources.

PUBLISHED FAMILY HISTORIES

For years, published family histories were the only type of family history that existed. In *The Genealogist's Computer Companion,* I related how genealogists, compiling before computers, would wait to publish their family history until they were sure of all the information. This sometimes offers a better genealogy, because the researcher tried hard to make the book as accurate and complete as possible, though sometimes it meant no genealogy was published if the researcher died before completing the project. Like everything else in genealogy, though, the published family history differs in how the information is presented and in what records were used. You may also wonder at how complete the family history is.

Whenever you are using a published family history, start first by reading the introductory material, if there is any. This is often where the author or compiler will describe the work, effort, and hours that went into the book you are now holding in your hands. Too frequently we aim for the index of the book to search for names and then head to the referenced pages. We never stop to read why the person compiled this family history in the first place. Understanding why the book was compiled can offer insight into the accuracy and care with which the research was completed.

Tip

Published family histories have been published for more than a hundred years, though the number has increased within the last one hundred years or so. Today, many individuals are now self-publishing histories rather than

AN INTERNATIONAL HOBBY

Compiled family histories are not limited to the United States (see Figure 8-2 below). They are published all over the world, with those in other countries usually published in the native tongue. A publication for those interested in the Swedish ancestry of a variety of celebrities is Bo Lindwall's *24 Famous Swedish Americans and their Ancestors* (Sveriges Släktforskarförbund, 1996).

Figure 8-2
Just because the ancestry goes to another country doesn't mean it can't be researched, as seen here with the maternal line of actress Melanie Griffith.

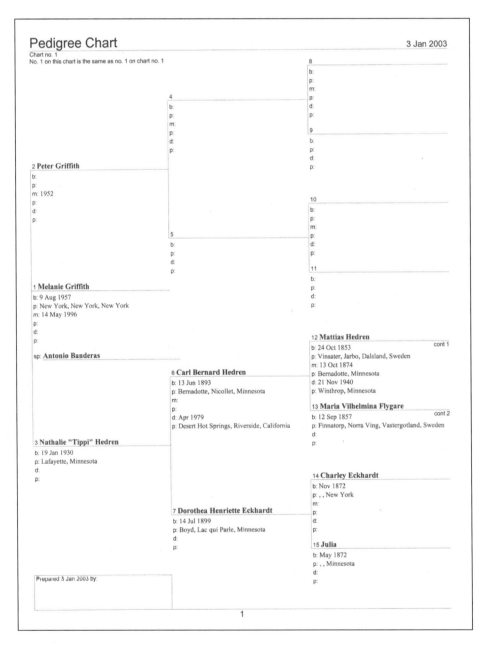

going through the vanity presses. With the current high quality and affordable personal printers and copy centers now available, it is no longer necessary to have someone typeset and print the family history.

Many published family histories from the late 1800s are still in existence. Used book stores may locate such books for you to purchase, but most family historians tend to rely on the holdings of libraries for their access to these books. Public libraries with large genealogical collections will often have a section devoted to the family histories donated or purchased over the years.

There are some libraries genealogists should always make a point to visit when they can. These libraries are either devoted to genealogy or have amassed a large collection of genealogical books. They include:

- Family History Library, Salt Lake City, Utah
- The National Archives, Washington, DC <www.archives.gov/index .html>
- New England Historic Genealogical Society Library, Boston, Massachusetts
- The Daughters of the American Revolution (DAR) Library, Washington, DC <www.dar.org/library/default.html>
- Allen County Public Library, Fort Wayne, Indiana
- Sutro Library, a branch of the California State Library, San Francisco, California <www.library.ca.gov/index.cfm>
- Newberry Library, Chicago, Illinois <www.newberry.org/nl/newberry home.html>

There are many other useful libraries with excellent genealogical collections. You may find that there is a genealogical society with a library near your residence, or if you are traveling, you may want to see if you can plan a visit to any local libraries that may cater to genealogy.

If you cannot easily travel to these libraries, it is possible that the books you need may be borrowed through your public library's interlibrary loan program. In most cases, reference books such as published family histories must be viewed while you are on the premises of your public library. With such restrictions, not all books can be viewed using interlibrary loan. In such instances, if you can locate the book in question through the catalogs of one of the libraries above, not all of which have made available an online catalog, you may need to hire a professional researcher to visit the repository and complete the research for you.

Another method of locating and viewing published family histories is to find them on microfilm. While the Family History Library in Salt Lake City, Utah, has many shelves full of published family history books, they also have a large collection of these volumes on microfilm or microfiche. These microform resources can be loaned to your local Family History Center (FHC), where you can view it for thirty days, with renewal extensions available. While Family History Centers are generally located in local chapels of

For More Info

FAMILY HISTORY HELP

If you are planning a trip to Salt Lake City and want to get the most out of your time at the Family History Library, you can't go wrong by reading *Your Guide to the Family History Library* by Paula Stuart Warren and James W. Warren (Cincinnati: Betterway Books, 2001).

Money Saver

Research Tip

YOUR REACH CAN BE FAR

If you need to hire a professional genealogist, check out the Association of Professional Genealogists <www.apgen.org> and the Board for Certification of Genealogists <www.bcgcertification.org> to find a researcher.

Warning

The Church of Jesus Christ of Latter-day Saints, they are open to the public. Through a local FHC, you have access to most of the microform resources available at the main library, as well as a number of computerized genealogical databases. For a nominal fee that covers the postage and handling of the microfilm, you can then view all manner of records, including some published family histories.

Thanks to the computer technology now available, you may find what you need on the Internet. The next section will discuss compiled genealogies that are designed to be published directly to the Internet, rather than appearing in book form. However, many previously published books about family histories, now in public domain since their copyright has expired, have been scanned and made available through various online subscription sites such as Ancestry.com and Genealogy.com.

This information is being made available on the Internet through two different ways: optical character recognition (OCR) and digitization. OCR uses a scanner that scans the page from the book and then runs that image through a program that reads the page and converts what it sees into text, much like you and I would read the page and type into our word processing program. However, this system doesn't always recognize a letter or a word for what it is.

The digitization process also scans the page from the book, but it leaves that scan as an image. What you see is like a photocopy of the original page of the book. The benefit is that there is no chance of additional typos or errors being introduced onto the page during the process. The downside, though, is that any indexes that accompany such a digitized volume can generally only point you to the page, not the exact line of the page in which the name can be found.

I mention the OCR and digitization of published family histories here rather than with those family histories published directly to the Web for a couple of reasons. First, these works were originally published as printed books. **Both printed books and histories published directly to the Web are open to errors for different reasons, and while many published genealogies are excellent and reliable, there are an equal number of published genealogies that are not.** The second reason that I mention them here is to get you thinking about alternative methods of accessing information. While I have already suggested interlibrary loan as a way to get access to some published genealogies, those for which the copyright has expired may now be available online, adding a degree of convenience to your research that you would not have if you need to visit the public library to read the book.

WEB PUBLISHED GENEALOGIES

The Web published genealogy is a different animal from his typeset ancestor. Today's genealogy software programs allow you to publish information electronically without needing to understand the Internet or the degree to which you're making the information available. In some ways this is a bonus—information gets published without our having to learn anything technical. In other ways it is a problem—some people are not controlling the information they publish, sometimes resulting in angered relatives with hurt feelings.

Those family histories that are published to the Internet are all done using one of the genealogy programs presently available, many of them listed in chapter two. These programs are designed to take the information you have entered and create a narrative style report, which is then uploaded to the Internet. Some upload automatically and go to a site predetermined by the program. Others allow you to upload the files that have been created to any Web space you have, either through your local Internet Service Provider or another Web site designed to display pages.

One of the biggest problems with Internet published genealogy is the lack of cited sources. There is seldom any way of knowing where the shared information was found and as a result no way of knowing how reliable the information posted is. To make matters worse, most people are so mesmerized by the Internet that they seldom question the validity of the information they find online. Instead they simply type in the information found, or download a GEDCOM file if the publisher of the information has included one, add it to their own database, and go merrily on their way.

To borrow a phrase from Robby the Robot: "Danger, danger, Will Robinson!" **Information on the Internet is no more or less reliable than what we find in the family histories we use in libraries.** The problem is that few genealogists verify the information they find on the Internet, and as a result there is a vicious cycle of perpetuated and passed-along errors.

Whenever you find a Web site that includes a lineage to which you can connect, take the time to truly evaluate what has been shared. **Don't just dump the information into your database.** Create a separate database file with that family information so that it is kept separate from your research until you have time to check the accuracy of the information against primary, original sources. If the person who published the information on the Internet hasn't shared sources, don't be afraid to e-mail her and ask where she got the date or place you were unaware of. You are not being rude when you do this. You are not saying you doubt her work. You are saying that you did not know this information and would like to know where she found it so you can check the records as well.

If the Web site includes source citations, usually denoted by superscripted numbers after names, dates, or places, it is a good idea to examine them (see Figure 8-3 on page 158). Some genealogy programs will link these so that you can easily click on them and be taken to that exact source. You can then use the Back button in your browser to return to the narrative of the lineage. A good source citation should mean you have no doubt where the information came from and could go right to the source yourself, assuming it isn't a personal letter or diary in a private collection. A good researcher will not rely only on the research of others but will use the records discussed in chapter seven as the basis of his research. In some instances he may

Library/Archive Source

THE NEHGCS LENDING LIBRARY

Don't live in Boston but need resources from the New England Historic Genealogical Society? The Lending Library is the answer, if you are a member. Search the Lending Library catalog at the NEHGS Web site <www.newenglanda ncestors.org/>.

Warning

Important

Below is an article compiled by someone with a simple interest in knowing Larry Hagman's ancestry. The research described is a wonderful case study and a great way to learn how to do research.

LARRY HAGMAN'S SOUTHERN ROOTS

By James Pylant

© *2002—as posted on AncestorChronicles.com, used with permission*

In the long-running television series *Dallas*, ruthless Texan "J.R. Ewing" was portrayed by actor Larry Hagman, a native of the Lone Star State. Like his fictional counterpart, Hagman was from a prominent North Central Texas family, but there the similarity ends. Though "J.R." was a Dallasite, the famous actor was born in Fort Worth, Tarrant County. Larry Martin Hagman, the only child of Benjamin Jackson Hagman and Broadway legend Mary Martin, was born on 21 September 1931.[1]

Hagman attended school in his mother's hometown of Weatherford, in Parker County,[2] which adjoins Tarrant County on its western border. Mary Martin was sixteen years old when she wedded accountant Ben Hagman, but their marriage lasted only a few years. Several years following her divorce, she married Richard Halliday, a film editor and writer. They had one child, Heller Halliday.[3]

Mary Virginia Martin was born in Weatherford on 1 December 1913 and she died in Rancho Mirage, Riverside County, California, on 3 March 1990.[4] She had one older sister, Geraldine "Jerry" Martin, who was born on 3 September 1902, also in Weatherford.[5] They were the daughters of Preston Martin and the former Juanita Pressley. Preston Martin, whose law practice in that town spanned more than forty years, was a Mississippian, his birth occurring at Popular Creek, Choctaw County, on 6 April 1872.[6] He and Juanita Pressley, a music teacher, were married in Fort Worth on 10 August 1899.[7] His wife was a native Texan, born in Brenham, Washington County, on 27 May 1878.[8] Mr. Martin died on 20 December 1938 in Weatherford.[9] Mrs. Martin then joined her actress daughter in California, where she died at age sixty-six on 9 August 1944 in Los Angeles.[10]

Geraldine Martin, Mary Martin's sister, was the namesake of their paternal grandmother. James Alberta Martin and the former Geraldine Hearon, the parents of Preston Martin, were married on 19 September 1867 in Mississippi. Born on 7 September 1845, James A. Martin was a native of Alabama and lived in that state until, at age five, he moved with his parents to Popular Creek, Mississippi. He enlisted in the Confederate Army and served through Forrest's Cavalry, and after the war's end taught school and farmed in Mississippi until moving his family to Texas in 1877. Here, the Martins settled at Long's Creek, fifteen miles southeast of Weatherford, where James A. farmed and ranched until 1905, when the family moved to Weatherford. James A. Martin continued living in Parker County until age eighty-one, when he moved to Floydada, Floyd County. He lived four years, his death occurring there on 25 April 1931.[11] The Martins had nine children: Howard (born 1868), Assistant Attorney General of Texas; Lela (born 1870), who married W.M. Massie; Preston; Eugene H. (born 1874); Luther (born 1878); Barnard (born 1880); Andy J. (born 1883); James G. (born 1886); and Claude M., born 1888).[12]

According to C.M. Martin, his grandparents—the parents of James A. Martin—were Jackson Martin and the former Nancy Sawyer.[13] The 1860 Federal Census of Choctaw County, Mississippi, shows the Popular Creek household of forty-six-year-old Jackson Martin, a farmer and South Carolinian, with Alabama natives Nancy A., age thirty-six; teacher William L., age eighteen; James A., age fourteen, and Mississippi natives Andrew, age five; Lilley, age three; and Beulah, age eight months. Jackson Martin's real estate was valued at $3,000.00, while his personal property was estimated at $12,475.00.[14] The 1870 Federal Census shows Jackson Martin still farming in the same county, but his real estate was then valued at $1,500.00, while his personal property had dropped to $1,450.00. Jackson, age fifty-six, and Nancy, age forty-six, had four children in their household: sixteen-year-old Andrew; Lillie, age thirteen; *Buler* [Beulah], age ten, and *Isiac*, age four.[15] By then, James A. Martin had been married nearly three years and had a household of his own. At Popular Creek, James Martin, age twenty-five, a farmer, is shown with *Gerlden*, age twenty-three and two-year-old Howard and one year old *Liler*. His real estate was valued at $1,000.00, while his personal property was valued at $500.00.[16]

Although Choctaw County Courthouse lost much of its early records in two nineteenth century fires, the first book of deeds was found in recent years in an old smokehouse. Recorded in this volume is Jackson A. Martin's purchase of a mule, wagon, and yoke from S.S. Lott in February of 1868.[17]

Family tradition tells that both James A. Martin and Geraldine Hearon came from plantation-owning families, and that the Hearons were also merchants.[18] Geraldine Hearon was born on 26 January 1847 in Alabama and died in Parker County, Texas, on 4 October 1910.[19] According to the 1880 Census of Parker County, her father was a South Carolinian and her mother was a Tennessean.[20]

Also living in Choctaw County at the time of the 1860 Census was the large family of farmer Stephen Herron, a fifty-four-year-old South Carolinian. In this household were Elizabeth, age forty-two, born in Tennessee; Alabama natives Christopher C., age sixteen, and Milton, age fifteen, both farm laborers; *Jereldine*, age thirteen; *Baxtor*, age eleven; Luther, age nine; Alexander S., age seven; Mississippi natives Edna, age six, Adella, age four, and Marcus, a two year old. Stephen Herron's real estate was valued at $6,000.00, and his personal property was given at $15,000.00.[21]

Continued on next page

The Hearons migrated to Mississippi from Clarke County, Alabama, where they are shown on the 1850 Federal Census. At age forty-six, Stephen Hearon's occupation is listed as a merchant, thus supporting the Martin family tradition that the Hearons were merchants. His age is forty-six, and again South Carolina is recorded as his birthplace. His real estate was valued at $1,500.00. Also listed were Elizabeth, age thirty-two, born in Tennessee; and children Christopher C., age seven; John, age six; Milton, age four; Geraldine, age three; Baxter, age one; and four month-old Luther. Another resident of the Hearon household was a twenty year old named Jno. Holder. Enumerated above Stephen Hearon was James Hearon, age seventy, a farmer from North Carolina, and fifty-eight-year-old Minerva, a Virginian.[22]

Clarke County is where Stephen Hearon and Elizabeth Black were married a decade earlier on 6 February 1840.[23] Larry Hagman's roots run deep in that southwestern Alabama county, and his Hearon kinfolks are found abundantly in its records. Further research might untangle the relationships and intermarriages with other old Clarke County families.

1. Texas Birth Index <www.rootsweb.com> listed the birth of Larry Martin Hagman, born 21 September 1931, Tarrant County, son of Benjamin Jack Hagman and Mary Virginia Martin. Note: This database has been removed from Rootsweb. Susan L. Stetler, ed., *Biography Almanac* (Detroit: Gale Research, 1986), Vol. I, p. 734, gives the same birth date and lists Fort Worth as the birthplace. However, *Who's Who in America, 1984–85*, Vol. I, p. 1339, states Weatherford was Hagman's birthplace.

2. In an article in the *Weatherford Democrat*, Mon., 23 June 1986, Larry Hagman said Jim Wright (later the U.S. Speaker) was his boxing instructor in high school in Weatherford.

3. Obituary of Mary Martin, *Fort Worth Star-Telegram*, Mon., 5 November 1990.

4. *Ibid.*, which states "some reports placed the date [of her birth] one year later." *Biography Almanac*, Vol. II, p. 1095, gives 1 December 1914 as her birth date.

5. Obituary of Mrs. Jerry Martin Andrews, *Weatherford Democrat*, 10 May 1979. Her full name is given as "Jerry Geraldine Andrews," as informant on the death certificate of Juanita Pressley Martin, no. 12559, California State Department of Health Services, Sacramento. Her tombstone inscription in Greenwood City Cemetery, in Weatherford, states "Andrews/ Geraldine Martin/Born Sept. 3, 1902/Died 10 May 1979," as copied by the compiler in February 2002.

6. Obituary of Preston Martin, *Weatherford Democrat*, 23 December 1938.

7. Obituary of Juanita Pressley Martin, *Weatherford Democrat*, 17 Aug. 1944.

8. Juanita Pressley Martin, California state death certificate 12559.

9. Preston Martin obituary, 23 December 1938.

10. Juanita Martin obituary, 17 August 1944.

11. Obituary of J.A. Martin, *Weatherford Democrat*, Fri., 1 May 1931. A biographical sketch of James Martin in the Parker County Historical Commission's *History of Parker County* (Weatherford, Texas: the commission, 1980), p. 431, states that his middle name was Alberta. The biography was compiled by Don W. Martin, a grandson.

12. J.A. Martin's obituary names surviving children as Mrs. W.M. Massie, J.C., Claude M., Bernard, Preston, Eugene, and Luther Martin. "Two sons, Howard and Andy, died several years ago." Farmer Jas. A. Martin (age thirty-four) and wife Geraldine (age thirty-three), both Alabama natives, with children Howard, age eleven; Lela, age ten; Preston, age eight; Eugene, age six; Luther, age two; and Bernard, age four months (born in January), are shown in the 1880 Federal Census of Parker County, Texas, population schedule, Justice Precinct 6, enumeration district 189, supervisor's district 3, p. 458B, dwelling 16, family 16; National Archives microfilm T9, roll 1322. (Hereafter, National Archives is

designated as NA.) J.A. Martin, age fifty-four (born Sept. 1845), wife, G., age fifty-three (born Jan. 1847), and sons E.H., age twenty-six (born May 1874), Luther, age twenty-two (born Mar. 1878), Bernard, age twenty (born Jan. 1880), Jas. G., age fourteen (born Mar. 1886), and Claude M., age eleven (born Nov. 1888) appear in the 1900 Federal Census of Parker County, Texas, population schedule, Precinct 6, enumeration district 77, supervisor's district 3, p. 237A, sheet 4, dwelling 65, family 65; NA microfilm T623, roll 1664. J.A. Martin was farming on his own land, while his three oldest sons were listed as farm laborers. His wife was the mother of twelve children, only nine of whom were living. Howard Martin's obituary in the Weatherford *Daily Herald*, Sat., 2 April 1906, states that he was the "assistant attorney general of Texas."

13. James A. Martin, death certificate, no. 18296, Texas Department of Health, Austin.
14. Jackson Martin household, 1860 Federal Census, Choctaw County, Mississippi, population schedule, Huntsville post office, p. 117, dwelling 835, family 805; NA microfilm M653, roll 579.
15. Jackson Martin household, 1870 Federal Census of Choctaw County, Mississippi, Township 18, Range 7, p. 280; NA microfilm M593, roll 725.
16. James Martin household, 1870 Federal Census of Choctaw County, Mississippi, Popular Creek, p. 260, dwelling 8, family 8.
17. Betty C. Wiltshire, *Abstracts of Choctaw County, Mississippi Records* (the author: 1993), p. 93.
18. Parker County Historical Commission, *History of Parker County*, p. 431.
19. Dates of birth and death from tombstone inscription of Geraldine Martin, Greenwood City Cemetery, Weatherford, Texas, as copied by the compiler in February, 2002. Place of death from obituary of Mrs. Geraldine Martin in the *Daily Herald*, Wed., 5 October 1910.
20. 1880 Federal Census, Parker County, Texas, population schedule, Justice Precinct 6, enumeration district 189, supervisor's district 3, p. 458B, dwelling 16, family 16.
21. Stephen Herron household, 1860 Federal Census, Choctaw County, Mississippi, population schedule, p. 17, dwelling 110, family 107.
22. Stephen Hearon household, 1850 Federal Census, Clarke County, Alabama, population schedule, p. 206, dwelling [blank], family 20; NA microfilm M432, roll 3.
23. *Marriage Records*, Vol. B., p. 49, Clarke County, Alabama.

begin with the research of others and then verify that research with his own research. If he cites both types of resources, then you can feel confident that he's done quite a bit of research but perhaps has not as yet verified everything.

The Internet allows researchers the flexibility to publish the lineage in progress. With this flexibility comes the possibility that misinformation will be published. After all, we are human, which means we are prone to mistakes, and those mistakes may go undiscovered for some time. **Even if the researcher has shared the sources used in compiling the research she publishes to the Internet, it is still important to verify that research and see what you get out of the records.** Did you come to the same conclusion as the other researcher based on what the records told you? Were you able to find other records that supported the conclusions? Did other records conflict with the information published on the Internet?

If you do use information found online, be sure to print it out. If you don't and return to that Web site later, it is possible that the site will no longer exist or that the information will have been changed. Having a printed copy, which usually includes a date and time stamp at the bottom of each page, allows you to compare the printout with the site on subsequent

Important

157

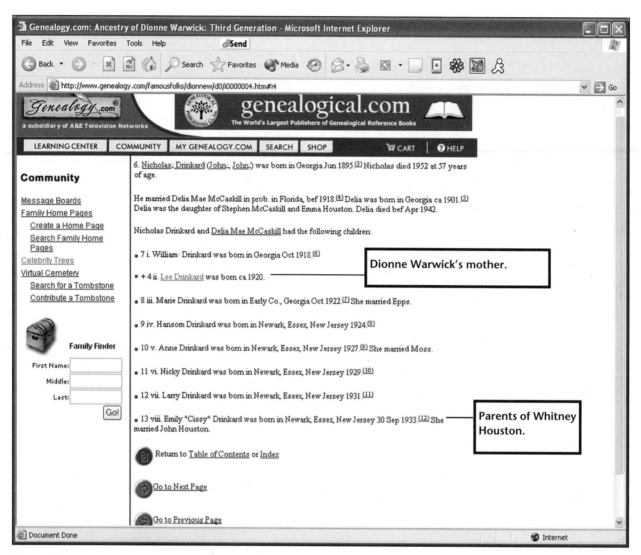

Figure 8-3
Internet genealogies offer a jump start to your research as seen here with the family history of Dionne Warwick. © 2002 Genealogy.-com. Used with permission.

visits to see if the information has been updated. If it has, did the research alter any facts that you were relying on in your own research? If so, you may need to go back to the library or another repository to see if you can prove or disprove the information now shared.

Compiled genealogies that are published in a narrative style are easier for me to follow. This could be because I am more familiar with the old printed genealogies, and therefore I am more comfortable with something that resembles them. When I work with those designed in a pedigree style, resembling a pedigree chart, there are times I get lost or skip a generation. All that clicking back and forth from linked name to linked name sometimes results in me overlooking someone. Pedigree-styled Web sites often require me to print out ten or twelve pages or may not actually show a family unit, but instead treat everyone as a single individual, with parents' and spouse's

---

RESOLVING CONFLICT

There will be times when you will discover that the documents or resources you have found on an individual give conflicting information. Then you will have to look at the records in question and decide which is more likely to be the most accurate for the conflicting data. This is something that comes with experience. The more research you do and the more you read, the more you will understand the limitations for certain record types. For instance, the information supplied on a death certificate for the birth date and parents' names of the deceased may be more suspect than the same information found on the marriage license. An original document is usually more reliable than a published, compiled family history.

---

information requiring another click of my mouse to view dates and places for the parents' or spouses' events.

GEDCOM DATABASES

GEDCOM stands for GEnealogical Data COMmunication, and it's designed to allow a genealogical software program to read data entered in a different way in a different database, and vice versa. The importing of information this way is not completely without problems, as the different genealogical programs handle different special features. It is better, though, than having to retype all the information.

Such databases are flourishing. Millions of names can be searched in a single database in just a few seconds. Of course, in order to get the most from these databases, there are a few things to keep in mind:

- It is best if you have more than just the name of a person. At the very least, you should have the name of a spouse or at least one parent. It is better if you have the name, date and place of birth, and date and place of death.
- You may find more than one entry for the individual on whom you have run the search. It is a good idea to check all hits that come up.
- While it is good to know more than just a name, it is sometimes better to type in just the name of the person first. If you get too many hits, you can then begin to use the other information you know to help eliminate some of the hits.
- Different GEDCOM databases offer different abilities in the results that are shared.

There are a number of different GEDCOM databases, some larger than others, and some more familiar to researchers than others. The more familiar the site is, the better—GEDCOM databases rely on submissions by researchers to grow. **Most of these databases are available free of charge.**

- Ancestry World Tree/WorldConnect—When Ancestry.com purchased

Money Saver

RootsWeb.com, they combined their Ancestry World Tree with Roots-Web's WorldConnect. Regardless of which site you are on, you are actually researching the same GEDCOM database. It can be reached through Ancestry.com <www.ancestry.com/> or RootsWeb.com <www.rootsweb.com/>.

- World Family Tree—The GEDCOM database compiled by Genealogy-.com was originally on CD-ROMs and is now available through a subscription on the Web site. It can be reached by signing up at Genealogy.com <www.genealogy.com/>.

- Ancestral File—This is an older database made available by the Family History Library. It was originally published on CD-ROM and accessible only through local Family History Centers and the Family History Library. Today it is freely available on the Family History Library's Web site <www.familysearch.org/>.

- Pedigree Resource File—This is the newer database compiled by GEDCOM submissions sent to the Family History Library. While the actual GEDCOM files must presently be purchased on CD-ROM, the basic information and lineage links can be searched and viewed online at the Family History Library's Web site <www.familysearch.org/>.

SEARCHING GEDCOM DATABASES

Most GEDCOM databases can be searched individually or as part of a larger set of databases available at the site in question. There will be times when you may want to do a blanket search of all the databases available at a site. If you are searching at Ancestry.com or Genealogy.com it is probable that many of the hits found in the other databases will be unavailable to you unless you have paid to subscribe to them. Even if you have subscribed to Genealogy.com's World Family Tree, you still may not be able to access the other databases. A lot will depend on the type of subscription you have. Other sites, such as FamilySearch, are searchable for free, regardless of which database you are searching or if you're doing a blanket search.

Some of the databases allow you to limit or expand your search by including certain terms or characters. If you're searching for a common surname, there will likely be times when there are just too many hits to go through them one at a time. In these cases, knowing more about the person is important because you can use the additional information to narrow the search by including the year of birth or the place of birth. Remember, though, that the more information you add to a search engine, the more you run the risk of excluding the person you were looking for. When you begin to add additional information, go slowly. Start with one addition, such as the year of birth, and run the search. If there are still too many hits, then add the place of birth and so on. There is always a chance that you know more about the person you are searching for than the person who submitted the name to the GEDCOM database.

WHY CAN'T IT BE FREE?

Genealogy is the only hobby I am aware of where everyone wants it all to be free. If I play tennis then I know I will need to purchase a racket and tennis shoes. If I like boating, then I can expect to pay a hefty price for a boat and the maintenance involved in its upkeep. Genealogy is a hobby like any other—we just tend to have a little more control over where our money goes. The reality is that while the Internet is a marvelous resource, it costs a lot of money to keep it going. I am not surprised to find that I must pay for the data I am seeking. Presently I pay subscriptions to about ten different sites, including genealogy sites, military databases, and celebrity information sites. The information I can find online usually saves me a great deal of time in the preliminary stages of any research, which allows me to devote my time and travel to just those things I need. Preparing online this way actually helps save me money, because I no longer need to drive up to the library for every aspect of my research.

In some cases, you can expand your search by using a wild card search. **A wild card is a character, such as the asterisk, known in computing as the star (*), that tells the search engine to replace the star with up to five letters, any five letters it finds.** For example, you could do a search for STAND*, and the search would find, if the names were in the database, STANDERFER, STANDIFOR, STANDFORD, STANDEFER, STANDIFER, and so on.

\di'fin\ *vb*

Definitions

Not all searchable databases can support the wild card. Some may offer a wildcard search in one section of the database but not in another. To find out what character the database recognizes for a wild card and how it must be used, you will need to read the online help or FAQ (Frequently Asked Questions) file as each database is different and how and when you can use the wildcard is likely to differ.

FINDING COMPILED GENEALOGIES

Finding a compiled genealogy depends on the kind of compiled genealogy you are looking for and on what you can use to search for it. The compiled genealogies that are found in the GEDCOM databases are usually only searchable by visiting the site that makes them available. You may be able to locate those published on the Internet through general Internet search engines. To find a specific book, you can take advantage of online library catalogs.

Compiled family histories such as the GEDCOM databases or the books that have since been computerized are usually found in "member only" areas. These areas are not accessible by regular Internet search engines, so the only way to find out what is available in these compiled family histories is to visit the specific Web site responsible for the database. And remember, while you may be able to run a search to see how many hits the database(s) offers, you may have to be a paying member to actually view the information.

When you are looking for Web published family histories, the best option is one of the many general search engines. To get the most out of an Internet search engine, you need to understand what it is searching. Generally speaking, for whatever you've typed in, the engine searches a database of Web pages with certain terms and perhaps the words on one to five layers of Web pages. Search engines often have guidelines of how you need to enter a phrase or how to narrow your search by adding or excluding words. The best way to learn about the search engine you like is to read the online help or FAQ file.

There are many different search engines available on the Internet. While we like to believe that they were put there just for us to find solutions to all of our genealogical nightmares, the reality is that other people use them to find other things. Because of this, there will always be times when the search you run comes up with totally unrelated searches. **I often start my search with the name of the individual I am looking for and then some term to help narrow it down.** If I am looking for a biography on a celebrity, for instance, to see what has been published online about that person, I will use the name and the term *biography*, so I am using a phrase and a required term

Tip

"Tom Cruise" biography

If I have found a few generations and there is a particularly unique name on the family tree, I will often use that name as a way of searching for anyone else who might have shared genealogy on the Internet. Try to find the most obscure name on the tree that is actually a direct relation to the person you are searching for. If that name comes up in a search, chances are there is something about that lineage available on the Internet.

Some of the more popular search engines include

Internet Source

SAVE YOUR SEARCHES

Copernic Agent <www.copernic.com/en/index.htm> is a Web search engine on your computer that allows you to save the searches you have done to be pulled up later, which is not possible when running a general search at Google.com or other online search engine sites.

- AltaVista
- HotBot
- Google
- Ask Jeeves/Ask.com
- Excite
- AlltheWeb
- Dogpile

ONLINE LIBRARY CATALOGS

Libraries and archives are beginning to harness the power of the Internet. This must cut down some of the phone calls and general questions libraries used to get about their holdings.

I can often find a Web site for a library or archive by simply using a general search engine and typing in the name of the library as a phrase and then adding the state. There are other ways, though, to find library catalogs. Some directories are devoted to the various libraries with online catalogs. I encourage you to use a general search engine as well as these directories.

FINDING ONLINE LIBRARY CATALOGS	
Libweb Library WWW Servers http://sunsite.berkeley.edu/Libweb/	Updated nightly and currently has links to more than 6,100 pages to libraries in more than 100 countries.
LibDex www.libdex.com/	The Library Index that has indexed the library catalogues of more than 18,000 libraries. Index includes library catalogues, Web sites, and Friends of Libraries pages.
Gateway to Library Catalogs www.loc.gov/z3950/	Offers links to a number of online library catalogs, including the Library of Congress.
Library of Congress: State Libraries http://lcweb.loc.gov/global/library/statelib.html	Offers links to the state libraries—valuable and often overlooked resources for genealogists.
Directory of Genealogy Libraries in the U.S. www.gwest.org/gen_libs.htm	An impressive list of links to those libraries with genealogical collections, including public libraries.

The general search engine will show you any Web page for that library, even if the library doesn't have an online catalog. Some of these directories will not list any library or archive site that doesn't have an online catalog.

Through these online library catalogs and the OCLC (Online Computer Library Center, Inc.), a subscriber-only firm to which libraries can belong, you will find you have more than enough catalogs to search for published family histories. Don't forget those libraries mentioned earlier in this chapter and the online subscription sites.

TAKING THE NEXT STEP

Now that we have discussed original records and published resources, it is time to look at how to use these resources to go beyond a direct lineage. Seldom will you discover a descent from a famous individual, and if you are related to a celebrity of today, then you know that relationship is a cousinship and you will need to branch out, reaching beyond your direct lineage to find the connection.

NINE

Branching Out

For More Info

MORE CLUSTER GENEALOGY

For a look at the cluster genealogy concept in detail, see Emily Anne Croom's *The Sleuth Book for Genealogists* (Cincinnati: Betterway Books, 2000).

Most people researching their family tree are trying to take their own personal ancestry back generation by generation. Because they are using this approach, the concentration of research time is often on the direct lineage. While siblings may be discovered and included in the genealogy software database and on the subsequent family group sheets, most of the time the researcher is obsessed with adding another generation to the pedigree chart, which is simply a direct lineage back from some individual.

Whereas there is nothing wrong with this approach, if you are looking for a connection to a famous individual, you must expand your research to include more. It is only by looking more extensively into the lives of siblings and female lineages that you are likely to uncover the connection. And when trying to connect to a famous individual, you need to not only branch out on your own research but to also branch out when working on the tree of the celebrity.

"CLUSTER" GENEALOGY

Cluster genealogy is the act of researching beyond the direct lineage. It could mean researching the siblings and the spouses of the siblings. It could mean researching the families of those who signed as witnesses on deeds or wills. Instead of focusing on just one person and hoping that the records you can find on that one person will be the answer to all your questions, the research needs to be expanded to include many more people who are directly and indirectly related to your direct ancestor. Of course the first thing you need to do is to define the cluster for the research you are trying to accomplish.

\di'fin\ *vb*

Definitions

I think of genealogical research as clusters within larger clusters. I have applied this thinking in two ways: with the people themselves and with the locality in which the ancestor is living. In the first case, I look to see what types of clusters of people are associated with my ancestor. In the second case, I look to see what clusters of localities are somehow connected to the person I am researching and begin to broaden that cluster.

A CLUSTER OF PEOPLE

Most people who have heard the term "cluster genealogy" think in these terms—the people. There are levels of clusters, though, from the immediate family, to the extended family, and finally to the community in which the subject is living and with whom there has been interaction. Every person is a piece to the final puzzle. Research them all, and you will soon discover you have put together a massive picture of the true family tree.

While it can help you stay focused, concentrating just on a direct line is a narrowing experience. If your family tree is anything like mine or some of the other ones I have worked on, you will soon discover that your ancestor was the one who never appears in the records. For instance, in the census from 1860 to 1880, can I find my third great-grandfather? Nope. Can I find his siblings? Of course. Now, in this case it could have had something to do with his less than sterling character when it came to matters of law. Yes, I am talking about colorful Benjamin Standerfer. Although I am now convinced that Benjamin was placed on my tree to expose me to the necessities of cluster genealogy.

Unfortunately, we often do not take the time to venture out beyond our immediate ancestor. I understand there is only so much time we can devote to this hobby. We want to get the most for our time, and it is easy to think that focusing attention on a sibling of your ancestor may be wasting time. In the end, though, it could actually save you time by helping you find records that list the names of the next generation. Of course, you need to prove that the two individuals are related in order to accomplish this.

With a recent foray into the family history of actor Bob Newhart, I found myself again returning to the cluster genealogy approach. I had gone through the steps of looking for biographies about him and was quite pleased with the information I found online. I then turned my attention to the census records, other online databases including the SSDI (as found at RootsWeb.com), and the Illinois Death Index <www2.sos.state.il.us/departments/archives/idphdeathindex.html>. I had also found a brief compiled genealogy of Bob Newhart on one of the GEDCOM database sites. With each step, I was recording possible records that I needed to check and seeing what records were available at the Family History Library and which would allow me quick access.

One of the first records that I wanted to look up was a death record for a David Newhart, who I had been led to believe from the information found in the compiled genealogy was Bob Newhart's paternal grandfather. Research in the death records revealed that the man was too old to be a possible match. So I had to ask myself if it was possible that his death was not recorded. While it was, I began to wonder if the information I had found in the compiled genealogy was off somehow.

A return to the 1920 and 1910 Soundex allowed me to view all of the Newharts in the state of Illinois. The Soundex revealed why I hadn't been able to find Bob Newhart's father, George David Newhart, under a listing for a

Case Study

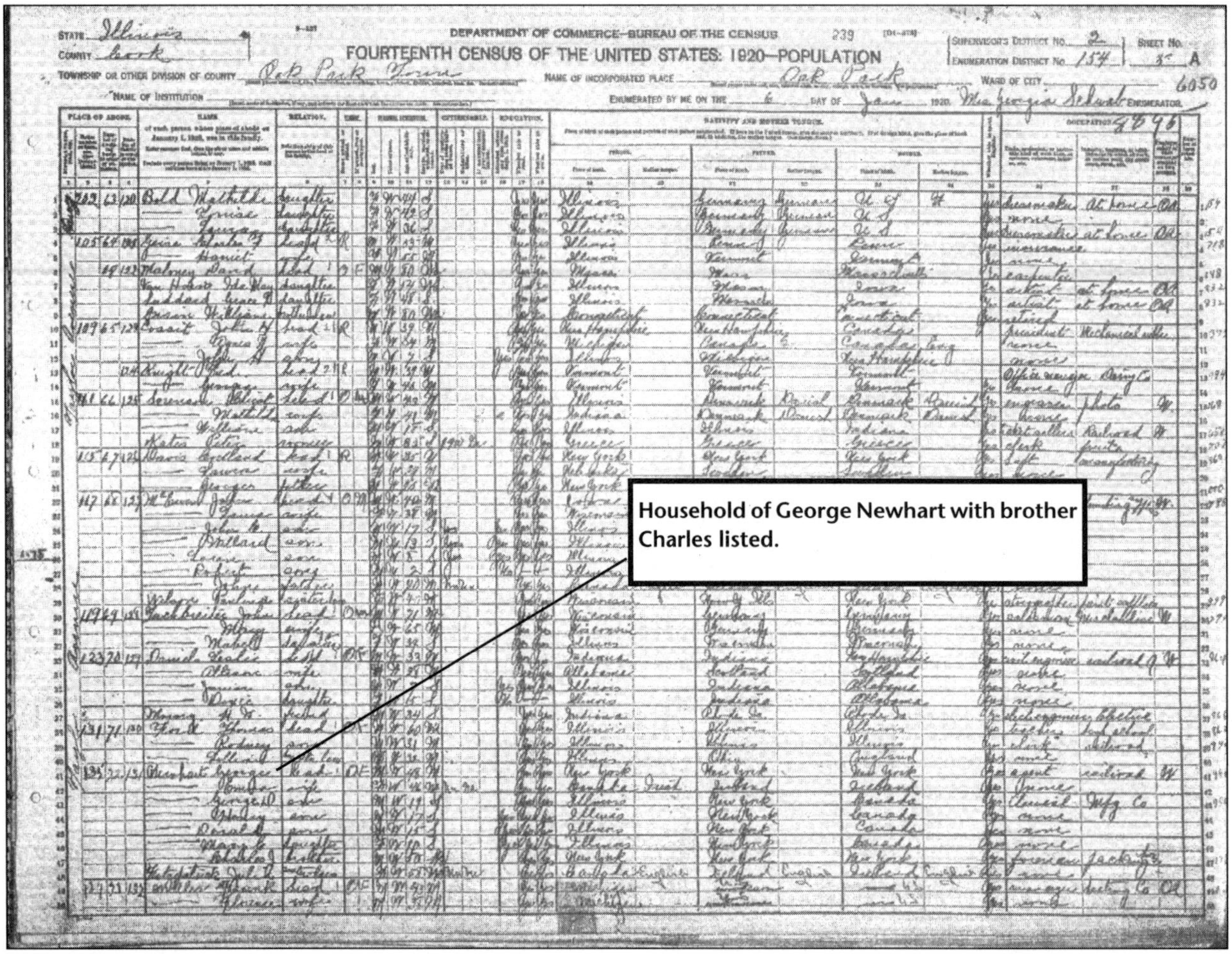

Household of George Newhart with brother Charles listed.

Figure 9-1
1920 census for George Newhart, Bob Newhart's grandfather. (Oak Park, Cook Co., Illinois, T625, roll 361, Enumeration District 154, sheet 5A).

head of family named David. The 1910 and 1920 census showed George D. Newhart as a son of George M. Newhart and his wife Emma. Also living with George M. in the 1920 census was his brother Charles. (See Figure 9-1 above.) This made it easier to locate the family in the 1880 census.

In working in the Illinois Death Index, I had come across a Henry D. Newhart who died in 1927, in Chicago, Cook Co., Illinois. Though I had no real proof that Henry was related to the family, a copy of the death certificate was made. The death certificate listed Henry's birth as Constableville, New York, and his parents as David Newhart and Caroline Marcy. It was the names of the parents that piqued my interest in this particular death certificate as the compiled genealogy I located online listed a David and Caroline [--?--] Newhart. Was it possible then that the compiled genealogy was simply missing a generation? After all, the first two generations had both been named George—Bob Newhart's birth name was George Robert Newhart.

In reexamining the information already found, it appeared that three brothers had been identified. I had George M. Newhart with a brother

Charles, both born in New York, like Henry. Henry was born 1 December 1865. Charles J., according to the 1920 census, was born about 1870, and George M. was born about 1872.

When I searched the 1880 census index as found on the FamilySearch.org site, I discovered a family that had three brothers: Henry (b. about 1865), Charles (b. about 1868), and George (b. about 1872). They were living in the household of a David Newhart and his wife Carrie in Lewis County, New York.

Ideally we would love to be able to have all of the records we find say with certainty that George M. Newhart is the son of David Newhart and Caroline Marcy. This is a research project I have recently undertaken and I may finally find such definitive records. Until that time, though, I feel I have made a strong enough case to believe that George David Newhart's father is George M. Newhart, not David, and that, in fact, David is George M. Newhart's father.

By applying the cluster genealogy approach, I paid attention to the similarities of that death certificate on Henry D. Newhart. I checked out Henry's death certificate simply because the date and place of death seemed to be in the same vicinity both in place and time as other Newhart information. Through looking for David Newhart, I kept my research options open. In fact, when I saw the index entry as Henry D. Newhart, I originally suspected that he had gone by his middle name and that this was David. It wasn't until I began to look at the death certificate that I saw I might be missing a generation.

Also, had I not thought to grab a copy of Henry's death certificate at the time, I would probably have gone back to get it after I found the 1880 census entry. Without it I would not have known what Caroline's maiden name was (see Figure 9-2 on page 168).

While the Newhart research was a rather simple cluster genealogy application, the research accomplished in the Carradine wills (see "Where There's a Will" on page 169) was the only way to make the family connection as there were no other records available to prove the relationship of those individuals. Had I not bothered to look at the other wills, I would have gone away with what I thought was a lineage that couldn't be continued (see Figure 9-3 on page 170).

A CLUSTER OF PLACES

When I was new to genealogy, I attended a lecture at one of the annual conferences held by the National Genealogical Society. It was devoted to what I now refer to as a "cluster of places" approach. I wish I could remember who the lecturer was so I could publicly acknowledge her here. What I took away from that lecture was a way of branching out when I couldn't find the individuals in the place I expected. For instance, **if I can't find an ancestor in the county in which I expect him, this lecturer's suggestion was to look at a county map and see what counties border the one I have already exhausted.** I began to systematically go

Research Tip

through those counties and rule them out as potential alternatives. Sometimes, I take an old-fashioned compass to pinpoint the center of the county I originally suspected and draw a circle that encompasses the bordering counties. If I still don't find anything in those counties, I may draw a larger circle and begin to look at those counties as well.

If I still can't find information on the family in question, I begin to think I have taken a wrong turn somewhere. At this point I take a step back and see if I need to return to the "cluster of people" approach to exhaust all the records on the children of the previous generation. Often it is this backtracking that eventually breaks the brick wall and sends me once again on my way with the research.

WHY THE CLUSTER APPROACH?

While you may already see a useful application for cluster genealogy as far as your own research is concerned—the more people with potential records

ANCESTRY OF BOB NEWHART
Generation 1
1   **Bob Newhart** was born George Robert Newhart in Oak Park, Cook, Illinois, 5 Sept. 1929. He married Julia Quinn 12 Jan. 1964.
Generation 2
2   **George David Newhart** was born in Illinois, 26 Aug. 1900. He married Julia Pauline Burns ca. 1927. George died Sept. 1985 in Arlington Heights, Cook, Illinois.
3   **Julia Pauline Burns** was born in Illinois, 1 Oct. 1900. She died 21 June 1994 in Wheeling, Cook, Illinois.
Generation 3
4   **George M. Newhart** was born in New York, July 1871. He married Emma F. O'Connor in Chicago, Cook, Illinois, 4 Oct. 1899. George died 9 Nov. 1948 in Oak Park, Cook, Illinois.
5   **Emma F. O'Connor** was born in Canada, July 1871.
6   **John Joseph Burns** was born in Maysville, Mason, Kentucky, Mar. 1863. He married Laura Aloysius Shea ca. 1893. John died ca. 1945 in Chicago, Cook, Illinois.
7   **Laura Aloysius Shea** was born in Maysville, Mason, Kentucky, May 1863. She died ca. 1943.
Generation 4
8   **David Newhart** was born in Eaton County, New York, Jan. 1840. He married Caroline Marcy ca. 1865.
9   **Caroline Marcy** was born in New York, Nov. 1844.
12   **Thomas Burns** married Hanora Grady.
13   **Hanora Grady** was born in Ireland, May 1830.
14   **John Shea** was born in Rochester, New York, Oct. 1838. He married Margaret Sheehan before 1856. John died 18 June 1894 in Maysville, Mason, Kentucky.
15   **Margaret Sheehan** was born in Ireland, Mar. 1832.
Generation 5
28   **Henry Shea** was born in Ireland, 1797. He married Ann Rossiter. Henry died June 1845 in Maysville, Mason, Kentucky.
29   **Ann Rossiter** was born in Ireland, 1795. She married Henry Shea.

Figure 9-2
Ahnentafel of Bob Newhart showing initial results after research described.

WHERE THERE'S A WILL . . .

Sometimes it is only through the records of the other family members that you discover the true picture of the next generation. Take the Carradine family. I had been able to trace the lineage back to Rev. Beverly Carradine with ease, but although I had his parents' names, Henry Francis Carradine and Mary Caroline Hewitt, I was having trouble determining who the parents of Henry Francis Carradine were. I found a number of entries for wills and instead of stopping when I found the will of Mary Carradine, I checked them all out and eventually was able to piece the family together.

The will of Mary Carradine, dated 15 Sept. 1813, among other things mentioned grandchildren Eliza Carradine, Henry Francis Carradine, Martha Ann Carradine, and George R. Carradine. It also mentioned her son George R. Carradine, but did not appear to list the parents of her grandchildren.

The will of David Carradine, dated July 1818, mentioned brothers George R. Carradine, Parker Carradine, and Richard Carradine. It specifically mentioned "the children of George & Richard" but did not mention these children by name.

The will of Parker Carradine, dated 5 Mar. 1819 mentioned, among others, his brother's children, including George's daughters Eliza and Martha Ann, and his sons, though they were not named individually.

By combining the information of all three of these wills I was able to establish that Henry Francis Carradine was the son of George R. Carradine and the grandson of Mary. There is still a lot of work to do on this line, but every little bit helps.

you can check the better your chances of moving back a generation—when it comes to connecting to another person's genealogy it becomes more than just a bonus—it becomes a necessity.

Why? Your relationship to the other person is most likely to be that of a cousin. Because it is that of a cousin, at some point you will find at least one generation in which you must have identified two siblings. Without this connection, you will be unable to prove the relationship to the other person. While a cousinship is a given if you are talking about a relationship with a living celebrity, it is also the general rule with historic personalities as well. You have a much better chance of being a cousin of such an individual than you do of being descended directly (until you get back into the 1700s or earlier). How close the cousinship may be is dependent on how far back—how many generations—you have to go to find the common ancestor. The common ancestor is the parent of the siblings from which you and the other person descend.

Working with the cluster genealogy approach as you work back from generation to generation actually prepares you for the next step in the pro-

For More Info

BOUNDARY BASICS

Places are listed as they existed at the time the event took place. If you need help in identifying the county for a given year, check out William Dollarhide and William Thorndale's *Map Guide to the U.S. Federal Censuses, 1790–1920* (Baltimore: GPC, 1987) or AniMap <http://goldbug.com>.

David Carradine's last will and Testament. In the Name of God. Amen
I David Carradine of the State of Mississippi and County of Jefferson and
now being in perfect mind and memory thanks be given to God for his
being well convinced of the uncertainty of life and knowing all men [illegible]
ance to die, do make this my last will and Testament, revoking all
former wills. first recommend my soul to God who gave it, and my bo[illegible]
to the dust from whence it came. Secondly. It is my will and desire
that all my just debts and funeral expenses be paid. — Thirdly. It is
my will and desire that my Executor whom I shall hereafter [illegible]
after giving reasonable notice, dispose of my whole estate consisting of the
following property. To wit, one tract of land whereon I now live containing
of six hundred and thirty seven acres, about sixty head of cattle, three
head of horses, hogs &c on a credit of two years, my Executors take bond
with approved security with Interest from the date until paid, and the
money arising from said sale, the one half to go to my dearest broth[illegible]
George R Carradine's Children, to be equally divided amongst them,
and in case of the death of either them, survivors to draw the part of the
deceased brother or sister, shall have an equal proportion amongst them, the
money arising from the sail when collected the one half to be deposited in ban[illegible]

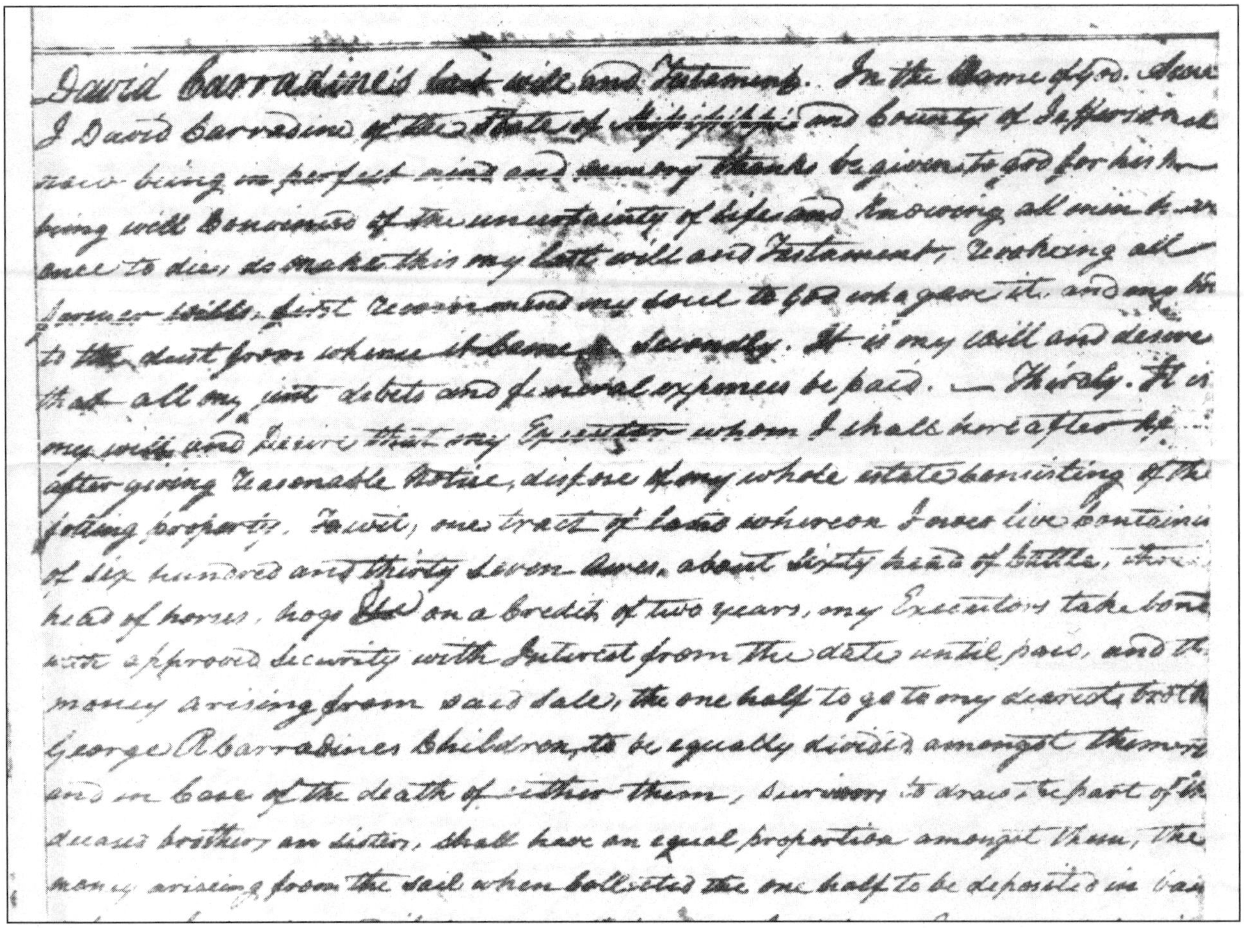

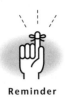

Figure 9-3
Using the wills of the Carradines in Jefferson County, Mississippi, I was able to piece together part of the family tree (Will Book A, 1800–1833, FHL #1939756).

cess of making the connection to a celebrity. Once you have worked back, you are likely to have to turn around and work forward. And when you are working forward you will be working completely in a cluster methodology because you will need to bring forward each child until you pick up your line and the line of the celebrity.

RESEARCHING INTO THE FUTURE

Reminder

So many genealogists have spent all their time researching back one generation at a time that they often have a hard time turning it around. The mindset is that finding the death or marriage certificate leads to the birth information and the parents' names. Throughout this book I have frequently reminded you that genealogists always work from the known to the unknown. This principle can also be applied when you reverse the lineage to show descendants rather than ancestors.

Remember that the cluster approach involves everyone in the family. The point is to amass documents on everyone in the family. Each document begins to supply an answer or a partial answer to the big family history question. When you get all the pieces to the question, you have the complete answer. While I would like to tell you that all of the pieces exist, I suspect you have already figured out from some of the examples in this book that there are times when the records will work against you. It is for this precise reason that you should strive to become proficient in cluster genealogy.

A cluster genealogy project is a perfect project for a genealogical project. What better way to keep track of all the individuals you are finding and the records and resources that are supplying you with the information? As you identify individuals in familial units, the genealogy program offers you an easy way to enter them and then locate a specific person as you progress through the records.

Another valuable tool when you are working with many different people and many different records is a program such as Clooz <www.clooz.com>. The Clooz program is called an electronic filing cabinet. While your genealogy program helps you to arrange individuals into family units linking parents to children, husbands to wives, and so forth, Clooz links individuals through the documents that they share. By removing the blood or marriage connection that a genealogy program wants, you may find that you can better evaluate the information you find on the records.

I use both systems. There are times when I enter everything into my genealogy software and other times when I take advantage of Clooz's templates and unique method of recording those individuals found in the records. I have had many family historians tell me that Clooz took some getting used to. I completely understand where they are coming from, since most of us have been trained to compile our families from day one. Think about the first forms we talked about—the family group sheet and the pedigree chart. From the very beginning of this hobby, we are taught to think in terms of families. Clooz wants you to think in terms of records, for instance, how many records that George M. Newhart was found in.

Tip

If you do decide to put everyone into your genealogy software, I suggest keeping it separate from your personal database during this all-encompassing phase. The focus of this database is to trace all the descendants of the individual you think you and the other person share. Eventually, if the records have been kind, you will find the direct lineage to your ancestor and to that of the other person. At that point, you should be able to identify those two lines and the siblings on each generation for inclusion in a GEDCOM file, which you could then load into your personal database.

While I have been talking a lot about finding a relationship to a famous person, the approaches mentioned throughout this chapter apply regardless of who you are trying to find a connection to. All of the records, with the exception of those specifically mentioned in chapter six, can be used for any type of research. Though some of the resources mentioned in chapter six may not mention your ancestor specifically, they shouldn't

For More Info

BEGINNER'S LUCK

If you are just getting started, be sure to read Emily Anne Croom's *Unpuzzling Your Past* (Cincinnati: Betterway Books, 2001).

Reminder

For More Info

EVERYTHING'S RELATIVE

Confused by relationship terms? You will want to read Jackie Arnold's *Kinship: It's All Relative* (Baltimore: Genealogical Publishing Company, 2000).

be overlooked, as they may still give you insight into the world and events that affect your ancestor.

As you begin to trace your lineage and that of the celebrity or historical figure, you may discover there are variations on the theme and the records you may have available—yet another reason to take a little time to read up on the records peculiar or unique to your research based on the date and place in which you are researching. I truly believe that the best resource for getting this history and record knowledge in a nutshell is the Research Outlines found at the FamilySearch Web site <www.familysearch.org>.

CONTEMPORARY OR HISTORICAL RELATIVE

When researching a contemporary relative, you usually have to research the lineage of that person back a greater number of generations. Remember, many of the published genealogies were done in the late 1800s and the early 1900s, and those genealogies generally stopped just before the year they were published. Some of the more recent genealogies are stopping at about 1900, both in an effort to protect the privacy of those who are still living and because the compilers felt that there were enough twentieth century records, such as vital records and census records, that the researcher should be able to use to get back to 1900.

Regardless of why the tree doesn't go into the late 1900s, **if you are trying to connect to a person born in the 1900s, you know you will have to spend some research time building a tree for that person that goes back far enough to begin to use these published resources, at least as clues.** (See Figure 9-4 on page 173.) While you may have an idea of what surname connects you, it is still a good idea to be as thorough as possible as you build the family tree. Should you discover your previous assumption is wrong, you may still find a different lineage that the two of you share.

COUSINS OR COUSINS REMOVED?

If you identify the common ancestor, and you may still need to try some of the tricks discussed in chapter ten before you do get that far, then it comes time to determine just what the relationship is between yourself and the other person. While there are many obscure relationships that are possible, when sisters of one family marry brothers of another family, for instance, most of the time you will be concerned with *cousins* and *cousins removed*.

Another method you can use is a chart where one person is identified along the left of the chart and the other person is identified along the top of the chart. You then see where the two meet and that should tell you the relationship (see Figures 9-5 on page 175 and 9-6 on page 176). There are a number of Web sites that have this chart available, and you may find it easier than the system described on page 174 when it comes to figuring out a relationship. We all like to stay with what we know, because we feel

Pedigree Chart

Chart no. 1
No. 1 on this chart is the same as no. 1 on chart no. 1

23 Dec 2002

2 Harry Lowe Crosby
b: 28 Nov 1870
p: Olympia, Thurston, Washington
m: 4 Jan 1894
p: Tacoma, Pierce, Washington
d:
p:

4 Nathaniel Crosby
b: 1835
p: Massachusetts
m:
p: prob. Tumwater, Thurston, Washington
d:
p:

8 Nathaniel Crosby
cont 2
b: 3 Nov 1810
p: East Brewster, Massachusetts
m: 1831
p: Wiscasset, Lincoln, Maine
d:
p:

9 Mary Lincoln
b:
p:
d:
p:

5 Cordelia Smith
b: abt 1839
p: Indiana
d: bef 3 Oct 1904
p:

10
b:
p:
m:
p:
d:
p:

11
b:
p:
d:
p:

1 Bing Crosby
b: 3 May 1903
p: Tacoma, Pierce, Washington
m: 24 Oct 1957
p: Las Vegas, Clark, Nevada
d: 14 Oct 1977
p: Madrid, Spain

sp: **Kathryn Grant**

6 Dennis Jr. Harrigan
b: 6 Sep 1832
p: Williamstown, New Brunswick
m: 1867
p: Newcastle, New Brunswick
d: 18 Sep 1915
p: Tacoma, Pierce, Washington

12 Dennis Harrigan
b: abt 1781
p:
m: bef 1809
p:
d: abt 1860
p:

13 Catherine Driscoll
b: 1791
p:
d: abt 1864
p:

3 Catherine Harrigan
b: 7 Feb 1873
p: Stillwater, Washington, Minnesota
d: 1964
p:

7 Catherine Ahearn
b: 1 Mar 1835
p: Newcastle, New Brunswick
d: 25 Oct 1918
p: prob. Tacoma, Pierce, Washington

14 John Ahearn
b: abt 1798
p: prob. County Cork, Ireland
m: 24 Jun 1827
p: Newcastle, New Brunswick
d: aft 1871
p:

15 Ann Meighan
b:
p: Ireland
d: 10 Jul 1869
p: South Esk, New Brunswick

Prepared 23 Dec 2002 by:

Figure 9-4
Once you build a preliminary pedigree, such as this one for crooner Bing Crosby, you are ready to look for published genealogies.

comfortable, so I will continue to draw charts like the one above while others will continue to use the cousin finder charts. There are a lot of different sites offering these charts:

- A chart for Figuring Relationships <http://lewisgenealogy.com/relate.html>
- The Gene Pool: A Chart for Figuring Relationships <www.rootsweb.com/~genepool/cousins.htm>
- A Chart of Consanguinity <www.geocities.com/BourbonStreet/1769/>
- Cousin Number Counter <www.geocities.com/Heartland/Prairie/1956/cousin.html>

FIGURING OUT YOUR RELATIONSHIP

When I first got interested in genealogy I was as confused as everyone else about the difference between a cousin and a cousin who was removed. It wasn't until I picked up a little book, *The Genesis of Your Genealogy: The Step-by-Step Instruction for the Beginner in Family History* by Elizabeth L. Nichols, AG (Logan: Everton Publishers, 1981), that it began to make sense. To this day, I use a chart similar to the one you see below when I am trying to figure out the relationship of two individuals who share a common ancestor.

Relationship of Glenn Close and Brooke Shields

Charles Arthur Moore

Charles Arthur Moore Jr.	Siblings	Mary Elsie Moore
Betinne Moore	First cousins	Marina Torlonia
Glenn Close	Second cousins	Francis A. Shields
	Second cousins, once removed	Brooke Shields

In general, as each side of the chart has a person listed, you count in cousins—first cousins, second cousins and so forth. So that is why you see that Betinne Moore and Marina Torlonia are first cousins and Glenn Close and Francis A. Shields are second cousins. You add one number for each additional generation away from the common ancestor.

When the one side of the chart has run out of generations and the other one still has some, you stop adding a number to the cousins and begin to count in "removeds." Again, you add one number for each additional generation away from the last person on the other side of the chart.

In the example above, because there is only one additional generation after Glenn Close to get to Brooke Shields, there was only one removed. So Glenn Close and Brooke Shields are second cousins, once removed.

GETTING OVER THE BREAK

Despite your best intentions, at this point you may find you still have not been able to bridge the gap between what you know about either your lineage or that of the celebrity. You are certain that the two lines share a common ancestor. The key now is in proving it. There are a few additional things you can try in an effort to make that connection.

A COUSIN FINDER CHART

Identify the common ancestor in the box at the upper left, then record the descent of one of the individuals along the top, one name per column. Next, record the descent of the other person along the left, one name per row. Follow from the last name on the top and the left until they meet. Where they meet is the relationship.

	Common Ancestor	1. Son/Dau	2. Grandson/ dau	3. Great grand- son/dau	4. 2great grand- son/dau	5. 3great grand- son/dau	6. 4great grand- son/dau
1.	Son/Dau	Brother/Sister	Nephew/ Niece	Grand nephew/ niece	Great grand nephew/ niece	2great grand nephew/ niece	3great grand nephew/ niece
2.	Grandson/ dau	Nephew/ Niece	1st cousin	1st cousin once removed	1st cousin twice removed	1st cousin three times removed	1st cousin four times removed
3.	Great grand- son/dau	Grand nephew/ niece	1st cousin once removed	2d cousin	2d cousin once removed	2d cousin twice removed	2d cousin three times removed
4.	2great grand- son/dau	Great grand nephew/ niece	1st cousin twice removed	2d cousin once removed	3d cousin	3d cousin once removed	3d cousin twice removed
5.	3great grand- son/dau	2great grand nephew/ niece	1st cousin three times removed	2d cousin twice removed	3d cousin once removed	4th cousin	4th cousin once removed
6.	4great grand- son/dau	3great grand nephew/ niece	1st cousin four times removed	2d cousin three times removed	3d cousin twice removed	4th cousin once removed	5th cousin

Figure 9-5

APPLYING THE COUSIN FINDER CHART

If we take the relationship of Glenn Close and Brooke Shields and insert it into the chart, it would look like this:

	Charles Arthur Moore Common Ancestor	1. Charles Arthur Moore, Jr. Son/Dau	2. Betinne Moore Grandson/dau	3. Glenn Close Great grandson/dau	4. 2great grandson/dau	5. 3great grandson/dau	6. 4great grandson/dau
1. Mary Elsie Moore	Son/Dau	Brother/Sister	Nephew/Niece	Grand nephew/niece	Great grand nephew/niece	2great grand nephew/niece	3great grand nephew/niece
2. Marina Torlonia	Grandson/dau	Nephew/Niece	1st cousin	1st cousin once removed	1st cousin twice removed	1st cousin three times removed	1st cousin four times removed
3. Francis A. Shields	Great grandson/dau	Grand nephew/niece	1st cousin once removed	2d cousin	2d cousin once removed	2d cousin twice removed	2d cousin three times removed
4. Brooke Shields	2great grandson/dau	Great grand nephew/niece	1st cousin twice removed	**2d cousin once removed**	3d cousin	3d cousin once removed	3d cousin twice removed
5.	3great grandson/dau	2great grand nephew/niece	1st cousin three times removed	2nd cousin twice removed	3d cousin once removed	4th cousin	4th cousin once removed
6.	4great grandson/dau	3great grand nephew/niece	1st cousin four times removed	2nd cousin three times removed	3d cousin twice removed	4th cousin once removed	5th cousin

Figure 9-6

TEN

Building Bridges

U p to this point most of what has been shared has had to do with the researching of either your ancestry or that of the celebrity. There hasn't been much said about how you begin to bring the two together. Sometimes, the connection will jump right out at you, usually when you are researching the celebrity's lineage. You may immediately recognize the common ancestor from your own research. More often, though, one or the other lineage has not yet been as thoroughly researched and you need to ask yourself where you are in the research on both and if anything is beginning to look like it connects.

In addition to showing themselves through the surnames that have already been found, connections may begin to show in the other surnames you are seeing, common to both lineages. More often, your first indication of which surnames you need to concentrate on comes from the fact that both genealogies will share certain common localities. Depending on when the ancestors were living in the area, they may have intermarried, or you may discover that the connection is further back and that the families arrived in the new locality together, having come from some town or state as a group.

You may be thinking that such connections should be obvious, but we often pigeonhole the research we do. Even if your goal is to find a connection, you may still find yourself ignoring one lineage as you work on the other. You may be concentrating on a line you think will reveal the connection, when it turns out that the connection is on another line. You may be concentrating on the paternal line only to later discover that the connection is through one of the maternal lines. **Too often the maternal lines are ignored, yet they are often the clue to many different relationships because of the new surnames being added to the pedigree.**

This need to narrow the research is generally encouraged when researching a family tree. Trying to search for too many surnames and lines often results in mistakes, overlooked entries in indexes, or misevaluation of the information found. Eventually there are too many names, and research that tries to include all the surnames is overwhelming and ineffectual. As you work back to each successive generation, you are doubling the number of

Important

DAUGHTERING OUT

When working in Italian records, which I love, notice that a woman retains her maiden name all through her life. Even when she dies, she dies with her maiden name. You may find it frustrating when you are working in the records of the United States and the British Isles, among a few others, that when a woman gets married, she loses her maiden name completely. She is born and married under one surname. After her marriage all the records that may record her, such as land deeds, her probate, and her death record, will all list her with her married name. If you cannot find a record that lists her maiden name, usually the death certificate, then the research of that female is often stalled. Quite frustrating.

By the same token, because the woman's name changes and the children all carry the surname of the father in many cultures, if you descend from a daughter, the surname is said to "daughter out" in your lineage. The surname ceases to exist after the marriage of that daughter, at least on your pedigree or on a descendant chart of your direct line.

If a line "daughters out," this means that there was a generation in which there were only female children, so there is no chance for the surname to be carried on since there are no male children.

individuals you need to look for and adding a new surname for each couple you add on your pedigree chart.

As a result, the need to narrow or focus your research becomes a safety valve—a way of staying organized—to limit your thoughts to what is at hand, which is whatever lineage you are concentrating on at that moment. When trying to find a common ancestor, the problem with such an approach is that you may narrow the research so much that you do not see the potential for a connection or you do not pursue some of the lines. It may turn out that it is one of the ignored lines where you could finally find the connection.

EVALUATING WHERE YOUR RESEARCH STANDS

The first thing to do is to look at your own research and decide where you are in that research (see Figure 10-1 on page 179). You may want to ask yourself the following questions as you look at your database or charts.

- How many lines have you been able to follow back?
- How many generations have you taken these lines back?
- How many female lines have you been able to identify and research?
- Have you exhausted all records and resources on the lines where they now stand?

Reminder

When trying to determine the possibility of a connection between your ancestry and that of someone who has left their mark, you will generally find that such connec-

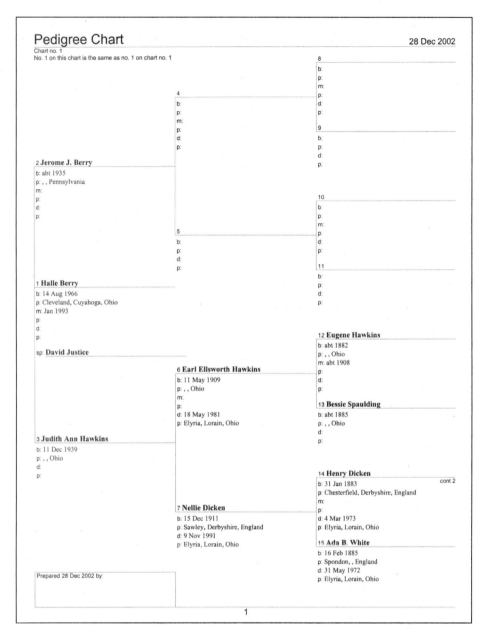

Pedigree Chart   28 Dec 2002
Chart no. 1
No. 1 on this chart is the same as no. 1 on chart no. 1

8
b:
p:
m:
p:
d:
p:

4
b:
p:
m:
p:
d:
p:

9
b:
p:
d:
p:

2 Jerome J. Berry
b: abt 1935
p: , , Pennsylvania
m:
p:
d:
p:

10
b:
p:
m:
p:
d:
p:

5
b:
p:
d:
p:

11
b:
p:
d:
p:

1 Halle Berry
b: 14 Aug 1966
p: Cleveland, Cuyahoga, Ohio
m: Jan 1993
p:
d:
p:

sp: David Justice

12 Eugene Hawkins
b: abt 1882
p: , , Ohio
m: abt 1908
p:
d:
p:

6 Earl Ellsworth Hawkins
b: 11 May 1909
p: , , Ohio
m:
p:
d: 18 May 1981
p: Elyria, Lorain, Ohio

13 Bessie Spaulding
b: abt 1885
p: , , Ohio
d:
p:

3 Judith Ann Hawkins
b: 11 Dec 1939
p: , , Ohio
d:
p:

14 Henry Dicken   cont 2
b: 31 Jan 1883
p: Chesterfield, Derbyshire, England
m:
p:
d: 4 Mar 1973
p: Elyria, Lorain, Ohio

7 Nellie Dicken
b: 15 Dec 1911
p: Sawley, Derbyshire, England
d: 9 Nov 1991
p: Elyria, Lorain, Ohio

15 Ada B. White
b: 16 Feb 1885
p: Spondon, , England
d: 31 May 1972
p: Elyria, Lorain, Ohio

Prepared 28 Dec 2002 by:

1

Figure 10-1
The pedigree chart may help you focus your thoughts.

Halle Berry
Ronald Asadorian/SplashNews

tions are usually back more than the four generations displayed in the pedigree chart shown. In many instances the connection is not found until you have traced the lineage back to early colonial inhabitants.

You may find that using the timeline that we discussed in chapter one works well here, especially when you have to research so far back on both lines. Following the years and localities already known and comparing them with your own personal lineage timeline may result in certain similarities you previously overlooked now jumping out. In addition to possibly seeing some similarities, the compiling of the timeline also forces you to review the records and research done on each line, and that may also refresh your memory about a certain surname, locality, or event that both lines share.

> ## POTENTIAL FOR COUSINS
>
> The ancestry of most notable American figures, five or six generations back, is very much the same as that of their less "distinguished" contemporaries. Often these latter, however, are themselves forebears of later notables, since most Americans of colonial ancestry (Puritan, Quaker and/or Tidewater esp.) can claim between 500 and 2,000 "household name" figures among 8th–12th cousins.
>
> Gary Boyd Roberts
> "Some Personal Notes—Or Why I Trace the Ancestry of Notable Figures"
> ©NEHGS, used with permission.

There are certain pockets of time and locality where you may discover a higher than average number of connections.

Why is it that you may find so many connections when you have traced back to the early 1700s or the 1600s? Think about the limited number of families who arrived in the "New World" and add the fact that travel was often long and difficult. As a result, if there were ten families in a community, it is likely that those of marrying age in the one family turned to look at the other nine families for an eligible partner. From these initial families, you may now find millions of people living in the United States who, if they persevere enough with their research, find that they are descended from these ten families.

GO WEST, YOUNG MAN—TRACE EAST, YOUNG RESEARCHER

When it comes to researching in the United States, remember that many lines go east. The United States began as thirteen independent colonies in the 1600s. As more immigrants arrived, especially after the American Revolution, and communities began to fill, at least by the standards of the day, folks began to look west for more opportunities. In this time if you had land you were rich. Many of the immigrants who moved west were in search of land to call their own. Those who had been serfs in the old country had been trained almost from birth that land ownership signaled success. When they arrived in America and discovered that all the land in the settled communities had been taken, they looked west to the large expanses that had begun to open as a result of exploration and war.

As a "baby genealogist," to borrow the term from a colleague—a term I think aptly describes our knowledge and experience when we first begin to research our family history—I concentrated on my maternal line. This was not by accident. My parents had divorced when I was young, and I had not had any contact with the paternal side of my family. Additionally, my maternal grandmother had joined the Daughters of the American Revolution (DAR). To join that society—a lineage society—she had to compile a line of descent from an accepted patriot of the American Revolution. For me, this meant that I had a working model with many generations at least on one line to jump-start my own research. In fact, when I first started to research, I took her DAR application and began to re-create the research she had done using the sources she cited in her application to see if I came up with the same ancestry as she did.

Over the years, before she died, we corresponded, and she sent me a few more things. After her death my grandfather went through the house, and he sent me box after box of anything he thought I might find of interest, including photographs, deeds, letters, pedigree charts, copies from obscure books, and more. I admit, I am one of the lucky ones in many ways. I got interested in this hobby before the older generations had passed away. I also had a grandfather who was always willing to encourage any passion, and he also found a great way to clean out the house without throwing things away.

Among the papers he sent, I found a letter from a professional genealogist addressed to my grandmother. It was a lineage that connected her to Plymouth Colony. I knew from our discussions that she had always hoped to find a connection to the *Mayflower*. Her ancestors had been in New England, primarily in Massachusetts, since the early 1600s, just not early enough.

As I took classes and began to spread my genealogical wings, I turned to what I thought would be a difficult research—my father's lineage. While it has been easy in some areas, there are plenty of lines that have stumped me for years. One such line took me about ten years to crack, and when it was all said and done it took me back to William Brewster of the *Mayflower*. I am convinced that when I made that connection my grandmother was rolling over in her grave. While I have the elusive *Mayflower* lineage now, it is not through her; instead it is through my father, a man that she naturally considered worthless and no good after he and her daughter were divorced.

You just never know where your connection will come from when it comes to a famous individual. My grandmother was convinced that because of all her Massachusetts connections she had to have a *Mayflower* lineage. I'm not done researching all of her lines, and so there is still a little hope, but while her ancestors were there for three hundred years, they all seemed to arrive just after the *Mayflower*, most coming during the Great Migration. My father's lineage on the other hand has led me a merry chase—it actually continues to do so—across the United States, truly going from sea to shining sea. With each new state that the lines enter and each new surname I gather in my research, I discover new potentials for relationships. His lines trace back to most of the original thirteen colonies, opening me up to many more relationships than that of my mother's lines, which were centralized in New England, more specifically in Massachusetts. Of course, it is through my

Notes

DESCENDED FROM A PATRIOT

The Daughters of the American Revolution (DAR) is a lineage society. To belong, you must prove your descent from a patriot who offered acceptable service. This is not limited to soldiers; there are many other ways our ancestors offered service during the American Revolution, such as supplying food or horses to the troops. You can find out more about the DAR on their Web site <www.dar.org/>.

Definitions

THE GREAT MIGRATION

The Great Migration is a term used frequently whenever large groups of people migrate, from the south to the north, from the east to the west. In this case, it is referring to the early immigrants who arrived in New England during the years 1620 to 1640.

mother's side that I find many accused witches along with a few other color-ful characters, not to mention that had America lost the American Revolution, I would have a few people who instead of being claimed patriots would instead be traitors.

Even if you find that some of your grandparents or great-grandparents were first generation immigrants, coming during that wave of immigration to the United States from the late 1800s through to the middle 1900s, it is still possible that you have a connection. Think about who our grandparents and great-grandparents may have married. While some stayed within their ethnic community when it came time to look for a spouse, others did look elsewhere. And do not think that because your ancestors were not early Americans that there are no famous individuals for you to claim. **Many of those in early Hollywood trace to ethnic immigrants in the 1800s.** Some of the biggest stars in Hollywood, such as Marlene Dietrich and Audrey Hepburn, were themselves of European birth (see Figure 10-2 on page 183).

Another perfect example of how place of birth can be deceiving is Diana, Princess of Wales. While she seemed to be all that was British, she had a great-grandmother who was American, an American with early colonial ancestry. As a result there are millions of people who have a distant relationship to the Princess, and millions more, as we saw through our look at royalty, peerage, and nobility in chapter five, who may have a connection there as well. A search on the online *Burke's Peerage* Web site <www.burkes-peerage.net> revealed Diana's entry, as I expected because she held a royal title. As her entry mentioned her children, I was redirected to a special section with information about the present Royal Family. As a result of Diana's ancestry, both her ties to America and her English ancestry, the future King of England has many distant cousins in the United States. Through his parents' royal and noble ancestry he also is related to many Europeans as well.

Writer Gary Boyd Roberts defined distant as being eighth to twelfth cousins (see "Royal Cousins" below). Most will find their connection to another to fall into the "distant" category. It brings out an important point about the number of generations back that you must research to find the connection in

Reminder

ROYAL COUSINS

In addition to the royal descents of perhaps 150 million or more Americans, probably 30 million of us (a group that may largely be subsumed in the preceding 150 million) are distantly related (8th–12th cousins) to the late Princess of Wales and her sons, Princes William and Henry.

"Comments on Royal Descents, Royal Cousins, and the British Royal Family"
Gary Boyd Roberts
©2002 NEHGS, used with permission.

ANCESTRY OF AUDREY HEPBURN

Don't let the fact that the ancestor or celebrity in question was born in a foreign country scare you. There are many guides and aids to help you with the language difference, and sometimes the records are full of information that allows you to compile an extensive family tree as seen here with just part of actress Audrey Hepburn's tree.

Generation 1

1   **Audrey Hepburn** was born Audrey Kathleen Ruston in Brussels, Belgium, 4 May 1929. Audrey died 20 Jan. 1993 in Tolochenaz, Switzerland.

Generation 2

2   **Joseph Victor Anthony Hepburn-Ruston** married Ella Van Heemstra, 24 Sept. 1926. Joseph was divorced from Ella Van Heemstra 1938.

3   **Ella Van Heemstra** was born 1900.

Generation 3

6   **Arnoud Jan Anne Aleid Van Heemstra** was born in Vreeland, Utecht, Netherlands, 22 July 1871. He married Elbrig Willemine Henritte Van Asbeck 26 Mar. 1896. Arnoud died 30 July 1957.

7   **Elbrig Willemine Henritte Van Asbeck** was born in Almelo, Ovrysl, Netherlands, 15 July 1873.

Generation 4

12   **Willem Hendrick Johan Van Heemstra** was born in Irnsum, Friesland, Netherlands, 23 July 1841. He married Wilhelmina Cornelia De Beaufort in Utrecht, Utrecht, Netherlands, 11 Oct. 1866. Willem died 27 Oct. 1909 in Doorn, Utrecht, Netherlands.

13   **Wilhelmina Cornelia De Beaufort** was born in Leusden, Utrecht, Netherlands, 26 July 1843. She died 8 Jan. 1927 in Doorn, Utrecht, Netherlands.

14   **Gerrit Ferdinand Van Asbeck** was born in Leeuwarden, Friesland, Netherlands, 4 Jan. 1820. He married Caroline Van Hogendorp in 's-Gravenhage, Zuid-Holland, Netherlands, 22 Apr. 1854. Gerrit died 9 Jan. 1905 in 's-Gravenhage, Zuid-Holland, Netherlands.

15   **Caroline Van Hogendorp** was born in Amsterdam, Noord-Holland, Netherlands, 2 Feb. 1831. She died 4 Apr. 1919.

Generation 5

24   **Frans Julius Johan Van Heemstra.** Frans was born in Groningen, Groningen, Netherlands, 15 July 1811. He married Henrietta Philippina Jacoba Van Pallandt in Sassenheim, Zuid-Holland, Netherlands, 28 June 1837. Frans died 19 Feb. 1878 in 's-Gravenhage, Zuid-Holland, Netherlands, at 66 years of age.

25   **Henrietta Philippina Jacoba Van Pallandt** was born in Sassenheim, Zuid-Holland, Netherlands, 27 Nov. 1810. She died 18 Nov. 1881 in Sassenheim, Zuid-Holland, Netherlands.

26   **Arnoud Jan De Beaufort** was born in Utrecht, Utrecht, Netherlands, 23 Apr. 1799. He was baptized in Utrecht, Utrecht, Netherlands, 2 June 1799. He married Anna Aleida Stoop in Amsterdam, Noord-Holland, Netherlands, 6 May 1841. Arnoud died 1 July 1866 in Leusden, Utrecht, Netherlands.

27   **Anna Aleida Stoop** was born in Amsterdam, Noord-Holland, Netherlands, 16 Aug. 1812. She died 3 June 1885 in Utrecht, Utrecht, Netherlands.

28   **Tjalling Minne Watze Van Asbeck** was born in Netherlands, ca. 1800. He married Elbrig Van Bienema.

29   **Elbrig Van Bienema** was born in Netherlands, ca. 1800.

30   **Dirk Van Hogendorp** was born in Amsterdam, Noord-Holland, Netherlands, 18 Dec. 1797. He was baptized in Amsterdam, Noord-Holland, Netherlands, 31 Dec. 1797. He married Marianne C Van Hogendorp in Velp, Gelderland, Netherlands, 2 Apr. 1830. Dirk died 18 Mar. 1845 in 's-Gravenhage, Zuid-Holland, Netherlands.

31   **Marianne C Van Hogendorp** was born in Amsterdam, Noord-Holland, Netherlands, 1 Dec. 1805. She was baptized in Amsterdam, Noord-Holland, Netherlands, 15 Dec. 1805. She died 8 June 1878 in 's-Gravenhage, Zuid-Holland, Netherlands.

Figure 10-2 continued on next page

Generation 6	
48	**Willem Hendrik Van Heemstra** was born in Netherlands, ca. 1785. He married Johanna Balthazarina Van Idsinga.
49	**Johanna Balthazarina Van Idsinga** was born in Netherlands, ca. 1789.
50	**Gijsbert Jan Anna Adolph Van Pallandt** was born in Ommon, Overijsel, Netherlands, 27 May 1783. He was baptized in Ommon, Overijsel, Netherlands, 1 June 1783. He married Cornelia Martina Van Der Goes in 's-Gravenhage, Zuid-Holland, Netherlands, 19 Sept. 1809. Gijsbert died 26 Oct. 1863 in Sassenheim, Zuid-Holland, Netherlands.
51	**Cornelia Martina Van Der Goes** was born in 's-Gravenhage, Zuid-Holland, Netherlands, 12 Feb. 1780. She was baptized in 's-Gravenhage, Zuid-Holland, Netherlands, 13 Feb. 1780. She died 26 Nov. 1859 in Sassenheim, Zuid-Holland, Netherlands.
52	**Willem Hendrik De Beaufort** was born in Ijselstein, Utrecht, Netherlands, 12 July 1775. He married Cornelia Anna Van Westrenen in Domkerck, Utrecht, Utrecht, Netherlands, 9 Oct. 1796. Willem died 21 Apr. 1829 in Utrecht, Utrecht, Netherlands.
53	**Cornelia Anna Van Westrenen** was born in Utrecht, Utrecht, Netherlands, 7 Jan. 1777. She was baptized in Janskerk, Utrecht, Utrecht, Netherlands, 12 Jan. 1777. She died 28 Dec. 1839 in Leusden, Utrecht, Netherlands.
54	**Joannes Bernardus Stoop** was born in Amsterdam, Noord-Holland, Netherlands, ca. 1786. He married Margaretha Laurentia Brender A Brandis.
55	**Margaretha Laurentia Brender A Brandis** was born in Amsterdam, Noord-Holland, Netherlands, ca. 1790.
60	**Gijsbert Karel Van Hogendorp** was born in Rotterdam, Zuid-Holland, Netherlands, 27 Oct. 1762. He married Hester Clifford in Rotterdam, Zuid-Holland, Netherlands, 4 May 1789. Gijsbert died 5 Aug. 1834 in 's-Gravenhage, Zuid-Holland, Netherlands.
61	**Hester Clifford** was born in Amsterdam, Noord-Holland, Netherlands, 14 May 1766. She died 4 Nov. 1826 in 's-Gravenhage, Zuid-Holland, Netherlands.
62	**Willem Van Hogendorp** was born ca. 1779. He married Hermina Clara Bonn.
63	**Hermina Clara Bonn** was born ca. 1783.
Generation 7	
100	**Adolph Warner Van Pallandt** was born in Ommon, Overijsel, Netherlands, 15 Dec. 1745. He was baptized in Ommon, Overijsel, Netherlands, 18 Dec. 1745. He married Anna Elisabeth Schimmelpenninck Van Der Oije in Voorst, Gelderland, Netherlands, 15 Apr. 1777. Adolph died 7 Dec. 1823 in Ommon, Overijsel, Netherlands.
101	**Anna Elisabeth Schimmelpenninck Van Der Oije** was born in Arnhem, Gelderland, Netherlands, 11 Dec. 1752. She was baptized in Arnhem, Gelderland, Netherlands, 14 Dec. 1752. She died 28 Dec. 1822 in Ommon, Overijsel, Netherlands.
102	**Philip Jac Van Der Goes** was born ca. 1754. He married Henriette Van Kreschmar.
103	**Henriette Van Kreschmar** was born ca. 1758.
104	**Joachim Ferdinand De Beaufont** was born in Hulst, Zeeland, Netherlands, 22 Apr. 1719. He was baptized in Hulst, Zeeland, Netherlands, 24 Apr. 1719. He married Anna Digna Van Gelre in Hontenisse, Zeeland, Netherlands, 7 Oct. 1763. Joachim died 11 May 1807 in Zeist, Utrecht, Netherlands.
105	**Anna Digna Van Gelre** was born in Zierikee, Zeeland, Netherlands, 14 Oct. 1734. She was baptized in Zierikee, Zeeland, Netherlands, 17 Oct. 1734. She died 22 Apr. 1779 in Ijselstein, Utrecht, Netherlands.
106	**Aernoud Jan Van Westrhenen** was born in Utrecht, Utrecht, Netherlands, 1750. He married Antonia Charlotte Godin.
107	**Antonia Charlotte Godin** was born in Utrecht, Utrecht, Netherlands, 1756. She was baptized in Utrecht, Utrecht, Netherlands, 22 Aug. 1756.

Figure 10-2

120	**Willem Van Hogendorp** was born in Netherlands, ca. 1736. He married Carolina W Van Haren.
121	**Carolina W Van Haren** was born in Netherlands, ca. 1740.
122	**George Clifford** married Johanna Bouwens. George was born in Amsterdam, Noord-Holland, Netherlands, 10 Oct. 1743. He married Hester Hooft in Amsterdam, Noord-Holland, Netherlands, 12 May 1765. George died 7 June 1776 in Amsterdam, Noord-Holland, Netherlands.
123	**Hester Hooft** was born in Amsterdam, Noord-Holland, Netherlands, 29 Jan. 1748. She died 16 Apr. 1795 in Amsterdam, Noord-Holland, Netherlands.

Generation 8

200	**August Leopold Van Pallandt** was born in Zwollerkerspel, Overijsel, Netherlands, 14 May 1701. He was baptized in Windesheim, Overijsel, Netherlands, 15 May 1701. He married Anna Elisabeth Van Haersolte in Hellendoorn, Overijsel, Netherlands, 4 Dec. 1744. August died 24 Nov. 1779 in Ommon, Overijsel, Netherlands.
201	**Anna Elisabeth Van Haersolte** was born 1715. She was baptized in Zwolle, Overijesl, Netherlands, 1 Feb. 1715. She died 18 Apr. 1790 in Hellendoorn, Overijsel, Netherlands.
202	**Andries Schinnelpennick Van Der Oije** was born in Zutphen, Gelderland, Netherlands, 1705. He was baptized in Zutphen, Gelderland, Netherlands, 11 Oct. 1705. He married Woltera Geerturida Van Wijnbergen in Voorst, Gelderland, Netherlands, 13 May 1749. Andries died 18 Nov. 1776 in Arnhem, Gelderland, Netherlands.
203	**Woltera Geerturida Van Wijnbergen** was born 1723. She was baptized in Voorst, Gelderland, Netherlands, 4 July 1723. She died 14 June 1798 in Voorst, Gelderland, Netherlands.
208	**Pieter Benjamin De Beaufort** was born in Hulst, Zeeland, Netherlands, 29 Sept. 1688. He was baptized in Hulst, Zeeland, Netherlands, 2 Oct. 1688. He married Bennudina Van Amama in Hontenisse, Zeeland, Netherlands, 18 June 1714. Pieter died 31 July 1777 in 's-Gravenhage, Zuid-Holland, Netherlands. His body was interred 7 Aug. 1777 in Hulst, Zeeland, Netherlands.
209	**Bennudina Van Amama** was born 1683. She was baptized in Leeuwarden, Friesland, Netherlands, 2 Sept. 1683. She died before 17 Apr. 1733. Her body was interred 17 Apr. 1733 in Hulst, Zeeland, Netherlands.
210	**Jan Herman Van Gelre** was born 1702. He was baptized in Zierikee, Zeeland, Netherlands, 7 Sept. 1702. He married Anna Margaretha Ockersse in Zierikee, Zeeland, Netherlands, 10 Jan. 1730. Jan died 13 May 1739 in Zierikee, Zeeland, Netherlands.
211	**Anna Margaretha Ockersse** was born in Zierikee, Zeeland, Netherlands, 8 Sept. 1707. She died 22 Mar. 1753 in Zierikee, Zeeland, Netherlands.
212	**Jan Andre Van Westrhenen** was born in Utrecht, Utrecht, Netherlands, ca. 1719. He married Paulina Lukretia Godin.
213	**Paulina Lukretia Godin** was born 1720. She was baptized in Utrecht, Utrecht, Netherlands, 1 May 1720.
214	**Pieter Anthonie Godin** was born in Utrecht, Utrecht, Netherlands, 14 Apr. 1726. He married Isabella Lucretia Barchman Wuijtiers in Amsterdam, Noord-Holland, Netherlands, 30 May 1751. Pieter died 7 July 1776 in Utrecht, Utrecht, Netherlands.
215	**Isabella Lucretia Barchman Wuijtiers** was born in Utrecht, Utrecht, Netherlands, 14 Jan. 1731. She was baptized in Domkerck, Utrecht, Utrecht, Netherlands, 17 Jan. 1731. She died 23 Jan. 1780 in Loosduinen, Zuid-Holland, Netherlands.
244	**Henry Clifford** was born in Amsterdam, Noord-Holland, Netherlands, 27 June 1711. He married Adriana Margaretha Van Marselis in Amsterdam, Noord-Holland, Netherlands, 19 Dec. 1742. Henry died 24 Oct. 1787 in Amsterdam, Noord-Holland, Netherlands.
245	**Adriana Margaretha Van Marselis** was born in Amsterdam, Noord-Holland, Netherlands, 11 May 1723. She died 1 Nov. 1763 in Amsterdam, Noord-Holland, Netherlands.

Figure 10-2 continued on next page

Generation 9	
400	**Adolph Werner Van Pallandt** married Agnes Amalia Van Pallandt.
401	**Agnes Amalia Van Pallandt**
402	**Antonij Adolph Van Haersolte** married Catharina Van Haersolte.
403	**Catharina Van Haersolte**
404	**Gerard Jurrien Schimmelpenninck Van Der Oije** married Cornelia Constancia Van Middachten.
405	**Cornelia Constancia Van Middachten**
406	**Dithmar Van Wijnbergen** married Anna Elisabeth Schimmelpenninck.
407	**Anna Elisabeth Schimmelpenninck**
416	**Pieter De Beaufort** married Anna Van Serooskerken.
417	**Anna Van Serooskerken**
418	**Joachim Van Amama** married Petronella De Vriese.
419	**Petronella De Vriese**
420	**Pieter Van Gelre** married Quirina De Keijser.
421	**Quirina De Keijser**
422	**Willem Ockersse** married Jacoba De Witte.
423	**Jacoba De Witte**
424	**Jan Jacob Van Westrhenen** married Catharina Johanna Mammuchet Van Hoederinge.
425	**Catharina Johanna Mammuchet Van Hoederinge**
426	**Isaac Ferdinand Godin** married Johanna Magdalena Voet Van Winsen.
427	**Johanna Magdalena Voet Van Winsen**
430	**Jan Caral Barchman Wuijtiers** married Johanna Maria De Wildt.
431	**Johanna Maria De Wildt**
488	**George Clifford** married Johanna Bouwens.
489	**Johanna Bouwens**
490	**Francois Van Marselis** married Anthonia Muljssart.
491	**Anthonia Muljssart**

Figure 10-2

some instances. If you discover that you are an eighth cousin of the Princess of Wales, that means that the connection is nine generations back. If you are a twelfth cousin, the connection is a distant thirteen generations back in history. Averaging about 25 years per generation, that means you will have researched back some 325 years, so the connection will be found in the late 1600s. For many, the connection to her or someone else may be much further back. During those generations you will find that it is seldom a direct paternal connection. Most of us will discover that our connection is the result of many twists and turns through female lineages and surnames we uncover.

BRIDGING THROUGH CLUSTERS

Because of these twists and turns, we must spend some time looking at the others in each family. Finding female surnames is one of the most frustrating aspects of research for many genealogists, especially in the mid to early

1800s in the United States when many of the records we rely on so heavily were not yet recorded, such as birth and death records. If they were recorded, they were not as thorough as they would eventually become, which means that the name we need is not always found with the first records we find.

In the last chapter we discussed the cluster genealogy approach. Perhaps when you think about the number of generations you may need to investigate before you make the connection, it becomes clearer as to why that approach is so important. Gaps in the cluster approach, though, may prove fatal in making the connection to the famous individual, even when the surname says it must be so.

Unfortunately, as I discussed earlier, the Internet has added to our research problems when it comes to the cluster genealogy approach and the gaps. **Too many of us are limiting our research to just what we find on the Internet.** It is not the only tool that I use, and it shouldn't be the only tool you use. In researching the family history of author Stephen King, I found out how true this can be.

As I mentioned in chapter eight, I have certain online compiled genealogies that I check first to see if any research has been done on the celebrities already. No sense recreating everything if I don't have to. Given the tight research schedules I often have, anything that helps me shoot out of the gate at a gallop is a good thing.

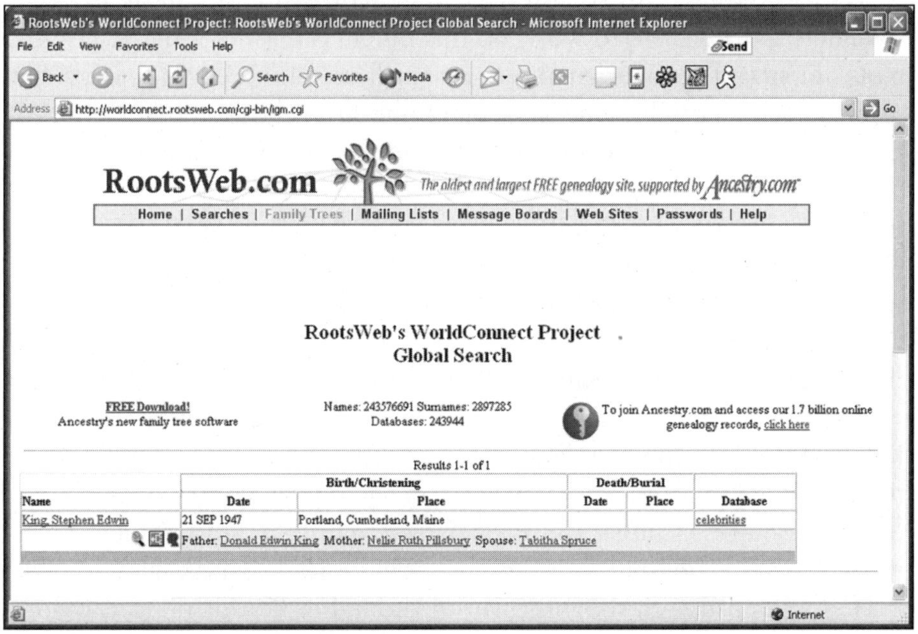

Warning

Figure 10-3
You never know who you will find in compiled databases like WorldConnect. © 2000–2002 MyFamily.com, Inc. Screen shot from Ancestry.com. Used with permission.

In searching RootsWeb's WorldConnect <http://searches.rootsweb.com/>, I discovered that someone had placed some information about Stephen King's ancestry in this GEDCOM database (see Figure 10-3 above). The pedigree icon in the index indicated this, but I had to check to see if it was more than just his parents, also listed in the index. Unfortunately there are many celebrities in

Case Study

Internet Source

THE TIP OF THE ICEBERG

While both Ancestry.com and Genealogy.com have become well known for their census digitization, that is just one of the areas in which they are acquiring records to make available online. Each site offers unique records and resources, that when used together, can make your initial research more productive.

these GEDCOM databases that have little or no genealogy beyond the names of the parents of the celebrity. This particular entry took Stephen's maternal Pillsbury line back to his great-great-grandfather Charles L. Pillsbury. What struck me about the Pillsbury line and had me off searching for more than just Stephen's ancestry, was the Pillsbury surname.

If you watch any television, you have seen the Pillsbury company's commercials with the bubbly and giggly dough boy. **I suspected that, given the New England connection of both the founders of the flour company and Stephen King's Pillsbury family, I would find a connection.** My initial research online, though, had me wondering when the information I found on Stephen's Pillsbury lineage seemed to stop in 1810 with the birth of his great-great-grandfather Charles C. Pillsbury. Had I stopped here I would not have discovered the connection.

Many people use the WorldConnect database because it has so many people (at this writing, almost 300 million names) and because it is free. Not all of the available GEDCOM databases can claim this, and each one is likely to offer you different information.

For instance, after finding this lineage on Stephen King in WorldConnect, I turned to some of the others, including the Pedigree Resource File at the FamilySearch Web site <www.familysearch.org/>. When typing in "Stephen King" and the birth year of 1947, I came up with some hits, but not for the Stephen King that I was interested in, and I found nothing in Pedigree Resource File or Ancestral File, the two GEDCOM databases available there.

As I was getting ready to visit the Family History Library in Utah, I knew I would have a chance to work on this line in published genealogies and, more importantly, in original records such as vital records and probate records, including wills. One particular published genealogy that I was eager to look at was *The Pillsbury Genealogy*, more traditionally known as *Ancestry of Charles Stinson Pillsbury and John Sargent Pillsbury* by Mary Lovering Holman (Concord: Rumford Press, 1938–1942). In my own New England research, I had seen many lines outlined in this two-volume work. I was curious to see what it would tell me about the Pillsbury line and also wanted to check some other books on the Pillsbury line as well as some of the surnames in Stephen King's ancestry.

In researching the lineage further, I did find the connection between Stephen King and the flour company founders. Interestingly enough, though, it wasn't through the Pillsbury genealogy by Holman but instead through a combination of other resources including the original town records for Scarborough, Maine, where Charles C. Pillsbury was born (see Figure 10-4 on page 189).

Had I stopped with the information I found in WorldConnect, I would not have been able to prove the relationship. His pedigree would still have been informative as it was posted on the Genealogy.com site. With a little additional research, branching out to different records and resources, not only was I able to extend that particular line, but others as well. In the final version, as was published on Genealogy.com, I was able to establish the relationship I had suspected (see Figure 10-5 on page 189).

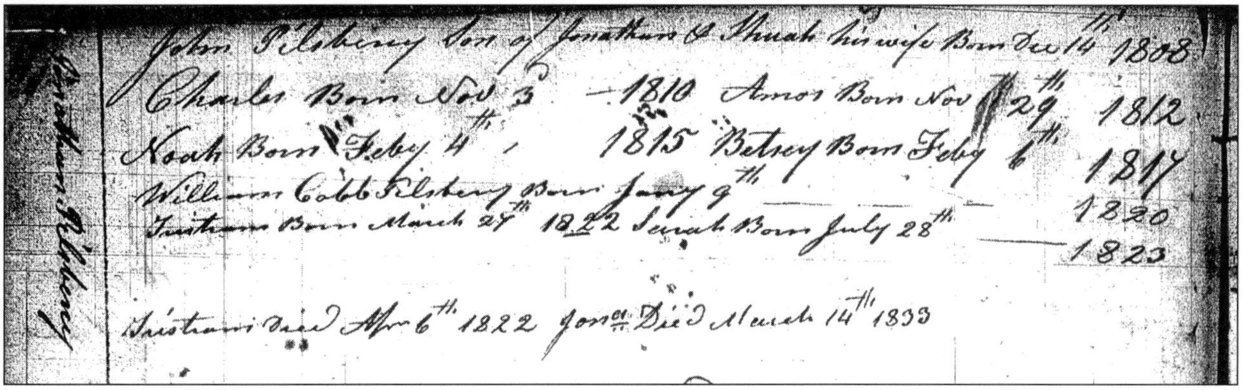

Jonathan Pillsbury

John Pillsbury Son of Jonathan & Shuah his wife Born Dec 14th 1808
Charles Born Nov 3 — 1810 Amos Born Nov 29th 1812
Noah Born Feby 4th 1815 Betsey Born Feby 6th 1817
William Cobb Pillsbury Born Jany 9th — 1820
Tristram Born March 24th 1822 Sarah Born July 28th — 1823
Tristram died Apr 6th 1822 Jona. Died March 14th 1833

Figure 10-4
Original records help verify a genealogy found elsewhere. (Scarborough, Cumberland, Maine, town records.)

STEPHEN KING AND THE PILLSBURY DOUGHBOY

After researching online and in many published and original resources, I was able to determine the relationship of Stephen King to the founders of the Pillsbury Flour Company, Charles Arthur Pillsbury and his uncle John Sargent Pillsbury.

William Pillsbury

Joe Pillsbury	Siblings	Moses Pillsbury
Josiah Pillsbury	1st cousins	Caleb Pillsbury
David Pillsbury	2d cousins	Caleb Pillsbury
Jonathan Pillsbury	3d cousins	Micajah Pillsbury
Charles C. Pillsbury	4th cousins	John Pillsbury
Howard L. Pillsbury	5th cousins	**John Sargent Pillsbury** and George Alfred Pillsbury
Guy H. Pillsbury	6th cousins	**Charles Arthur Pillsbury** (son of George)
Nellie Ruth Pillsbury	6th cousins once removed	
Stephen King	6th cousins twice removed	

The chart shows Stephen's relationship to Charles Arthur Pillsbury, his 6th cousin twice removed. Stephen's relationship to the other founder, John Sargent Pillsbury, would be 5th cousins, three times removed.

Figure 10-5

Warning

RESEARCHER BEWARE

Of course, there are times when the information you are given is incorrect. This is one of the downsides to research found on the Internet. While some researchers have taken the time to verify the information they have compiled and are now sharing, **more often than not, I find that the information either has not been verified, or the person sharing has not double-checked the information for errors.**

In a perfect world, when we find a pedigree chart or a compiled genealogy published online, we will also find that sources have been included. Unfortunately this is not always the case. In most instances I find that sources have been omitted, which is a shame, both for the person doing the research and for those who helped contribute to the research as it was published.

Finding misinformation may lead you to think that certain records need not be checked, cause you to narrow your research to a year range that is not actually appropriate, or lead you to think that records do not exist when in fact they do. This happens more frequently than we would like to think, and is actually not necessarily limited to the research published online or on CD-ROM. There have been times when I have found mistakes in the published and accepted genealogies that are only disproved after a researcher has gone the extra mile in using original records and the cluster research approach to get the broad picture. There are no clues to help you know something is wrong. This is why researching in original records yourself is so important. It is only when you find discrepancies in the original records that you are alerted to misinformation in published genealogies.

When I was researching the tree of Brad Pitt, I found some extensive research that had been posted about his tree to WorldConnect. Again, I printed this out and used it as the basis of my initial research in original records. Having the compiled research done by the other researcher helped me to narrow my research to given localities. The problem was the research of Brad's maternal line, the Hillhouse line. The information posted on the Internet showed that Elijah Boyd Hillhouse, Brad's maternal third great-grandfather, was born 15 August 1813 in Giles County, Tennessee, and died 17 May 1860 in Lawrence County, Missouri, and that Elijah's wife, Ann Bowie Gibson, was born about 1816 in Tennessee and died in September 1859 in Mount Vernon, Lawrence, Missouri.

Unfortunately we often accept an entry such as this because there are complete dates and the places listed the counties. Had either of the death dates been listed as "about" or "circa" then most genealogists would wonder if there was additional research that might better establish the date. For me the death dates affected my research in that I stopped looking for Elijah in the census indexes after 1850 since I didn't expect to find him. I didn't even think that I would be able to find his wife, since it appeared that she had predeceased him. On both counts I was wrong. In fact, I didn't discover my error until I was looking into the possible will of Elijah's and Ann's son, Elijah B. Hillhouse Jr.

THE WILL OF ELIJAH HILLHOUSE

The will of Elijah B. Hillhouse, born 15 Aug. 1813, Giles County, Tennessee, was found in Lawrence County, Missouri, in Will Book 2, on pages 96 and 97:

Mt. Vernon, Mo. Aug. 26, 1895

Being of sound mind and memory and understanding do make my last will and testament in manner and form following

I want my wife Ann B. Hillhouse to have five hundred dollars ($50000) and at her death her "affects" to be equally divided between my heirs. Then I want the balance of my "affects" to be equally divided between my heirs namely Elizabeth J. Midlin, James H. Hillhouse, Geo. S. Hillhouse, William R. Hillhouse, Elijah B. Hillhouse, John L. Hillhouse, Francis M. Hillhouse, Christopher C. Hillhouse, or his heirs, Nancy M. Thomas or her heirs, Cornelius P. Hillhouse and I want Geo. S. Hillhouse to execute my will.

E.B. Hillhouse

Witness: R.S. Young, Sade Young

This will and its mention of all the children and his wife not only told me that Elijah was still alive in 1895, but that his family didn't die until after that. Right now research indicates that he died sometime between 26 Aug. 1895 and 11 Nov. 1899, the date when the witnesses appeared in the probate court to state that it was indeed Elijah's will and that they had seen him sign it.

Once I realized I was on the wrong path as far as the information went in regard to when Elijah B. Hillhouse Sr. died, I returned to the census and other records, this time in search of Elijah Hillhouse Sr. I had already found that with his son the name was often written as just initials, which meant that when I was searching any computerized indexes that I had to search first with the full given name and then using the just the letter *E*. A similar approach was necessary for the father as well.

Additional research on the Brad Pitt lineage reminded me of how important those original records can be. In the above instance, the original research showed me that the already compiled and published genealogy found online for Brad Pitt was inaccurate at the time I was working on the tree. The compiler has since updated his information to reflect the dates given by the will. I also found that it is in the original records where we will find the clues that help push back the generations.

In the case of Etta Coleman Williams, Brad's great-grandmother, who married Emory A. Hillhouse, nothing else was known about Etta other than the fact that she was born 18 October 1888. Given the year of birth, and the unusual first name, I went looking in the 1900 census index. I found

Etta C. Williams, born Oct. 1888, living with Henry T. Williams and his wife Addie M. According to the 1900 census Henry T. Williams and Addie (who in later census records was enumerated as Ida) were married circa 1883. A search of the marriages for Lawrence County, Missouri, revealed the marriage of a Henry T. Williams and Ida Isbell.

Fortunately for me, both Henry and Ida were under age, Henry under twenty-one and Ida under eighteen when they married. I say fortunately because this meant that both of them had to get parental permission and the names of the parents who gave permission were included on the license (see Figure 10-6 on page 193). This gave me additional names and allowed me to take the ancestry back even further.

Combining the compiled genealogy I found online with the additional research in original records allowed me to compile a relatively decent genealogy on Brad Pitt in a short amount of time (see Figure 10-7 on page 194). Of course, like all genealogy projects, this tree is far from finished. It continues to be an ongoing project that gets worked on as time and records permit.

MUST YOU VERIFY ALL THE INFORMATION?

Throughout this book you have seen many pedigrees and Ahnentafels compiled and displayed. I have mentioned that I often launch a new tree by seeing what else has been published. Of course, I then turn to original records to verify what I found and to hopefully continue the research. You have also heard me talk about not having to re-create the wheel. So, the question remains: Should you verify all the information you find?

In a perfect world, yes. Of course, in a perfect world, the compiled genealogy that you find online would have all the sources cited for each piece of information. And in a perfect world our ancestors would be right where they should be and all the records would have survived. In a perfect world I would not be convinced that my great-grandmother had contrived to disappear from the records just so she could sit up there and enjoy the show as I try to locate her. However, it's not a perfect world. Because it isn't, we appreciate any help we can get. We shouldn't always have to do things from scratch. That's what I mean when I talk about not having to re-create the wheel.

In my mind, re-creating the wheel means compiling the genealogy of the initial individual with no help from any published or preresearched source. All of the information is found in original records that you have found on your own, working from one record to the next. We already do enough of that when we first get started in genealogy and often on those lines that no one else seems to be interested in. So, whenever we can, we should take the help we find and be thankful for it.

This doesn't mean that you should just download the GEDCOM file and dump it into your database, never bothering to check and see all of the individuals who are included in the database or what sources, if any, have

Figure 10-6
Marriage records often hold clues to the parents of the bride and groom, as seen here. (Lawrence County, Missouri marriages.)

been used for the information. **When you do this, you are begging for trouble.** You are opening yourself up to the passing on of misinformation. You will probably find that it is harder to get a grasp on where you are in the research and what records you need to check.

If I do download a GEDCOM file, I don't import it directly into my database. Instead I create a new database file into which it gets imported. This allows me to create reports and view the information and individuals

Warning

ANCESTRY OF BRAD PITT		
	Generation 1	
1	**Brad Pitt** was born in Shawnee, Pottawatomie, Oklahoma, 18 Dec. 1963. He married Jennifer Aniston in Malibu Beach, Los Angeles, California, 29 July 2000.	
	Generation 2	
2	**William A. Pitt** was born in Cleveland County, Oklahoma, ca. 1940. He married Jane Etta Hillhouse in Jasper County, Missouri, 11 Aug. 1962.	
3	**Jane Etta Hillhouse** was born in Missouri, ca. 1942.	
	Generation 3	

4	**Alvin Monroe Pitt** was born in Oklahoma 7, Mar. 1913. He married Elizabeth Jean Brown. Alvin died 4 Mar. 1959 in Mobile, Mobile, Alabama.	
5	**Elizabeth Jean Brown** was born in Oklahama ca. 1922. She married Raymond Russell.	
6	**Hal Knox Hillhouse** was born in Mount Vernon, Lawrence, Missouri, 13 Mar. 1911. He married Clara M. Bell 25 Feb. 1934. Hal died Nov. 1976 in Webb City, Jasper, Missouri.	
7	**Clara M. Bell** was born in Missouri, ca. 1911. She married Hal Knox Hillhouse 25 Feb. 1934.	

Generation 4		
8	**Oliver Pitt**	
9	**Rosa Lee Dorris** was born in Arkansas ca. 1900. She married William M. Spooner in Union County, Arkansas, 8 Dec. 1924.	
10	**Lester B. Brown** was born in Oklahoma Sept. 1902. He married Una Valerie Coker ca. 1921.	
11	**Una Valerie Coker** was born in Sevierville, Sevier, Tennessee, 3 Mar. 1903. She married Charles Cerba. Una died 12 Nov. 1997 in Arlington, Tarrant, Texas. Her body was interred 15 Nov. 1997 in Tecumseh, Pottawatomie, Oklahoma, New Hope Cemetery.	
12	**Emery A. Hillhouse** was born in Mount Vernon, Lawrence, Missouri, 23 Sept. 1882. He married Etta Coleman Williams in Mount Vernon, Lawrence, Missouri, 18 Nov. 1906. Emery died 23 Jan. 1965 in Mount Vernon, Lawrence, Missouri.	
13	**Etta Coleman Williams** was born 18 Oct. 1888. She died Sept. 1982 in Mount Vernon, Lawrence, Missouri.	
14	**Finis A. Bell** was born in Cave Springs, Arkansas, 21 Nov. 1867. He married Lenora Jane Hammer in Mount Vernon, Lawrence, Missouri, 20 Nov. 1898. Finis died 4 Nov. 1918.	
15	**Lenora Jane Hammer** was born in Lawrence County, Missouri, 14 Dec. 1871. She died 21 Oct. 1942.	

Generation 5		
22	**Richard Ogle Coker** was born in Sevierville, Sevier, Tennessee, 27 July 1872. He married Laura Trotter in Sevier County, Tennessee, 15 Dec. 1892. Richard died 9 Aug. 1932 in Shawnee, Pottawatomie, Oklahoma.	
23	**Laura Trotter** was born in Sevierville, Sevier, Tennessee, 7 Feb. 1873. She died 16 Jan. 1952 in Shawnee, Pottawatomie, Oklahoma.	
24	**Elijah Boyd Hillhouse Jr.** was born in Lawrence County, Missouri, 25 Sept. 1843. He married Melinda B. Morris in Lawrence County, Missouri, 24 July 1867. Elijah died 24 Oct. 1909.	
25	**Melinda B. Morris** was born in Kentucky, 24 Dec. 1848. She died 20 Jan. 1930.	
26	**Henry T. Williams** was born in Missouri, June 1864. He married Ida M. Isbell in Mount Vernon, Lawrence, Missouri, 23 Dec. 1883.	
27	**Ida M. Isbell** was born in Missouri, Nov. 1866	
30	**Felix Emery Hammer** was born in Mount Vernon, Lawrence, Missouri, 14 Oct. 1845. He married Sarah Angeline Parker in Mount Vernon, Lawrence, Missouri, 2 Dec. 1866. Felix died 22 Oct. 1926 in Mount Vernon, Lawrence, Missouri.	
31	**Sarah Angeline Parker** was born in Warren County, Tennessee, 2 Oct. 1845. She died 18 Mar. 1926.	

Figure 10-7

Generation 6	
44	**James William Harvey Coker** was born in Yancey County, North Carolina, 4 June 1847. He married Matilda Ogle in Sevier County, Tennessee, 15 Mar. 1864. James died 18 May 1911 in Sevierville, Sevier, Tennessee.
45	**Matilda Ogle** was born in Sevier County, Tennessee, 8 Jan. 1848. She died 7 Jan. 1913 in Sevierville, Sevier, Tennessee.
46	**John M. Trotter** was born in Sevier County, Tennessee, 31 Dec. 1831. He married Tryphena Flynn. John died 19 June 1889 in Sevier County, Tennessee.
47	**Tryphena Flynn** was born in Tennessee, 20 June 1831. She died 12 Nov. 1901 in Sevier County, Tennessee.
48	**Elijah Boyd Hillhouse** was born in Giles County, Tennessee, 15 Aug. 1813. He married Ann Bowie Gibson. He made a will in Mount Vernon, Lawrence, Missouri, 26 Aug. 1895. Elijah died before 11 Nov. 1899.
49	**Ann Bowie Gibson** was born in Tennessee, ca. 1816.
50	**Jordan Morris** married Mary Button.
51	**Mary Button**
52	**Unknown Williams** married Sarah G. [--?--].
53	**Sarah G. [--?--]**
54	**Thomas R. Isbell**
60	**Enoch Lane Hammer** was born in Milford, Butler, Ohio, 3 Dec. 1809. He married Susanah Cartwrite Newby in McMinnville, Warren, Tennessee, 1 July 1828. Enoch died 31 Mar. 1864 in Mount Vernon, Lawrence, Missouri.
61	**Susanah Cartwrite Newby** was born in McMinnville, Warren, Tennessee, 23 July 1809. She died 7 Nov. 1860 in Mount Vernon, Lawrence, Missouri.
62	**John Parker** married Martha Jane Cherry.
63	**Martha Jane Cherry**
Generation 7	
90	**Elijah J.P. Ogle** was born in Tennessee, ca. 1822. He married Elizabeth Conner.
91	**Elizabeth Conner** was born in North Carolina, ca. 1824.
94	**George Flynn** was born in Tennessee, ca. 1801.
98	**Unknown Gibson** married Ann [--?--].
99	**Ann [--?--]** was born in North Carolina, ca. 1800.
120	**Aaron Hammer** was born in Randolph County, North Carolina, ca. 1778. He married Hester Lane in Randolph County, North Carolina, 26 Oct. 1801. Aaron died ca. 1856 in Lawrence County, Missouri.
121	**Hester Lane** was born in Randolph County, North Carolina, 7 Nov. 1780. She died ca. 1819 in Warren County, Tennessee.
122	**James Whaley Newby** married Orpha Frances Hopkins.
123	**Orpha Frances Hopkins**
Generation 8	
240	**Elisha Hammer** married Elizabeth [--?--].
241	**Elizabeth [--?--]**

Figure 10-7

included in the file to see what is known, what sources, if any, are cited, and get an overall feel for the lineage that I am most interested in. I say this because many of the GEDCOM files that you download may have individuals totally unrelated to the line you're researching. By creating a separate file, I can isolate the individuals I am most interested in, work to verify the information on them, and then, once I am sure of the accuracy of the data, create a new GEDCOM file of just those individuals to import into my own database.

Rather than creating a new GEDCOM file, though, I usually work off printed reports, most often the Ahnentafel report you have seen used throughout this book. I make notes and change information based on the records I use. In effect, as I am working off of the Ahnentafel, I am also adding the information to my own database, citing the original documents. In the cases in which I have not yet been able to verify all the information but I must create a tree for publication, I cite the GEDCOM file or the compiler of that GEDCOM file as my source. This lets those who are working off my published research know what I have been able to verify and what still needs to be researched.

When it comes to researching the surnames associated with celebrities, you will often find that there is already information that has been compiled. If you discover, through cluster genealogy, that you share certain surnames with the celebrity, it is possible that you may not have to completely research the celebrity.

Books such as Gary Boyd Roberts' *Notable Kin* (Santa Clarita, CA: Carl Boyer, 3d edition, 1998–1999), may supply part of the lineage, perhaps enough so that you know right away if you are related to that line. In his book, he often concentrates on those lines that go back to the *Mayflower* or other notable beginnings, rather than listing all the known individuals in each generation. This does not mean that the information doesn't exist.

Whenever possible, whether I am researching a celebrity or my own ancestry, I will check the various compiled genealogies we discussed in chapter eight. And don't forget to use the valuable indexes such as PERSI and AGBI. Indexes such as these help point us toward the right volumes or pages in resources, a task that may otherwise have seemed too daunting if we had to check each individually on our own. If nothing else, these indexes give us a place to start in our research.

BRIDGING TO PEOPLE

As we discussed earlier, genealogy works better when there are more people than just you researching the line in question—strength in numbers. Others may have access to records that you don't. So in addition to building bridges between your genealogy and that of the celebrity, you want to build bridges between yourself and other researchers.

When you find a compiled genealogy Web page about the lineage in which you are interested or you find that a person has submitted a GEDCOM file

For More Info

AMERICAN GENEALOGICAL-BIOGRAPHICAL INDEX (AGBI)

The *American Genealogical-Biographical Index* (AGBI) is a massive index to genealogies found in published sources. To find out more see my *The Genealogist's Computer Companion* (Cincinnati: Betterway Books, 2002).

that helped you, don't hesitate to contact that individual. Researchers like to know that the information they have published was useful. They like to hear from others who are researching the same lines—after all, they don't want to be the only person doing the research either.

The key to building bridges with other researchers is to not ask them for everything they have. Many already share all that they currently know either in the GEDCOM file or on a Web site. Others may only share a portion of the information so that you will contact them. They may be hoping to find another researcher who wants to correspond with them and take an active participation in the research. If you contact them and immediately ask for everything they know, it is likely they will not feel that you want to help them but instead simply take all that they have and run.

When you contact fellow researchers, start by thanking them for the information that they have already shared and tell them where you found it. Many researchers who share in one place will often share in more than one and they like to know where folks are finding the information they submitted or published. You should mention how you have found the information useful. Then, ask a simple question. Perhaps ask if they know of the parents of a particular individual, or if they have found the death date of one particular person. Tell them what you have been working on, let them know that you are willing to share, and that you're looking forward to working on this line together.

If you are new to research, don't be afraid to let researchers know. If I know a researcher is new to the hobby, I will take pains to explain records or resources that I have used, and will be sure to spell out acronyms when I use them the first time. If the person you are corresponding with knows you are new, he may be more willing to overlook some common mistakes, such as asking for everything.

PUTTING IT ALL TOGETHER

Before publishing your information or sharing it with the rest of the family, there are some things to keep in mind. In the upcoming chapters, we will look at how to handle the skeletons after you have found them, especially when the information was unsuspected. Should you share the information with the rest of your family and the world?

ELEVEN

Making Skeletons Dance

Writer Carolyn MacKenzie once said, "If you have a skeleton in your closet, take it out and dance with it." I suspect many of our families are afraid we will take MacKenzie's writing advice to heart when it comes to researching our family history. I know of many genealogists who have been discouraged in their research by family members. They have been told to leave things alone. They've been questioned about digging up the past. No one actually sets out to uncover a skeleton, certainly not with the intention of hurting the family. Some require our seeking out the records, while in other cases, the skeletons pop up when least expected.

Take, for instance, the deed record mentioned in chapter three. The woman researching Resolved Chace in Massachusetts was not expecting to find the record she did in the deed books. After all, we expect to find records of the exchanging of land or other property for money in the deed books, not a statement of someone's wrongdoing. Even though Resolved Chace gave an account of what took place, he admitted to accompanying John F. Stebing to the house of ill repute. Of course, this took place back in 1831, so even for those researching the Stebing surname, a lot of time has come and gone. However, it would still be a shock to expect another dry land deed and instead come up with such a recorded testimony. Had you or I found something similar about a living cousin or grandfather who we idolized, it would certainly be not only a shock, but perhaps also an embarrassment to the family and something that members would prefer we not mention again.

WHO WILL IT HURT?

Important

Before sharing any colorful detail you have uncovered in your research, there are a few questions you should ask yourself to make sure you are not hurting anyone in the family. In our zeal to uncover the family history, we sometimes forget that such information may hurt someone. Our intention is not to hurt anyone, but it can happen if we don't take a moment to evaluate what we have found and how others in the family may react to our discovery. So, before sharing with the world, ask yourself:

- How many generations ago did this happen?
- What was the nature of the skeleton?
- Is it something that is no longer considered scandalous?
- Is it something that today is considered scandalous or embarrassing, but in the past wasn't?
- How did you react when you first made the discovery?

Once you have answered these questions, you will probably have a better idea of the reaction you are likely to get from the family. Of course, there will always be one or two people who do not react the way you expected.

When I was researching Benjamin Standerfer, for instance, and made the big discovery of his larceny and divorce, and the reason for his divorce, I eagerly shared the information with my mother. I was excited—the individual in question was on my father's side, and it never entered my mind that my mother might be upset by the find. After sharing the information, I was a little surprised when I got a different reaction from her than anticipated. Her shock and dismay were not what I expected and I took a moment to remind her that he wasn't even on her lineage, if anyone should have been upset by Benjamin's activities, it should have been me since I share his genes to a degree. Because of the number of generations that separate him and me I was not threatened by his activities. In fact, I was in a way grateful for them because of the records they generated that helped me get a handle on when and where he was born. This gave me a base to work on when trying to connect him to potential parents.

HOW MANY GENERATIONS?

When you find a skeleton of any kind, you need to see how long ago the event took place. Is anyone who knew this individual alive today? If so, it is possible that the information needs to be kept quiet a little longer? People tend to get upset if you have unearthed the big family secret and want to shout it from the rooftops, especially if that family secret has to do with those living now.

In researching my own family tree, I discovered a disturbing trend of "premature" births of the first child in each generation of one particular line for about four generations. I didn't fudge the information. I recorded the date of birth of the first child as recorded on the records I found. I recorded the marriage date as I found it in the records as well, but I didn't call great attention to the fact. I know that for a number of generations there were some shotgun weddings, but the rest of the family didn't realize this, and I didn't want to upset anyone by sharing the trend. As we will see later on, there are ways of recording the information without drawing attention.

When we think about the privacy act that prevents us from accessing the census records of the United States until seventy-two years after the census was enumerated, we think about protecting the privacy of living individuals. We think in terms of identity theft and other modern-day privacy invasions. Yet, imagine if you were to learn your father was in prison when the census taker came through twenty years ago? What if you found yourself on the census and it indicated you were born a year before you thought you were? Could you handle such discoveries? However, if you locate a family member in prison in 1860, enough time has gone by that you are not as shaken by the discovery, at least not at first. Perhaps, though, the reason for the incarceration may be shocking enough to be upsetting.

WHAT WAS THE NATURE OF THE SKELETON?

As we saw in chapter three there are many different skeletons that we can uncover. Some of them no longer carry the stigma they once did. In fact, some of them are so intriguing that we almost prefer to find them in the family. However, other things you may uncover might not have been considered wrong at the time, but today are a big embarrassment to the family. Take, for example, slave owners. Even though many considered owning slaves wrong at the time, many more considered it to be a way of life. Today, though, your family members may feel uncomfortable at discovering a slave owner on the family tree.

In comparison to today's crimes, the crimes of the past may not seem so grave. For example, the eleven dollars Benjamin Standerfer stole then doesn't seem like as much as what today's thieves steal. Of course, looking at the equivalent of his eleven dollars in today's money it might put a different spin on the escapade. (When I visited The Inflation Calculator <www.we stegg.com/inflation/>, though, I learned Benjamin only stole about $187 in today's money, so still not a "big" amount.) Don't get me wrong—I am not advocating stealing—but Benjamin's crime is an example of something that at the time was viewed as awful, but when viewed against the travesties of today isn't necessarily on the same scale.

Had Benjamin stolen thousands of dollars or killed anyone in his attempts to steal the money, I am sure I would have reacted differently to the find. After all, large sums of money are harder to justify or explain away. You can't just say he was trying to provide for his family. And when people are killed as a result, you are forced to examine the possibility that the killing didn't bother him.

While it seems a murderer is someone we would never want to find on the family tree, when our cousin or ancestor is a famous criminal like Jesse James or Doc Holliday, the criminal events are somehow glossed over. While we would initially think murder is one of those skeletons we never want to mention, when the murderer has been idolized, it seems safe to mention him or her. In fact, I suspect that if you have found a connection to one of these famous gunslingers, it may be one of those facts the family actually does want to hear about.

Often, when we are trying to share the information we have found, our family either stares at us politely, not really listening, or they turn and run the other way when they see us coming. Tell them you've found a relationship to Jesse James or Billy the Kid and see how quickly their ears perk up. You may even catch them bragging about it later on.

While in most instances the severity of the crime is what upsets family members, we have seen that if that person is famous for their terrible deeds, their crimes are somehow dehumanized and thus acceptable. However, one scandal of old that, for the most part, is not considered unacceptable anymore, is the case of the illegitimate child.

In the past, girls who found themselves pregnant often disappeared from the time they began to show until after they had given birth to the baby. Sometimes the mother of the pregnant girl would take on responsibility for the new child; more often, though, the child was put up for adoption. Regardless, the pregnancy was seldom discussed, and if you did find out about it, you were told to forget what you knew. Today, many girls and women have babies out of wedlock. While some give the children up for adoption, things are more open than they used to be. The stigma has been removed, though your older family members may still react in "cover-up" mode should you mention something about a possible additional birth or a child born out of wedlock (see Figure 11-1 on page 202).

See Also

SET YOUR SITES ON ADOPTION

See "Adoption and Birth Certificates" on page 139 for a list of useful sites to aid you in your adoption research.

A CHANGE OF VALUES

The change in the acceptance of an unwed mother is an example of how changes in society's values can make the issues with a previously unacceptable skeleton almost passé. Those who were owners or traffickers of slaves, though, are now on the other end of that spectrum. In the past, they were accepted by the majority of the population. Even though abolitionists were trying to get the practice banned, and there are indications that when the United States was breaking away from England some tried to put a stop to it, there wasn't a stigma to owning slaves. Today that is not the case.

Most Anglo researchers who find their ancestry heading south before the Civil War have concerns about what they might find in regard to slave owners. You may discover in the census that you have an ancestor who lived in the South, perhaps an older man, who listed his occupation as a "planter." The term *planter* is just one of the occupations that generally means the person had a plantation of some type with at least a few slaves. Another, more subtle clue is the dramatic change in real estate value from 1860 to 1870.

What should you do if you discover a slave owner in your history? Yes, it was a terrible thing that happened, but as we have seen, it was not always viewed as such a terrible thing during the time of your ancestor. Take pride now that your family has since broken what could have been a vicious cycle.

SUSPECTED ANCESTRY OF JACK NICHOLSON

Because of the secrets which his biological mother and grandmother kept, it has been difficult to piece together the paternal lineage of Jack Nicholson. Jack did not find out until he was 37 that the individuals he thought were his parents were actually his grandparents. While his maternal line is known, Jack's paternal lineage is based on the fact that June and Don were married when she would have been pregnant with Jack.

© AMPAS

Generation 1

| 1 | Jack Nicholson was born in New York City, New York, New York, 22 Apr. 1937. |

Generation 2

| 2 | Don Furcillo-Rose was born probably in Monmouth County, New Jersey, 23 May 1909. He married June Frances Nicholson in Elkton, Cecil County, Maryland, 16 Oct. 1936. Don died 27 July 1997 in Ocean Grove, Monmouth County, New Jersey. |
| 3 | June Frances Nicholson was born in Pittsfield, Berkshire, Massachusetts, 5 Nov. 1918. She married Don Furcillo-Rose in Elkton, Cecil County, Maryland, 16 Oct. 1936. June died 31 July 1963 probably in California. Her body was interred in San Fernando, California, Mission Cemetery. |

Generation 3

4	Samuel R. Furcillo Furcella was born in Italy about 1886. He married Antoinette [--?--] probably in Monmouth County, New Jersey, about 1908.
5	Antoinette [--?--] was born in Monteforte Irpino, Italy, 25 Jan. 1890. She died Apr. 1961 in New Jersey.
6	John J. Nicholson was born in Staten Island, New York, about 1898. He married Ethel May Rhoads in Neptune Township, Monmouth County, New Jersey, 4 Aug. 1918. John died 24 July 1955 in Neptune Township, Monmouth County, New Jersey.
7	Ethel May Rhoads was born in Chester, Delaware County, Pennsylvania, 9 Mar. 1898. She died 6 Jan. 1970 in Monmouth County, New Jersey.

Generation 4

11	[--?--] Soma
12	Joseph Nicholson married Ella Lynch about 1895. Joseph died 1904.
13	Ella Lynch was born in County Cork, Ireland.
14	William J. Rhoads was born in Pennsylvania, Mar. 1878. He married Mary Alice Wilkinson ca. 1897.
15	Mary Alice Wilkinson was born in Pennsylvania, Mar. 1879. She died 16 Aug. 1904 in probably New Jersey.

Generation 5

24	Joseph J. Nicholson was born in England. He married Bridget Derrig in Kent, England, 1854. Joseph died about 1885 in England.
25	Bridget Derrig was born in Ireland, 13 Jan. 1835. She died 13 Aug. 1887 in Fall River, Bristol County, Massachusetts.
28	Alfred C. Rhoads was born in Pennsylvania, June 1851. He married Maggie ca. 1873.
29	Maggie was born in Pennsylvania, Aug. 1852.
30	J. John Wilkinson was born in England, ca. 1835. He married Ellen.
31	Ellen was born in Pennsylvania, ca. 1844.

Generation 6

| 61 | Alice |

Figure 11-1

SURPRISE!

Imagine being thirty-seven years old, taking a phone call from a writer doing a piece on you for a magazine, and then finding out that the writer has discovered that your mother is actually your grandmother and your sister is really your mother. That's what happened to Jack Nicholson. Born in 1937, he was riding high in 1974 when he was given this information. The writer agreed to do without the information from the article at that time, but it did eventually come out. Today there is a book written by a woman who says she is Jack's half-sister, as she and he supposedly share the same father. The book, *You Don't Know Jack: The Tale of a Father Once Removed* (Virtual Publishing, 2001) is written by Linda S. Allen and Donna Rose. Donna Rose is the child of Don Furcillo-Rose, the suspected father of Jack Nicholson. The book leaves a lot of questions, but does offer pictures of some of the documents that genealogists have come to rely on.

WHAT WAS YOUR REACTION?

When we are reading information in a record—perhaps looking at the occupations of people as we look line-by-line in the census—we have gut reactions to what we are seeing. How many of us take a minute longer when we discover we are looking at the census enumeration of the state penitentiary or the county jail? How many times have we hoped that the page number we were looking for doesn't end up right in the middle of that enumeration?

As you compile the information you have found about a particular ancestor, think about your initial reaction at the discovery of the skeleton. Were you shocked? Did it make you feel uncomfortable? Were there underlying circumstances that made you feel pity or sadness for what happened? With the exception of the understanding or pity you gain through your research, generally, the initial reaction you have about a person will be mirrored by your family. If you were appalled, then it is likely that your family will be also.

Sometimes the distance in years of the incident may color your reaction. I have reacted one way when the divorce was in the generation of my great-grandparents and another when the divorce took place five or six generations back. Perhaps my reaction was different because the individuals involved, instead of being compiled, almost mythical people, were people I knew personally. (See Figure 11-2 on page 204.)

SAINT OR SINNER?

There will be stories you unearth that will make you question if the individual was a saint or a sinner. Depending on which side of the situation you are on, your opinion of the event and how good the person was may be colored. In some instances the sinner is now a saint, and in other instances

Warning

DIVORCE IS DIVORCE, RIGHT?

Even if you think you are prepared for what you might find when researching a divorce, sometimes the absolute facts can be a little hard to take when you knew the individuals involved or the reason for the divorce is something we find unacceptable today.

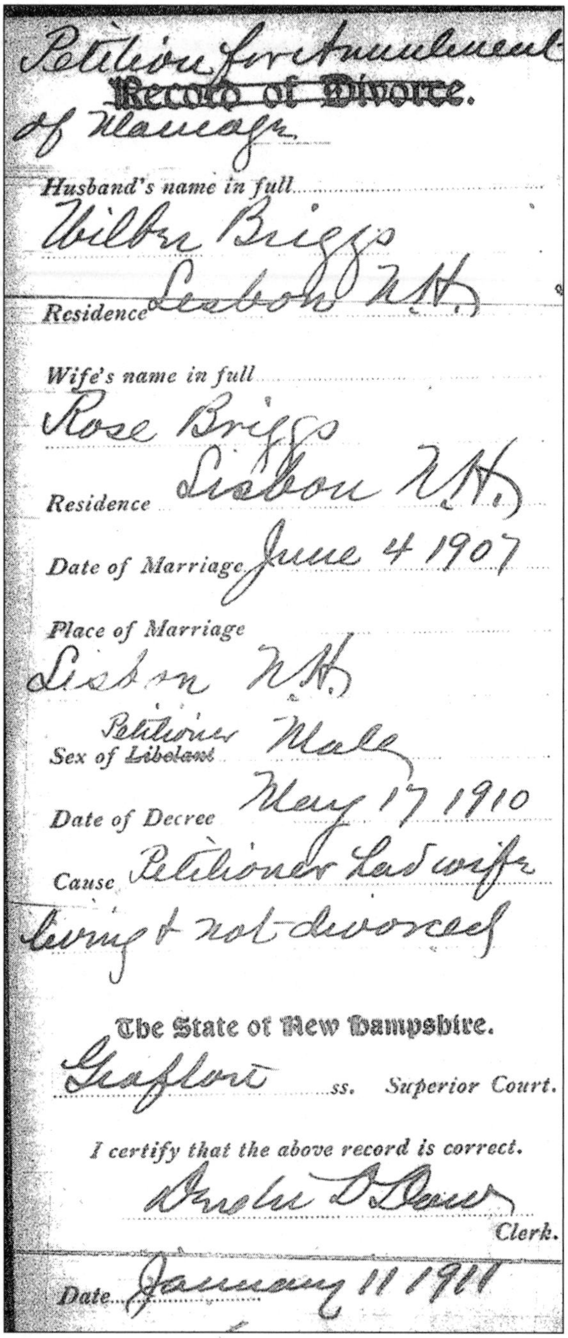

Figure 11-2
The index to divorces in New Hampshire sometimes gives you more information than you expected. Two wives?

someone held up as a hero may be viewed by another as a heel.

Today, those who have traced their ancestry to Salem Village, Massachusetts, see the suspicions of the time as an unmistakable hysteria that gripped the area. The type of spectral evidence that the girls could bring against a person had no alibi. While those hanged were not buried in hallowed ground and were, in some instances, excommunicated from the church, today we consider them martyrs for what they had to endure. In 1692 they and their families, to some degree, were considered evil. Today we marvel at what they went through.

THE STORY OF HANNAH

Hannah Dustin was born Hannah Webster Emerson in 1655. She was the daughter of Michael Emerson and the sister of Elizabeth Emerson, who had been hanged in Boston in 1693 for the deaths of her twin children. On 16 March 1697, Hannah was still in bed, having given birth six days earlier, when Indians attacked the town of Haverhill. Hannah's nurse, Mrs. Mary Neff, tried to save the baby, but she and the baby were captured by the Indians, as was Hannah. The three, along with other captives from the raid, were sent on a forced march north. On the way, Hannah was forced to watch as her baby was dashed against a tree (the baby was held by the feet and swung like a bat until the head hit the tree).

After some time, Hannah, Mrs. Neff, and their captors were met by another group of Indians, and the two women discovered a teenage boy, Samuel Leonardson, who had been captured sometime earlier. When it became clear that the three were being taken to Canada to be sold into slavery, they devised a plan to escape. The escape involved the killing of their captors. At some point, whether or not planned, the captors were also scalped on the night of the getaway.

Today, there are two statues that stand in honor of Hannah, the trials she endured, and her heroic escape. One can be found in New Hampshire on Dustin Island and the other in Haverhill, Massachusetts. There is also a poem by John Greenleaf Whittier, who grew up in Haverhill, in his *Legends of New England in Prose and Verse* which was published in 1831. To this day she is considered a heroine for enduring the terror that befell her and for the way she managed to escape.

Like the changes in views we discussed earlier, similar changes in thinking may leave people questioning the actions of a hero. Again, we are placing our present-day thinking on an event at which we were not present and can not completely understand. While we may not strike up the band, we also should not condemn the act and relegate the former hero to the new role of criminal.

To many, Hannah Dustin is a heroine. She endured a terrible fate, including having to watch the murder of her newborn child. This would be hard on anyone. Of course, when we hear this story we apply our present-day standards to the events. For instance, the dashing of the baby, which we consider nothing less than cold-blooded murder, was to the Indians a way of preventing the baby from suffering. While we can understand the captives' desire to escape and their feeling that they could only do it if they killed their captors, does the scalping do anything to negate Hannah's heroic status?

There are no clear answers to these questions because to answer them, you and I would be applying our present-day views to an event that took place more than three hundred years ago. I have often said to my children as they tried to tell me how a sibling should have acted, "You weren't there. You don't know what was going on and what was going through her head." We don't know what was going on; we have only the historical accounts, some of which we will discover are slanted to support the point or agenda of the author.

Hannah's terrible ordeal begs the question—saint or sinner? Or was she a combination of the two? And if a sinner, do you still shout from the rooftops that she is on your family tree?

IT'S *THE JERRY SPRINGER SHOW*

I am convinced that in some ways I am old school, a product of the child who is seen and not heard. I may be an adult with children of my own, but in many ways I still subscribe to the belief that I should be seen and not heard. I am astounded by the dirty laundry that is routinely aired on various talk shows and often wonder where the entertainment value and integrity is.

After seeing a few episodes of these shows, no one should be surprised by anything found on the family tree. Such programs almost glamorize the unwed mother who has no idea who the father is of her yet-to-be-born child. In my mother's day, such an admission would never have happened. Even in my day, you would have been hard-pressed to find a pregnant girl who was even talking about how she got pregnant.

There are times when it is better not to shout out your skeleton. This doesn't mean that you have to hide the information discovered; on the contrary, I discourage anyone from doing that. People have altered dates of marriage so as to hide the fact that the firstborn child was not already on the way at the time of the wedding. Others deny the cause of death of a family member because of the scandal involved as a result of the cause of death. I don't like to think of anyone purposely misleading people with their genealogical information, but neither is it always necessary for the skeletons to dance all the time.

Idea Generator

In some instances, if you don't call attention to the issue, the way I handled the trend of shotgun weddings in one family, the information can be published with none the wiser. In other situations, including the information in a footnote rather than the narrative is all that is needed.

If your family has reacted in a horrified manner at your discovery, that is a good indication of how they will react if you decide to share what you know with the world. Sharing your genealogy can usually be accomplished without hurting anyone in the family and at the same time without hurting the research either. Of course, there will always be exceptions to the rule, but generally speaking, you can stick to the names, dates, and places rather than expounding on the extracurricular activities of a particular ancestor. Supplying the names, dates, and places along with the familial connections will make it possible for another to find the same information you found but perhaps at a time when it no longer is upsetting to the rest of the family.

PUBLISHING FOR POSTERITY

For many who are researching their family history, the goal is to publish something in the end. The search for the ancestry is the act of finding out where a person has come from, of discovering the roots of that person, and her family. The publishing of the family history is like stating to the world, "I was here." When it comes to finding a celebrity on the family tree, the publisher of the information not only wants posterity to know he was here, but also wants those today to know that he is related to an actor, a president, or some other notable. He wants to create a published record of his family for future generations and future researchers. Like all the other issues surrounding the research of your ancestors, there are some issues you'll want to keep in mind as you consider publishing the family history.

TWELVE

Telling All

F amily history is a dual process. First, you spend time researching the family history, and then, you spend time publishing what you have found. Actually the two processes go hand in hand, the one building on the other. As you publish information, other researchers will contact you with information to share, which in turn helps you to do more research. Publishing has always been a part of the family history hobby to many people, though in the past the publishing options were more limited than they are today.

In the past, most of the published family histories were primarily text and were the result of the time- and energy-intensive process of typesetting of the book. Computers, in addition to offering software programs that allow us to record our information, now offer a myriad of methods for publishing the information we have compiled. We can still publish the information in a book that we either sell or give away, but by far, the most popular way to share genealogical information is now through the Internet. Of course, like anything new there have been some growing pains and some unexpected issues as a result of the publishing of the information online.

Because we access the Internet while sitting comfortably in our own home, we tend to forget that the information we share online doesn't stay just in our home, and that what we post to the Internet is available to all sorts of different people, many of whom never make their presence known. As a result, we may never even realize people are reading what we published. (When I mention *published* here, I am using it as a blanket term that includes any way in which we disseminate the information we have compiled about a family tree with others. When it comes to the Internet, this could include a published genealogy in the form of a Web site, a message to a mailing list or bulletin board, or the uploading of a GEDCOM file to one of the GEDCOM databases.)

As a publisher of information, there are certain things you should keep in mind regardless of how you are posting the information. There are other factors to consider based on the manner in which you are sharing the information online. And there are yet other issues to think about if you are publishing

Notes

in a more traditional manner, such as with a book, which will end up in libraries and as a result be around for a long time.

There are also some legal and ethical issues to keep in mind. When publishing your information online, there are additional concerns in regard to the protection of living individuals. There is also some misunderstanding as to whether or not publishing to the Internet is real publishing. Since it is, you need to understand the issues that govern the publishing of a book. Let's look at each of these issues.

IS IT COPYRIGHTED?

The biggest misunderstanding about genealogy has to do with the issue of copyright. Genealogists are often confused as to what they can and can't do with information they find in books, online resources, photocopies of documents, and digitized images of the census, just to name a few. Some err on the side of caution, afraid to publish anything, while others think that everything they do is covered under the fair use clause, so they are exempt from the copyright law. We will examine the fair use clause and copyright in greater detail in a moment.

First, let's look at what constitutes publishing. Before it was quite clear— if you printed a book you were publishing your family history. Today things are not as clear. The Internet is another form of publishing. It doesn't matter that you aren't holding the printed word in your hand; if you have posted information to the Internet, most especially if you have created a Web page, then you have published. As a result the information is covered by copyright laws, but understanding what is covered is often where the confusion arises.

Copyright was established to protect the creative works of authors, artists, musicians, and others, which today includes Web designers. After all, no one would put much work into creating something new if just anybody could take that hard work and call it his. Copyright was not designed to protect a creation forever or to keep people from using the information completely. Instead it was designed to limit what others could do with that creation (see Figure 12-1 on page 210).

Most of the time we think about copyrights as they apply to "real" books—you know, those fiction books we use to escape reality—or songs and movies. When it comes to genealogical information we often don't consider copyright. Actually, when it comes to genealogists, we seem to think that the copyright law doesn't apply to us.

I can't think of how many times I have brought up this subject or have been involved in a discussion of copyright with other genealogists. It isn't long before the rebuttal sentences begin. We may think that we don't have to abide by the copyright law, but we are not exempt. Since we are not infringing on a major company's revenue, no one is going after us. We have been lulled into a false sense of security that what we are doing is legal.

Believe me, I think I have heard all the reasons why a genealogist is exempt from the copyright act. The most common ones include.

MAILING LISTS VS. BULLETIN BOARDS

A *mailing list* allows you to send a single message to many people through a single e-mail address. The message arrives like regular e-mail. A *bulletin board* allows you to post a message on the Web so others can read it, much like posting a "for sale" sign on the bulletin board at the library or grocery store. The biggest difference between the two is that mailing list messages come to you and you go to a bulletin board.

COPYRIGHT QUESTIONS

The U.S. Copyright Office at the Library of Congress <www.loc.gov/copyright/> is the place to go for answers to questions about copyright. They offer detailed Frequently Asked Questions (FAQs) about getting a copyright, what the copyright protects, and more. There is also a searchable database where you can put in the name of an author and check on the copyright, though it is not complete.

Figure 12-1
The U.S. Copyright Web site.

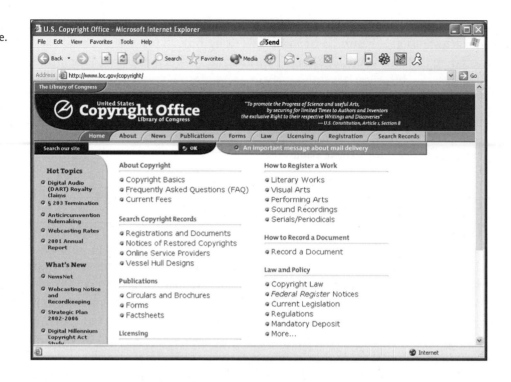

- I'm not charging any money for my research.
- It's just facts; you can't copyright facts.
- It's my family, so I deserve it.
- It's on the Internet, so it is in the public domain.
- There's no copyright statement on the Web site, so it is fair game.
- My research falls under the fair use clause.

Let's look at each of these to see how right genealogists are with their rebuttals.

I'm Not Making Any Money

Many genealogists think that if they aren't making any money on the information they took from someone's book or Web site, they have not infringed on the copyright of the other person. While monetary consideration can affect a court ruling, the fact that you are not making money does not exempt you from having to abide by the law.

A colleague of mine found an article she had written, which was published on a commercial Web site and was designed to drive traffic to that Web site, elsewhere. She made the discovery when she was using a general search engine and typed in the subject of her article—interested in seeing what else was available online. She was surprised to find her article pop up, not because she hadn't known it was on the Internet, but because of where she found it. She was further upset to discover that the person who had posted it had stripped her name out completely. It looked like the Web site owner had written the article. In contacting the individual to have him remove the article from his site, the individual responded that it wasn't a copyright infringement because he wasn't charging people to read the article.

Many times publishers of local genealogical newsletters or people compiling a Web site devoted to a specific subject request permission to reprint an article I wrote. Nine times out of ten, I gave permission provided that the reprinted article contained my name, information about where it was originally published, and the statement "Printed with permission." As a genealogist, I understand that knowledge is essential to our progressing. As an author, I understand the work that goes into that five hundred word or three thousand word piece. I have to weigh the sharing of knowledge against the work involved, the potential to sell the piece, and if I have actually been paid to write the article, the agreement I have with the publisher of the piece.

You Can't Copyright a Fact

Facts cannot be copyrighted. The fact that my name is Rhonda McClure or the fact that Benjamin Standerfer was born in 1841 cannot be copyrighted. As such the facts of a pedigree cannot be copyrighted. After all, if you and I independently work on the same lineage, and we have both done the research correctly, we should come up with the same facts. Both of us should have the same parents and grandparents. We should have found the exact same dates and places of birth and death. (See Figure 12-2 on page 212.)

By the same token, if I spend a little extra time compiling stories or enhancing the genealogy with anecdotes about the family, or take the time to visit cemeteries and get photographs of the tombstones, then the compiled genealogy as it now appears is covered by copyright.

Of course, if I rely on someone else's information in building my own genealogy, even though the facts are not copyrighted and as such are available for the taking, I ethically should be citing my sources. We talked about this earlier, and the responsibility of citing is even more critical when it comes to publishing on the Internet. There is so much misinformation out there that we should tell other researchers where we got what we are now sharing.

Important

It's My Family, I Deserve It

Genealogists are a unique breed. I can say this because I am one. For some reason we think we are entitled to everything that has mention of our family and that we shouldn't have to pay for any of it. As such, if we can make photocopies of a book at the library for a fraction of what it would cost to buy the book, then we justify it by saying it's family and we deserve the information. I have even seen genealogists take pad and paper into a vendor's booth at a genealogy conference and treat their books like a library.

Yes, it is your family. It is my family. If I have paid not only to get the photocopied documents, and ordered the microfilms, but have also paid to publish the book—a book you find useful—should you not pay for that book? Without that book, you would have to spend the same dollars as I did in getting the documents in question.

Figure 12-2
If the research has been done correctly, any genealogist should get the same lineage as this for Tom Hanks.

Tom Hanks
Mario Anzuoni/SplashNews

Pedigree Chart   11 Mar 2003
Chart no. 1
No. 1 on this chart is the same as no. 1 on chart no. 1

8 Daniel Boone HANKS
b: 10 Sep 1847
p: , , Kentucky
m: abt 1873   cont 2
p:
d:
p:

4 Ernest Buel HANKS
b: Sep 1890
p: , , California
m: 16 Jun 1917
p: Willows, Glenn Co., California
d: 14 May 1935
p: Willows, Glenn, California

9 Mary C. MEFFORD
b: Sep 1855
p: , , Missouri
d: 27 Aug 1923
p: , Tehama County, California

2 Amos Mefford HANKS
b: 4 Mar 1924
p: , Glenn County, California
m:
p:
d: 31 Jan 1992
p: , Alameda County, California

10 Amos BALL
b: 13 May 1849
p: Launceston, Cornwall, England
m: 23 Jun 1874
p: St. Helier, Jersey, Channel Islands
d: 27 Jan 1934
p: , Los Angeles County, California

5 Gladys Hilda BALL
b: 6 Mar 1888
p: Toledo, Tama, Iowa
d: 2 Jun 1965
p: , San Mateo County, California

11 Selina SCOBLE
b: 24 May 1849
p: Shaldon, Devon, England
d: 16 Jan 1907
p: Chicago, Cook, Illinois

1 Thomas J. HANKS
b: 9 Jul 1956
p: , Contra Costa Co., California
m:
p:
d:
p:

sp:

12 Manuel G. FRAGER
b: 19 Oct 1872
p: , , California
m:
p:
d: 14 Sep 1933
p: , Alameda County, California

6 Clarence P. FRAGER
b: 2 Nov 1903
p: , , California
m: abt 1925
p:
d: 16 Jan 1945
p: , Alameda County, California

13 Mary ENOS
b: abt 1880
p: , , California
d: 18 Dec 1930
p: , Alameda County, California

3 Janet Marylyn FRAGER
b: 18 Jan 1932
p: , Alameda County, California
d:
p:

14 Emanuel ROSE
b:
p:
m:
p:
d: bef 1920
p:

7 Elexio Norrine ROSE
b: 5 Feb 1907
p: , , California
d: 9 Feb 1955
p: , Alameda County, California

15 Nora E. A. BORGE
b: abt 1882
p: , , California
d:
p:

Prepared 11 Mar 2003 by:

1

I know, you are thinking about the fair use clause. While not the next item in our list of "rebuttals," let's go ahead and look at fair use since it may be what is coming to mind as the reason that you shouldn't have to buy the book.

Fair Use

The fair use clause was designed to allow those who were doing a commentary, parody, or review of the work to include specific small excerpts of the work in that commentary, parody, or review. I have used a couple in this book, attributing them not only to the author but mentioning the specific work I found it in as well. In addition to being mindful of how much of the work is used, you need also to remember to attribute that part of the work, either directly in your narrative or in a source citation footnote.

There are four standards by which the courts measure if information used falls under the fair use clause:

1. Is the purpose of your work commercial or noncommercial?
2. What is the nature of your work?
3. How much of the copyrighted work was used in relation to the whole work?
4. What is the effect of your use on the commercial value of the copyrighted work?

Notes

The third standard is often the one that folks try to use as their "out." There is no magic number to the amount of a work you can use. You can use a single sentence, and if it was the entire-work-in-a-nutshell type of sentence, it is possible a court would consider you to have exceeded the limitations of fair use. When in doubt, assume that you are not covered by the fair use clause. For more on fair use, see the pages on the U.S. Copyright Office Web site <www.loc.gov/copyright>.

PUBLIC DOMAIN

Genealogists confuse publicly available with public domain. The Internet makes a lot of information publicly available, but this does not mean that it is in the public domain. **Public domain is a term that indicates that a previously copyrighted work is no longer covered by copyright law.** Remember, copyright isn't forever; it does expire. In fact, many of the books now available in digitized format at sites such as Genealogy.com and Ancestry.com were in the public domain, which is what made them available to be scanned and digitized.

\di'fin\ *vb*

Definitions

Another reason that people often think that information found on the Internet is in the public domain is the lack of a copyright notice on the page. Again, this is a misunderstanding of the law, usually a result of the fact that we are used to seeing the copyright symbol on things that are seriously protected by copyright.

THERE WAS NO COPYRIGHT STATEMENT

While it is true that in the past it was a requirement of copyright law to put the statement on the work in order for it to be covered, that is no longer the case. Today, as soon as you create the work it is covered by copyright. An author can specifically designate their work as being in the public domain, but not finding a copyright symbol or statement on the site does not mean that it is in the public domain.

Believe me, I know it is confusing. In fact, that is why there are copyright lawyers and FAQ pages at the Copyright Office Web site. In most cases, if you innocently infringe on a copyright and make an effort to correct the issue when it is brought to your attention, you will not have any problems. In fact, genealogists usually just want to be recognized for their contribution to the community and to the research of that particular lineage or family.

MY NAME IS COPYRIGHTED

There has been a disturbing trend of late where genealogists are demanding the removal of "their ancestor's name" from a GEDCOM database or from a Web site. Recently a colleague received from a man a demand with the threat of legal action if the man's name was not removed from someone's database or Web site. The individual in question had a unique name, said that he had copyrighted his name, and that pursuant to copyright law, he had the authority to demand that they remove his name. While I am not a copyright attorney, I did find it interesting that the URL he included in his e-mail actually went to a portion of the Copyright Office's FAQ on names, in which the FAQ specifically says you can't copyright a personal name (see Copyright Office FAQ Copyright Protection, <www.copyright.gov/help/faq/faq-protect.html>.

Names, short phrases, titles, and slogans cannot be copyrighted. At the very best, it might be possible to get a trademark but there are guidelines and limitations in regard to this as well, especially when it comes to personal names. Generally you and I will not qualify for a trademark on our name.

INVASION OF PRIVACY AND IDENTITY THEFT

I think that the reaction of "you have my name" is actually a panicked response to a fear of invasion of privacy or the fear that your identity will be stolen. I completely understand that reaction. I have had it myself as I found my information in a GEDCOM database, more especially since I had never shared my date of birth or marriage or the names of my children with anyone. When I share genealogical data, I limit the information I share to just the lineage I have in common with the other researcher, and I have always stopped with the last generation of deceased individuals. So it was a little disconcerting to find my name, with my maiden surname horribly messed up, and the names of my children submitted by someone else.

Mine is a unique case, though, because most of the time we would have shared this information. When genealogical software programs first came out, and they had the magic of GEDCOM, we didn't think about security. Most of us didn't even begin to conceive of the idea that within a few short years we would be conversing online with the world. We shared our entire database in a GEDCOM file. The problem with this is that as soon as you have shared all that information with someone else, you have lost all control of where that information ends up. You cannot go to Ancestry.com and demand that they remove your family from a GEDCOM file submitted by another. If you gave that information to the other person, or to anyone who

For More Info

TRADEMARKED CELEBRITIES

While you can't copyright a name, you may find that some names are trademarked. To find out more about how celebrities such as Frank Sinatra had their name trademarked, visit the U.S. Patent and Trademark Office Web site at <www.uspto.gov/>.

Important

Notes

LIVING HISTORY

In the past it was necessary to purchase or download a special file that would look at your GEDCOM file and make the necessary changes to protect the living individuals. Today's genealogy software programs all come with an ability to protect living individuals. Some replace pertinent dates with the word "living" while others replace the whole name.

then passed it along to that person, the information is out and there is no way to recall it.

While I don't advocate sharing information about living individuals on the Internet, primarily because I don't know who is reading that information, I also have not heard of anyone who was able to show that their identity theft problem was a direct result of genealogical information.

Identity theft is a problem in today's society, but it takes more than your mother's maiden name to steal your identity. Think about it. When I deal with my bank I have to supply them with my name, my social security number, and my mother's maiden name. I sometimes have to supply them with additional information. I also know that many banks and other financial institutions are beginning to offer additional "identifying" words, such as your pet's name in place of the mother's maiden name. I have twice recently elected to use another identifying code word instead of my mother's maiden name.

The reality is that there is a lot of information out there about you, most of it available in much easier places to find than a genealogical site. By the same token, there is no reason to actively give the family a reason to be paranoid about the information you are gathering. After all, we have already discussed many surprises that the family may have to come to terms with already. Instead, consider creating a Web site that includes your end of line ancestors or that ends the descent from the immigrant ancestor with the last generation where everyone is deceased. Doing this still gets the information out and shows people where you are having research problems, but doesn't make any of the living relatives nervous, at least about your sharing their personal, and what they consider to be private, information.

Reminder

PUBLISHING THE SKELETONS

In the last chapter we looked at how to handle the skeletons that you may uncover in your research, at least when it comes to how you share that information with your family members. You would think that if a person chooses not to share the information with the family that they would likewise not publish the information online or in a book. Yet, in some cases you would be wrong.

Of course, while I understand protecting the family's feelings when it comes to the skeletons and embarrassments, I also don't want later researchers not to know about the family. I certainly don't advocate the fudging of dates of events because I believe in citing the sources of events and other information. Dates can't be fudged if you do this. By the same token, I hope never to publish a genealogy that mentions something like the Emerson genealogy did about Elizabeth Emerson: "Let the mantle of kindness cloak her sin."

Publishing on the Internet, though, exposes the information to a lot more people, and the family, if they didn't know about the scandal or early birth, may not appreciate having someone else tell them about it and then tell

INTERNET INTRUSIONS

If you are interested in finding out more about what is available online about you, you may want to check out Carole Lane's book *Naked in Cyberspace: How to Find Personal Information Online* (Medford: Information Today, 2002).

Warning

DEFAMATION OF CHARACTER

Defamation of character isn't something genealogists usually think about. If you find a black sheep in a celebrity's tree, make sure you are right, you can prove it, and that you are not sharing the information out of malice.

Notes

them where they found it. It is a fine line that must be walked. Some will try hard to walk it, while others will throw caution to the wind and simply post the information, all the information, that they find.

While publishing information online exposes it to the world, publishing it in a book gives it a certain permanence. While publishing it online may make it available to many, the information may actually be read by fewer, especially if the information is posted as a footnote or is something easily missed like the early birth of the first child. A lot of people who are searching for and incorporating the information found online don't bother to take the time to read everything they find. In fact, many of them simply download a GEDCOM file, dump the file into their database, and move on, never bothering to see what the file tells them. Those who take the time to get the book will sometimes read the footnotes or spend a little extra time thinking about the information and perhaps adding up the months from the marriage to the birth of the first child.

Before sharing any skeletons or other potentially embarrassing information about the family, think long and hard about the reaction you may get from the living family members. Make sure it is worth the possibility of ruining family relationships. In some families, the airing of the dirty laundry is something that isn't done. Other families simply don't care. Be sure you understand the potential reaction of your own family, as it should be one of the factors in your decision.

SHOUTING FROM THE ROOFTOPS—CELEBRITY RELATIONSHIPS

While there may be some trepidation at sharing the skeletons, there seldom seems to be hesitation in sharing a relationship with a celebrity, especially in the online genealogical community. It seems strange to me that published genealogies sometimes omit the famous individual or only briefly mention the name but omit the occupation, given the number of sites I have found where people are sharing in charts or other genealogical reports their relationship to a famous individual. Publishing has gone from the book to the Internet, and likewise the information shared and how it is shared has gone from one extreme to the other.

When sharing information about celebrities, both living and deceased, there are a few things you need to keep in mind. Some of them, you would think, would be common sense, while others are things that you shouldn't have to learn the hard way.

It is natural to get excited when you discover that you are related to a celebrity. If the actor or actress is still living, do not think that you will magically become his or her best friend. However, a connection is one of those quirky tidbits you can come across that remind the rest of the family that genealogy really is interesting after all. If your connection is to a historical individual, you may find that your kids are now a little more interested in history—you might also be a little more interested. You may find that

---

MOVIE STAR SITES

Often when posting information about a celebrity, it is natural to want to enhance your Web page with a photograph of the celebrity. To do this legally, you need to purchase the rights to that photograph. Here are some sites to start with. Be sure to tell them what you want to do with it because some sites price differently for images used on the Web. Additionally, some of these companies sell pictures just for your personal collection, not having the authority to sell you rights to use the pictures in any way.

- Celebrity Photos

- Celebrity Pictures, Search, Buy, Download

- Cinema & Celebrities

- Movie Star News

- MPTV—The Ultimate Hollywood Stock Photo Resource <www.mptv.net/main/main_elements/mainpage.htm>

- PhotoWorld <www.photowrld.com/page4lm.htm>

---

you better understand why the historical person chose to do what he did, or why your family did what it did as a result of the event.

Remember that the famous and infamous were all three-dimensional. Seldom do you find a person who was 100 percent good, and likewise, most of the bad guys of history had some good qualities as well. As you publish what you find, try hard to share all the facts instead of feeding into society's current approach of showing just the good or throwing light onto all the evils. Try not to let your personal ideals color how you see the celebrities and how you portray them in your research.

I don't know how often my mother used to tell me "You can pick your friends, but you are stuck with your family." While I may be stuck with them, I try not to judge them or put them on a pedestal. That is certainly easier to do with the faceless ancestor of two hundred years ago, but when the ancestor or relative, even from two hundred years ago, is famous, then you treat her differently. Try not to treat the person specially when posting the information, though it is certainly understandable that you would want to highlight that unique relationship on your Web site.

Of course, if the information you have found connects you to a living celebrity, there are certain publishing concerns to keep in mind. Remember, whether you publish in a book, a genealogical periodical, or on the Internet, you are publishing. We often don't understand all the legal issues and ramifications of publishing—copyright, right of privacy, and right of publicity—and may publish something in innocence that causes us some problems later on. Most of the copyright infringements I have seen genealogists commit have been innocent and a result of a misunderstanding or lack of knowledge of the laws.

While genealogy groups and individual genealogists are likely to nicely ask you to remove copyrighted material, because of the sheer number of abuses that celebrities must often deal with, they usually are not as forgiving, having their lawyer do their talking for them. This does not mean that if you are related to a famous individual that you cannot post that information—it just means you need to understand the laws that protect your information while also protecting the celebrity.

COPYRIGHT AGAIN

When you discover that you are related to a famous individual, whether alive or dead, you naturally want to do call attention to it on your site. It is understandable, therefore, that you would want to include a picture of the celebrity on your site. Because genealogists are often conditioned to using whatever we find with little regard to legalities, too often people use pictures they shouldn't. While I don't know of any genealogist who has been sued for using a picture of a celebrity on their Web site, you certainly don't want to be the test case.

There are legal ways to get pictures of celebrities to include on your Web site. In fact, you can purchase CDs full of photos of celebrities. Most of these CDs or Internet files have the stipulation that you need to use them on a noncommercial site. Usually this isn't a problem for genealogists, since most genealogists are doing the research as a hobby, with no receipt of monetary reimbursements (though our families—especially our spouses—may wish we did).

RIGHT OF PUBLICITY

While there are rules protecting the photos of celebrities that exist, the copyright in that instance protects the creation of the photo by the photographer. It should not surprise you, though, that there are also laws and rules that protect the "persona" of the famous. The use of the sports hero's face or name is sometimes protected through the "right of publicity."

At first glance it looks like the right of publicity would prevent you from sharing the information you have found. Instead it protects the celebrity from abuses of a commercial nature. A company cannot use the face of a celebrity for an ad when the purpose is to give those seeing the ad the impression that the celebrity is endorsing the product, unless of course the company has gotten the celebrity's permission, which usually means they have paid the celebrity for his involvement.

What you are publishing falls under the category of "public interest" and

Sources

\di'fin\ *vb*

Definitions

FIRST AMENDMENT PROTECTION

The *right of publicity* is what prevents people from using the "persona" of a celebrity in a way that looks like the celebrity is endorsing a product. This does not prevent sharing information about a celebrity's tree, as that is covered under the First Amendment.

"newsworthy." As a result your information is exempted from the right of publicity, and you can post the information freely. However, **if you have discovered a skeleton in the tree of a celebrity, make sure that your information is accurate before you post it, if you insist on posting it.** Depending on the skeleton, it is possible that the celebrity may not appreciate you sharing the information. And while the case could be made that it is newsworthy, if you are wrong you may have opened yourself up to some problems.

Everyone is interested in celebrities. Because they come into our homes each evening on the television or stare down at us larger than life from the movie screen, there are people who believe they have a real connection with celebrities. I understand celebrities' needs to distance themselves from that. When you share the family tree, you cement a relationship in some ways, so I encourage you to share the best information possible so that those who find it will not only find an accurate tree but will also learn how to publish a good family history.

DESIRED AND DEPENDABLE, NOT DRIVEL

Genealogy is a hobby to some, a fascination to others, and yes, an obsession to still others. I admit, I fall into that last category. I love the research, all aspects of research. I love learning more about different types of records and research methods. Today, I love the way the computer helps me to accomplish so much preliminary research, allowing me to devote quality research time to the records of whatever repository I am visiting.

I am dismayed when I use so many of the online resources only to discover that those posting the information seem to have spent no time compiling what they are sharing. Some of this is the result of the enthusiasm of novices, and I completely understand that. Unfortunately, more of it is the result of people not caring they are passing along bad genealogy, even if it is with good information, or people not understanding the destructiveness of passing on the bad genealogy.

Genealogy is a hobby and as such should be fun. People might say that if they have to follow all of those rules they can't have fun. I find that the rules remove some of the guesswork but also give me a constant to hold onto when my ancestors refuse to appear. Publishing a solid genealogical table, whether it is four generations or twenty-four generations, should be the goal. Publishing in today's world is not as difficult as it once was. Because we no longer need to worry about the details of the process of publishing, I sometimes think we have stopped taking pride in the entire aspect of it.

Share your information online and with your family. **Share it responsibly so that no one's feelings are hurt.** Share the information in such a way that fellow genealogists can work with your data instead of feeling like they have to fight against it. Cite your sources so that others know where you got the information (see Figure 12-3 on page 220). And if you do publish the information on the Internet, don't forget to print out at least a couple of copies of your genealogy to submit to libraries, especially the Family History

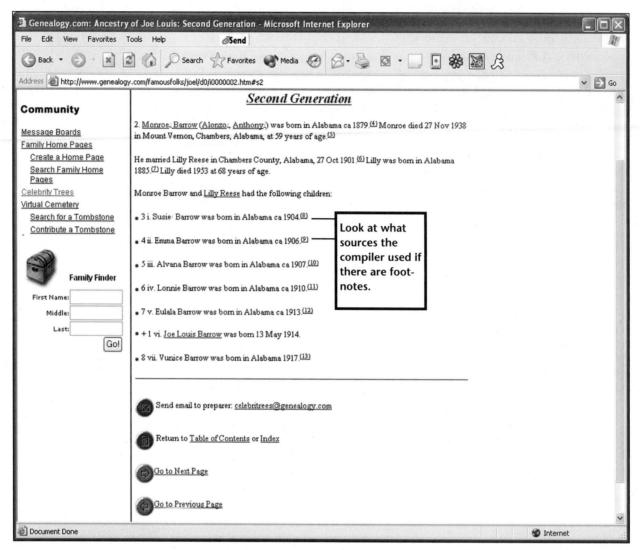

Figure 12-3
Look for footnotes on genealogy sites, such as those shown here in the ancestry of boxer Joe Louis. © 2002 Genealogy.com. Used with permission.

Library in Salt Lake City, so that when you are gone, your hard work lives on and others can thank you in their prayers as I have thanked so many researchers who went before me.

NOW THE ADVENTURE TRULY BEGINS

It is hard to believe that I have come to the end of this book. It has been an adventure taking you on the road that I travel with each new research project I undertake. Along the way, I have given you an introduction to the many different and valuable records and resources that are available online or through libraries, archives, and courthouses, as well as shared with you some of the projects I have compiled. I have shown you the expected and the unexpected, and how the unexpected may actually turn out to result in more records being available.

I have shared just a few of the famous and infamous individuals I have had the pleasure of researching. Each one brought new challenges either in record availability or in ethnic research idiosyncrasies. I have also shown you how important the Internet has become to all genealogical researchers. You have walked this path with me, and now the real adventure begins as you walk the path of your ancestry. May you find ancestors from all different walks of life. We have heard how America is a melting pot. I believe that each of us is a genealogical melting pot, having traits and tidbits from all those who have gone before us and contributed just a little to the person we have become. And yet, by the same token, none of our great ancestors has made us any greater nor our black sheep any darker. We are individuals, free to soar and become what we want while having the knowledge of our roots.

Enjoy the adventure of your lifetime.

FAMILY GROUP SHEET OF THE _____ **FAMILY** (Source #_____)

Source #_____ Full name of husband	Birth date
	Birthplace
His father	Death date
	Death place
His mother with maiden name	Burial place

Source #_____ Full maiden name of wife	Birth date
	Birthplace
Her father	Death date
	Death date
Her mother with maiden name	Burial place

Other spouses	Marriage date, place, etc.
Source #s	Source #s

Children of this marriage	Birthplace & date	Death date, place & burial place	Marriage date, place & spouse

SOURCE #_____   SOURCES (DOCUMENTATION)

Bibliography

Celebrity Resources

Brown, Adele Q. *What a Way to Go: Fabulous Funerals of the Famous and Infamous*. San Francisco: Chronicle Books, 2001.

Donnelly, Paul. *Fade to Black: A Book of Movie Obituaries*. New York: Omnibus Press, 2000.

Crawford, Tad & Tony Lyons. *The Writer's Legal Guide*, 2d ed. New York: Allworth Preso, 1998.

Kidd, Charles. *Debrett Goes to Hollywood*. New York, St. Martin's Press, 1986.

Masek, Mark J. *Hollywood Remains to Be Seen: a Guide to the Movie Stars' Final Homes*. Nashville, Tennessee: Cumberland House, 2001.

Mitchell, Corey. *Hollywood Death Scenes: True Crime and Tragedy in Paradise*. Chicago: Olmstead Press, 2001.

Parish, James Robert. *The Hollywood Book of Death*. Chicago: Contemporary Books, 2002.

Roberts, Gary Boyd. *Notable Kin*, 2 vol. Santa Clarita, California: Carl Boyes, 3d, 1998–1999.

Stewart, Ray, comp. & ed. *Immortals of the Screen*. New York: Bonanza Books, 1965.

Ethnic Resources

Burroughs, Tony. *Black Roots: A Beginner's Guide to Tracing the African American Family Tree*. New York: Fireside, 2001.

Carmack, Sharon DeBartolo. *A Genealogist's Guide to Discovering Your Immigrant & Ethnic Ancestors*. Cincinnati, Ohio: Betterway Books, 2000.

Kurzweil, Arthur. *From Generation to Generation: How to Trace Your Jewish Genealogy and Family History*, rev. ed. New York: HarperPerenniel, 1994.

Smith, Franklin Carter and Emily Anne Croom. *A Genealogist's Guide to Discovering Your African-American Ancestors*. Cincinnati, Ohio: Betterway Books, 2003.

Weiner, Miriam. *Jewish Roots in Poland*. Secaucus, New Jersey: Miriam Weiner Routes to Roots Foundation, and New York: YIVO Institute for Jewish Research, 1997.

———. *Jewish Roots in Ukraine and Moldova*. Secaucus, New Jersey: Miriam Weiner Routes to Roots Foundation, and New York: YIVO Institute for Jewish Research, 1999.

General Genealogy Sources

Bentley, Elizabeth Petty. *The Genealogist's Address Book*, 4th ed. Baltimore: Genealogical Publishing Co., 1998.

Carmack, Sharon DeBartolo. *A Genealogist's Guide to Discovering Your Female Ancestors*. Cincinnati: Betterway Books, 1998.

———. *The Genealogy Sourcebook*. Los Angeles: Lowell House, 1997.

———. *Organizing Your Family History Search: Efficient & Effective Ways to Gather and Protect Your Genealogical Research*. Cincinnati, Ohio: Betterway Books, 1999.

———. *Your Guide to Cemetery Research*. Cincinnati, Ohio: Betterway Books, 2002.

Everton, George B., comp. *The Handybook for Genealogists*, 8th ed. Logan, Utah: Everton Publishers, 1991.

Eichholz, Alice. *Ancestry's Red Book: American State, County, and Town Sources*. Salt Lake City: Ancestry, Inc., 1989.

Greenwood, Val D. *The Researcher's Guide to American Genealogy*, 3d ed. Baltimore: Genealogical Publishing Co., 2000.

Hinckley, Kathleen W. *Locating Lost Family Members and Friends*. Cincinnati: Betterway Books, 1999.

Jones, Linda and Paul Milner. *A Genealogist's Guide to Discovering Your Scottish Ancestors*. Cincinnati, Ohio: Betterway Books, 2002.

McClure, Rhonda. *The Complete Idiot's Guide to Online Genealogy*. 2d ed. Indianapolis, Indiana: Alpha Books, 2002.

———. *The Genealogist's Computer Companion*. Cincinnati, Ohio: Betterway Books, 2002.

Mills, Elizabeth Shown. *Evidence! Citation & Analysis for the Family Historian*. Baltimore: Genealogical Publishing Co., 1997.

Rose, Christine and Kay Germain Ingalls. *The Complete Idiot's Guide to Genealogy*. New York: Alpha Books, 1997.

Schaefer, Christina K. *The Hidden Half of the Family: A Sourcebook for Women's Genealogy*. Baltimore: Genealogical Publishing Co., 1999.

Szucs, Loretto Dennis and Sandra Hargreaves Luebking, eds. *The Archives: A Guide to the National Archives Field Branches*. Salt Lake City: Ancestry, Inc., 1988.

———, eds. *The Source: A Guidebook of American Genealogy*, rev. ed. Salt Lake City: Ancestry, Inc., 1997.

Royal and Notable Sources

Anselme de Saint Marie (Pierre de Guibours) *Histoire Généalogique et Chronologique de la Maison Royale de France*, 9 vols., 1726.

Aubert, Francoise Alexandre, *Dictionnaire de la Noblesse . . .* , 11 vols. 3d ed. Paris, France : Francois Alexandre Aubert, 1867.

Bickersteth, John and Robert W. Dunning. *Clerks of the Closet in the Royal Household: Five Hundred Years of Service to the Crown*. Wolfeboro, New Hampshire: Alan Sutton Publishing, Inc., 1991.

Bridger, Charles. *An Index to Printed Pedigrees Contained in County and Local Histories, The Herald's Visitations, and in the More Important Genealogical Collections*. London, England: John Russell Smith, 1867.

Burke, Bernard, Sir. *Burke's Genealogical and Heraldic History of the Landed Gentry*. London: Burke's Peerage, Limited, 1939.

———. *Royal Descents and Pedigrees of Founders' Kin*. London: Harrison, 1864.

Call, Michel L. *Royal Ancestors of Some American Families*. Salt Lake City, Utah: Michel L. Call, 1989.

Cokayne, George Edward. *The Complete Peerage Of England, Scotland, Ireland, Great Britain And The United Kingdom, Extant, Extinct, Or Dormant*, 13 vols. London: St. Catherine's Press, 1910–1959.

Dupont, Jacques Gaillot. *Cahiers de Saint Louis*, 28 vols. Angers, France: 1976–1978.

Filby, P. William. *American and British Genealogy and Heraldry: A Selected List of Books*. Chicago, Illinois: American Library Association, 1983–1987.

Foster, Joseph. *The Royal Lineage of Our Noble and Gentle Families*. 2 vols. London: Hatchards, 1887

Fox-Davies, Arthur C. *A Complete Guide to Heraldry*. London: Nelson, 1969.

Garcia Carraffa, Alberto, and Arthuro Garcia Carraffa, *Diccionario Heraldico y Genealogico de Appelidos Espanoles y Americanos*, 86 vols. Madrid, Spain: Nueva Impenta Radio, 1952–1963.

Gatfield, George. *Guide to Printed Books and Manuscripts Relating to English and Foreign Heraldry and Genealogy: Being a Classified Catalogue of Works of Those Branches of Literature*. Detroit, Michigan: Gale Research Company, 1966.

Gayo, Manoel Jose da Costa Felgueiras. *Nobilario de Familis da Portugal*, 33 vols. Braga, Portugal: Officinas Graficas de Pax, 1938–1942.

Herber, Mark D. *Ancestral Trails: The Complete Guide to British Genealogy and Family History*. Baltimore, Maryland: Genealogical Publishing Company, Inc., 1998.

Howard, Joseph Jackson. *Visitation of England and Wales*. London: 1893–1919.

Litta, Pampeo. *Famiglie Celebri Italiane*, 12 vols. Milan, Italy: Paolo Emilio Giusti, 1819–1871.

Marshall, George W. *An Index to the Pedigrees Contained in the Printed Heralds' Visitations*. London: Robert Hardwicke, 1866.

———. *The Genealogist's Guide*. Baltimore, Maryland: Genealogical Publishing Company, Inc., repr. 1980, 1903.

Nouvelle Biographie Générale depuis les Temps les Plus Réculés Jusqu'à 1850–60 avec le Renseignments Bibilgrahiques et l'Indication des Sources à Cansulter, publiée par Mm. Firmin Didot Frères sous la Direction de M. Le Dr. Hoefer. Copenhagen, Sweden, Rosenkilde et Bagger, 1967.

O'Hart, John. *The Irish and Anglo-Irish Landed Gentry*. Shannon, Ireland: University Press, 1969.

Paget, Gerald. *The Lineage and Ancestry of H.R.H. Prince Charles, Prince of Wales*, 2 vols. London, England: Charles Skilton, Ltd., 1977.

Roberts, Gary Boyd and William Addams Reitwiesner. *American Ancestors and Cousins of The Princess of Wales*. Baltimore, Maryland: Genealogical Publishing Company, Inc., 1984.

Roberts, Gary Boyd. *The Royal Descents of 500 Immigrants to the American Colonies of the United States Who Were Themselves Notable or Left Descendents Notable In American History*. Baltimore, Md.: Genealogical Publishing Company, 1993.

Ruvigny and Raineval, Marquis of. *Plantagenet Roll of the Blood Royal*. London: T.C. & E.C. Jack, 1907.

Stokvis, Anthony Marinus Hendrik Hohan. *Manuel d'Historie de genealogie et de Chronologie de Tous les Etats du Globe*, 4 vols. Leiden, Netherlands: B.M. Israel, 1966.

Sturdza, Mihail-Dimitri, *Dictinnaire Historique et Genealogique, des Grandes Families de Grece, d'Albanie et de Constatinople*. Paris, France: Mihail-Dimitrie Sturdza, 1983.

Tonge, Thomas. *Heraldic Visitations of the Northern Counties in 1530*. Durham, England: The Surtees Society, 1863.

Whitemore, John Beach. *A Genealogical Guide: An Index to British Pedigrees in Continuation of Marshall's Genealogist's Guide*. London: Walford Brothers, 1953.

———. *London Visitation Pedigrees, 1664*. London: 1940.

Index